The Beautiful Feet of
MISSIONS

The Beautiful Feet of
MISSIONS

An Overview of Modern Missions Thought

MIKE PETTENGILL

for

My wife Erin who is the most incredible
woman, mom, missionary, nurse I know
and keeps loving me for some strange reason.

*"How beautiful upon the mountains
are the feet of him who brings good news,
who publishes peace, who brings good news of
happiness, who publishes salvation,
who says to Zion, 'Your God reigns.'"*
- Isiah 52:7

*"And how are they to preach unless they are sent?
As it is written, 'How beautiful are the feet of
those who preach the good news!'"*
- Romans 10:15

Table of Contents

Preface

I spent 10-years living on the mission field, studied missions in seminary, read lots of missions books, attended conferences, mentored new missionaries, and preached countless times on God's call for his church to participate in global evangelism. The reality I have experienced is most laypeople in churches have not been properly trained on missions. The other sad truth is there are very few resources out there which can help train pastors, church leaders, and laypeople about global missions originating from the local church. Don't get me wrong, there are lots of books on missions and missionaries, but very little out there which sums it all up in one place.

My desire in researching and writing this book was to provide a missions primer for the modern church. The local church in the Western world today seems to have lost the foundational belief which insists the church exists to replicate the faith. The founding of the local church in Scripture was so disciples of Christ could be trained and sent into the world to seek the elect and to disciple and train them in the ways of the Lord.

Today's modern Western church has lost its focus on the world and turned itself into an institution which centers on making existing Christians better Christians. Largely, our local churches are not training their people to have a passion for reaching the lost. Church goers are not burdened to reach the lost, but instead are interested in Christian navel gazing.

Few of our pastors and church leaders are preaching or teaching frequently on global outreach. Missions and evangelism are not priorities in most pulpits. Few seminaries are mandating even one course on missions or evangelism for our future pastors. Because our churches are not centered on reaching the lost, our laypeople are woefully aware of just how important sharing the gospel is to God.

There are so many books which need to be written on global outreach, but at the forefront of my mind in writing this book was to try to plug the holes in the lives and theology of fellow disciples of Christ. This book is for both well-educated theologians and pew-sitters alike. It can also be equally used by churches which have never looked outside their front doors and churches which have burgeoning and healthy missions programs. Most churches are not doing missions. And, most of the churches which are doing missions are doing it poorly.

Like most missionaries I have made many mistakes. As a missionary, I tried to launch 20 new programs for every one that succeeded. My interactions with nationals, teammates, and supporters has been a mixed bag of grand mistakes with a couple of successes sprinkled in. Frequently I failed, and every once in a while, I allowed God to work through me. My wife and I have had hearts to mentor and disciple others on missions. We have always been vulnerable and honest with other missionaries and sending churches. Because of this, we have been privileged to hear the experiences of failures and successes by both senders and goers. We have become a central depository for the missions involvements of tens of thousands of people. We have heard from all sides what works and what doesn't.

Churches shouldn't be punished because our seminaries aren't training our pastors to preach on missions and congregants shouldn't suffer because they aren't being taught about missions. More importantly, the nations shouldn't suffer because we aren't properly taking the saving message of Christ to the lost.

This book should serve as the start of a conversation in our homes, churches, and seminaries. This book does not have all the proper methods for you (as a goer or sender) and your church. Many well-intentioned pastors and seminary professors will undoubtedly disagree with the contents in this book.

What this book does do is provide a platform to learn and talk more about missions. Some of the themes here are controversial in missiological studies. At the heart of this book is an attempt to glorify God by motivating his followers to do more to reach the elect in the nations. I pray, if you have not been involved in missions, this book motivates you to get involved in God's global mandate. I also pray, if you and your church are already involved in missions, this book will motivate you to stretch yourself, expand your influence, and maybe consider changing the way you've been doing missions.

Chapter One

Missions Through Scripture

From Genesis through Revelation the Bible is one story. It is a telling of God's plan to unite himself with his fallen creation. Too often we fail to see how the Scriptures tell a unified, sequential story. From the moment God drove man from the Garden to the time he scattered and divided them at the tower of Babel, Yahweh always planned to increase the number of his elect through Adam and unite them under Christ. God's linear plan was always to use his disciples to spread his name, expand his glory, and unify the remainder of his elect under his grace and mercy.

All 66 books of Scripture include aspects of reaching the lost to unite them with God. If we read the Bible with God's plan for reunification in mind we can see the texts as the singular, covenantal story they were intended to be. Too often, the Bible is viewed as a collection of moral fables or a series of disjointed eras of man's failed attempt to know an unknowable god.

The love of God for his people spelled out throughout the Bible. His consistent desire to reach his elect becomes more evident when we see God for the consistently gracious and loving Father he is. God's desire to commune with his children never waivers. It is our ever-evolving desire to find new ways to separate ourselves from our Lord which makes up the changing themes of Scripture.

This chapter takes a brief survey through several points in Scripture which are united by God's desire to use the saved to reach the lost. This should not be considered an exhaustive list, only waypoints along the linear path of God's outreach to the nations. Use these examples as a way to focus the lens which we view Scripture. The desire is this brief study into missions through Scripture will help you see all of the Bible as God's eternal plan to unite the elect, from every people group, with their Savior.

The Covenant with Abraham

Following the great flood God repopulated the earth through Shem, Ham and Japheth, the sons of Noah (Gen 9:18-19). God spread the decedents of Noah throughout the earth (Gen 10). The people of the earth were then given varying languages (Gen 11:7) and further dispersed throughout the world (Gen 11:8, 9). God had created a planet that was, for the first time, populated by humans who were spread out, spoke different languages and were from drastically diverse cultures.

In Genesis 12 God put into motion his will to establish his elect race of people and to ultimately use them to reach the plethora of nations he had fashioned in the previous chapters. The Abrahamic Covenant showed a loving God who pursued sinful man. It pointed toward the coming of God's son Jesus Christ. The covenant was God's plan to bless his faithful disciples and to enable the sinless Creator to commune with and reside among his sinful creation. The Abrahamic Covenant provided a blessing for the nations by establishing Israel as the light for the world and by ushering in the gospel of Jesus Christ as the only way to commune with the Lord.

The Abrahamic Covenant is presented by God to Abram in Genesis 12:1-3. It is established in Genesis 15:18-21 and affirmed in Genesis 17:1-21. The covenant is then renewed with Abraham's sons Isaac (Gen 26:2-5) and Jacob (Gen 28:10-17). This covenant between God and Abraham contains language that obligates both Abraham to God (Gen 17:9-15) and God to Abraham (Gen 17:4-8, 16). The Abrahamic Covenant indicates a pivotal point in redemptive history as Yahweh covenants with his elect. Christopher Wright said, "God's promise to Abraham is key to the rest of Scripture. It is the beginning of biblical mission and at the heart of the gospel."[1] God here formalizes a relation with his people that will result in Israel serving as a "light for the nations" (Isa 42:6) and turn the followers of Jesus into the disciple makers "of all nations" (Mat 28:19).

Abram is challenged to turn his back on all the world holds dear and follow the Lord unconditionally. John Calvin said, "when he is first called by God's command [Gen. 12:1], he is taken away from his country, parents, and friends, considered by men the sweetest things in life, as if God deliberately intended to strip him of all life's delights."[2] Abram's call is no different than that of modern disciples of Christ: obey the Lord and faithfully follow what he asks of us.

Throughout the OT it is plain to see the fulfillment of the promises to Abraham and his descendants through ethnic Israel. Israel was blessed and became a great nation. As

---

[1] "Why Righteousness Matters." Wright, Christopher J.H. // Christianity Today; Nov2015, Vol. 59 Issue 9, p56

[2] John Calvin, *Institutes of the Christian Religion 1 & 2*, ed. John T. McNeill, trans. Ford Lewis Battles, vol. 1, The Library of Christian Classics (Louisville, KY: Westminster John Knox Press, 2011), 437.

she remained faithful to God she received his blessings and her enemies received the curses of Yahweh. After Israel was delivered from Egypt the Lord purified her and when she was ready, God gave her the land he had promised.

It was Israel's disobedience and regular turning from God which resulted in the Abrahamic Covenant not being completely fulfilled in early Israel. Israel had been blessed by God only to see her blessings turn against her. Paul Kissling wrote, "While the Pentateuch prepares for the fulfillment of the promises to Abraham, the rest of the Old Testament tells the tragic story of how his descendants nearly saw its fulfillment only to see it lost through persistent disobedience and outright rebellion."[3] God's elect would have to wait for the birth of Christ to see how God would fulfill the Abrahamic Covenant.

Through God's gift of Jesus Christ, the descendent of Abraham, the NT shows a fulfillment of the Abrahamic Covenant in God's elect. Robert Raymond said that, "the blessing of the covenant of grace that believers enjoy today under the sanctions of the New Testament economy are founded upon the covenant God made with Abraham."[4] In the new covenant the blessings of the Abrahamic Covenant are provided to the nations. The families of the earth are blessed in Christ's salvific gospel. God's mission for the church (Ma. 28:18-20; Acts 1:8) is a partial fulfilling of the covenant.

God's promise to Abram of greatness and blessing for the families and nations of the world is seen as being fulfilled in his descendent, Jesus. As the obedient disciples of Christ answer their call to disciple and baptize the nations they are fulfilling the promise of blessings given to Abraham. It is the modern church of Jesus Christ which is called to be obedient and faithful to God and bless the nations through the grace and mercy found in the gospel of the Lord.

God calls his church to remain faithful and trust in him for its provision, so he can use his disciples to bless the nations. The kingdom of God is created through the sharing of the blessings of the Abrahamic Covenant with the families of the world. God's promises to Abraham are inseparable from the biblical understanding of the mission of God's church.

The response to God's call exemplified in Abraham points to God's desire for Israel and God's elect today. Martyn Lloyd-Jones said, "The characteristics of Abraham's life

---

[3] Paul Kissling, *Genesis, vol. 2, The College Press NIV Commentary* (Joplin, MO: College Press Publishing Company, 2009), 33.
[4] Robert L. Reymond, *Contending for the Faith: Lines in the Sand That Strengthen the Church* (Fearn, Ross-shire, UK: Christian Focus Publications, 2005), 192.

are still the essential characteristics of the Christian life into which we are called by this glorious Gospel. The first is that his life was a God-centered, God-controlled life."[5] Abraham learned that his true blessings were obtained when he sacrificed his life for God's glory.

Jesus is the fulfillment of the Abrahamic Covenant set by God. The seed of Abraham delivers God's grace and mercy to Israel, the Gentiles and the nations of the world. Jesus brings the blessings of the covenant to physical and spiritual Israel through the global mandate of the Christian church.

Leviticus 11 - Early Food Laws

God created and set apart his elect people to bring himself glory and so his grace and mercy can be on display in their lives and through their justification. Because God is holy and perfect he must commune with a people who are holy and set apart. Through Jesus Christ, today God's elect are justified through his atoning blood. Before Christ, God establish the food Law (Lev 11) to enable his elect to become ceremonially clean so they could commune with their perfect Creator.

The mission and the purpose of Israel was to be different from the world. God's elect have always been called to be a city on a hill (Mat 5:14; Pro 4:18; Isa 60:1-3), to provide a stark contrast between them and the world. The food laws of Leviticus 11 helped keep Israel physically separate from the rest of the world so as to enable them to remain spiritually clean and presentable to God. The lifting of the food laws, under Jesus, enabled God's people to more freely spread throughout the world and take Christ's gospel to other cultures.

Leviticus 11:2-40 lists all the types of animals that are clean and unclean to eat and explains how Israel was to remain spiritually clean. It would be understandable to initially conclude these food laws seem a little arbitrary and confusing. What is the reason God wants his people clean? While many have hypothesized why these food laws were given to God's elect, the answer is found in Leviticus 11:44-45. The reason Israel was given to follow the laws was, "For I am the Lord your God." (v. 44a). Obedience to God is mandated.

"For I am the Lord your God" is used six times in Scripture. Its first use occurs in Leviticus 11:44. Additionally, "I am holy" also appears in Scripture for the first time in

---

[5] David Martyn Lloyd-Jones, "The Life of Faith," in *Glorious Christianity*, 1st U.S. ed., vol. 4, Studies in the Book of Acts (Wheaton, IL: Crossway Books, 2004), 109.

verse 44. Likewise, the command to "be holy" is used 32 times in the ESV and here in verse 44 is one of the first occurrences of the phrase. Herman Bavinck said of verse 44, "He gave his people Israel a law that can be summed up by saying that Israel had to be a priestly kingdom and a holy nation." Verse 44 is a scriptural launching point for the close communion between God and his holy people.

The food laws of Leviticus 11 would have been an impediment for God's followers to interact with other nations. Limiting interaction with foreigners and travel to foreign lands improved the chance Israel would not be negatively influenced by foreign god's or customs.

Jesus dedicated much of his earthly ministry to informing Jews they were no longer to separate themselves from the world, but were to enter the world and take God's message of grace to the nations. Throughout the Gospels Jesus made it a point to eat with sinners. This upset many righteous Jews. The Pharisees pointed out how Jesus actions were contrary for Mosaic Law (Mat 9:10-13, 11:19; Mar 2:15-17; Luk 5:30, 15:1-2). In the mind of the Pharisees no Jew could act like this, let alone the Messiah.

The clearest illustration Jesus eliminated the food laws of Leviticus 11 exists with Peter's vision in Acts 10. Peter, a Jew, saw a vision from the Lord telling to eat the animals before him. When Peter protested due to the uncleanness of the animals God said, "What God has made clean, do not call common." (v. 15b) Peter ate with the gentile convert Cornelius and other non-Jews. Peter then brought God's word to the gentiles (v. 34-43) and they were converted (v. 44-48). Charles Spurgeon said of this chapter, "The apostle Peter was shown by the vision of a sheet let down from heaven, not only that all nations were now to receive the gospel message, but that all kinds of food were now clean, and that all the prohibitions which had formerly been laid upon them for legal purposes were now once for all withdrawn."[6] No longer could the elect of Israel claim the Levitical food laws were in place. The blood of Christ had changed things forever and God's grace and mercy was now to go beyond the nation of Israel.

Jesus mandates his disciples to share God's salvific message in Jerusalem, Judea, Samaria and the end of the earth (Acts 1:8). Without the chains of the food laws limiting them to places where they can remain clean, God's disciples are told by Christ to go out into the world (Mar 16:15), to disciple the other races (Mat 28:18-20) and proclaim God's glory to all nations (Luk 24:47).

---

[6] C. H. Spurgeon, "The Clean and the Unclean," in *The Metropolitan Tabernacle Pulpit Sermons, vol. 9* (London: Passmore & Alabaster, 1863), 145.

The mission of early Israel was to be holy as God was holy. Following Leviticus 11, combined with other aspects of the Mosaic Law, served to make Israel holy for worship, helped Israel to stand out from the rest of the world and limited Israel's ability to interact with other cultures and travel to foreign lands. Israel's mission to remain distinct and separate was advanced by Leviticus 11.

The blood of Christ paid for the sins of God's elect and made them holy so they could freely fellowship with God. Jesus mandated his followers to take his gospel to all the nations and to teach his ways to all the cultures of the world. Without the food laws to confine our interaction with other races Christians are now free to follow God's Great Commission and share the grace and mercy of Jesus Christ with people of other nations. It is now permissible, and mandated, for God's people to travel to, eat alongside, and socialize with the people of other cultures.

Leviticus 11 kept God's elect holy and separate. The elimination of the mandate to follow Leviticus 11 now enables God's elect to go into all of the world and proclaim God's glory.

Psalm 67 - Saving Power

Psalm 67 is a testament of God's people focusing on missions. Israel, in this psalm, is singing that not only will they be blessed, but that God will also focus his blessings on the Gentiles. The Israelites sing that God will bring himself greater glory by expanding his global influence. The focus of this psalm is God's people asking that his salvation and praise may spread throughout the earth. The universal perspective of Psalm 67 is remarkable. The global focus is quite visionary even when compared to the rest of Scripture.

The psalm reiterates the need of God's great mercy and calls for God to expand his glory throughout the globe. God's promise to Abraham (Gen 12:1-3), that "all families of the earth shall be blessed," is called upon in Psalm 67.

Psalm 67, at first read, could be viewed as a song of thanksgiving for a fruitful harvest. Instead, it is a prayer that God would bless Israel so the rest of the world can be inspired to come to know God. Each Israelite is a bit player in a grand story designed to go beyond his own influence and into the world. In this psalm each Jew wants God to be glorified beyond the boarders of Israel and in the world of the Gentiles.

The author of Psalm 67 is unknown, but it is assumed to have been written in the vicinity of 1500 - 1400 B.C. Thus the original audience of the psalm were likely the pre-exilic Jews. Helen Jefferson stated, "the cultic coloring of Ps 67, its vocabulary and style, all point to Canaanite influence. This supports the theory that Ps 67 is pre-exilic in origin."[7]

Eckhard Schnadel, in Early Christian Missions, concludes that OT Israelites did not engage in missions as NT Christians did later. Schnadel does not see any formal concept of disciple-driven missions or global evangelism in the Psalms. He does, however, see evident in the Psalms a divinely initiated desire that the world would soon worship Yahweh.

The emphasis of Psalm 67 is a call for missions. It calls for disciples of God to be blessed, not only for our own pleasure, but so our joy in God will reflect his glory to the nations. Lawrence Nemer stated, "The nations are sometimes chosen, according to the Psalmist, to be instruments of God's punishment; but ultimately, as recorded so marvelously in Psalm 67, they are to be witnesses of God's work among His people and are to come to worship Him in Jerusalem."[8]

Missions, in and of itself, is a concept that is focused not on man's actions but instead on God's. While man is involved in reaching the nations, he is only a tool in the hands of a master carpenter. Graeme Goldsworthy echoed this thought when he wrote, "Even the missionary focus of Psalm 67 emphasizes that God himself must act for the nations to be blessed."[9] It is God working to bring the nations to himself. God may work through man, but the results, and thus the glory, are God's alone.

Worshipers of God should not view blessings as rewards. Blessings are not always to bless us. They come to us not for what we have done, but what God has done. The purpose God blesses us is to bring glory to himself. It is so others in the world will see God more clearly. Carl Bosma writes, "The function of this signally important harvest is to catch the attention of the nations and move them to recognize and praise God. The particular history of God and Israel is meant to become a blessing for all."[10]

Only a small number of hymns have been inspired by Psalm 67. Martin Luther's hymn, "May God Bestow on Us His Grace" is one of them. The second stanza of Luther's hymn begins with these words, "Thine over all shall be the praise, and thanks of every nation, and all the world with joy shall raise, the voice of exultation." Oliver Rupprecht

---

[7] Helen Jefferson, "The Date of Psalm LXVII," Vetus Testamentum 12.2 (April 1962): 205.

[8] Lawrence Nemer, "Spirituality and the Missionary Vocation", in Missiology: An International Review 11.4 (1983), 427

[9] Graeme L. Goldsworthy, "The Great Indicative: An Aspect of a Biblical Theology of Missions" The Reformed Theological Review (No. 1, 1996) 8.

[10] Eep Talstra and Carl Bosma, "Psalm 67: Blessing, Harvest and History" Calvin Theological Journal (No. 36, 2001) 313.

stated of this hymn, "What missionary can be timid after hearing or singing Luther's great missionary hymn, 'May God Bestow on Us His Grace,' based on Psalm 67?"[11] The words inspired by God in Psalm 67 have and will continue to have a great impact on disciples of Christ as they respond by going out amongst the nations.

Psalm 67 shows the people of God are to be concerned with not only their own lives nor the circumstances within their own borders. God's disciples are to be concerned about the eternal condition of all races, tongues and tribes. God does not bless his chosen people because they are good or worthy. God's elect receive blessings so they can share those blessings with others and draw attention to the greatness and mercy of God.

In this psalm, it is evident we have a God who is concerned about all nations and he wishes to draw them to himself. God's followers, in order to bring him glory, are called to also have a burden for other nations.

Jonah - God in Control

Most everyone is familiar with the Book of Jonah. Ask almost any Sunday school student and they'll tell you Jonah is about a big fish, or a worm, or a reluctant missionary, or the bad people of Nineveh. In reality, the Book of Jonah is about none of those things. Yes, they are all players in the tale. However, the book Jonah is about something completely different. Jonah is a book written to remind us that our merciful and gracious God is in control.

Many commentators claim Jonah is a fictional tale and that it just can't have any historical significance. Liberal theologians believe the story, complete with big fish, worm and runaway profit, is too fanciful to be real. Frankly, if a person believes in the Immaculate Conception and Jesus raising the dead, it should be no great stretch to imagine God sending a fish to redirect Jonah. Even many of those who believe in biblical inerrancy are starting to see Jonah as allegorical.

However, the best way to authenticate the Bible is by checking it against itself. The verse found in 2 Kings 14:25 mentions Jonah by name. That verse says Jonah was a son, a prophet and haled from Gath-hepher. The New Testament mentions Jonah by name 10 times. In fact, every time Jonah's name is used in the New Testament it is spoken by Jesus. Jesus references Jonah's tale as a prophecy pointing to his own resurrection (Mat 12:40)

---

[11] Oliver C. Rupprecht, "Timeless Treasure: Luther's Psalm Hymns" Concordia Theological Quarterly (No. 2, April 1883) 138.

and Jesus mentions Jonah's interaction with Nineveh as a historical event (Luk 11:29). According to Jesus, Jonah and Nineveh were true.

God speaks the first words in the Book of Jonah (1:1-2) and he speaks the final words (4:10-11). Cartoons, church VBS and most sermons focus on the actors of the story (Jonah, fish, etc,). Few resources focus on God as the central character in the Book of Jonah. It was God who sent the storm to halt Jonah (1:4). God likely controlled the lots falling to Jonah (1:7). God sent the big fish to save Jonah (1:17). God instructed the fish to vomit Jonah onto land (2:10). God provided the plant to give shade for Jonah (4:6). God appointed the worm to destroy the plant (4:7). God sent the wind to discomfort Jonah (4:8). And, lest we forget, it was God who sent Jonah in the first place and God who saved the people of Nineveh. Jonah is a book about God and his sovereignty.

Nineveh was the capital of the Assyrian empire. History tells us the Assyrians were a brutal people who were notoriously cruel to their enemies. The Assyrians and the Israelites lived in close proximity and had battled in the past. The city of Nineveh was large and was a pagan culture, which would not have taken kindly to a Jew telling them to seek salvation from his God.

Jonah is the only character mentioned in the book by name. He ran from God's command to go to Nineveh and prophecy to the people there. The reader doesn't learn the reason Jonah fled in the direction of Tarshis until chapter four. Jonah fled, not because he feared the Ninevites or doubted his own abilities, but because he did not want God to show mercy on the people of Nineveh. Jonah had enjoyed God's mercy toward Israel and he sought it for himself (chapters 2 and 4). However, Jonah did not want God to show mercy to the Assyrian people. Jonah had deemed them unworthy of the mercy he himself had enjoyed. With God's help, Jonah did find his way to Nineveh. Although, Scripture reveals Jonah's important prophetic message consisted of only eight words (in the translated English). Not exactly an impassioned plea for repentance.

The book concludes with God asking Jonah, "should not I pity Nineveh?" Of the 66 books of the Bible only two end with a question: Nahum and Jonah, both of which deal with Nineveh. The reason the Book of Jonah ends in a question, with an unfulfilling literary ending, is to pose the moral dilemma to the reader. Reader, should God show his boundless grace and mercy to the cruel enemies of God's chosen people?

What is it we place ahead of God's glory? There are thousands of unreached people groups and billions of people who do not claim Jesus as their Lord. Do we place our comfort, security, family, or fear of failure ahead of God's Great Commission? Have we, like Jonah, made the determination we will run from Gods command to share his gospel with those across the street and around the globe?

Jonah reminds us God is in control. He is sovereign and only he controls outcomes. God didn't need Jonah to preach to Nineveh, but in his great pleasure he chose to use his sinful servant. God does not need to use us to call his elect to himself, but it pleases him to do so. Embrace your calling to share the gospel with the lost, not because you fear a big fish, but because you desire to see God's glory multiplied on the earth.

Matthew 28:18-20 - Mission for the Church

The mission of the Christian church is found in the Great Commission. In Matthew 28:18-20 Jesus instructs the corporate body to make disciples of non-believers, baptize them and teach them God's ways. Only then will more people be in fellowship, be instructed and actively praising God. When this happens, God will receive greater glory.

Christ having authority over peoples and nations was not an original idea and was likely used by Jesus to cause the Jews to think of Daniel 7:13 and its declaration of dominion and glory over "peoples, nations and languages." Christ had earlier declared authority had been given to him by the Father (Mat 11:27), but in the Great Commission the authority to teach is passed from Christ to his disciples for the first time. The disciples and the corporate church are now endowed with the great authority given to them by Jesus Christ. This gives great boldness and confidence to the church and the disciples knowing God's plan will be fulfilled through their actions.

The church must go out into the world. The church must travel where the lost reside. Even in this technologically advanced age a disciple cannot be made over the internet or only by phone. The church must go and must send disciples out into the streets and into the jungles to reach the lost. The going action is presupposed by the making of disciples. Disciples cannot be made unless someone has gone.

The making of disciples is an active process in which the church must participate. It is not only a man or two who disciple for a season, but the entire church is to continuously participate in making disciples across the street and around the world. While great glory can come to God by showing a film or handing out tracts, that is not disciple making. If a person raises their hand, comes to the front of the church or says a prayer, the work has only just begun. Disciple making is a hard, lengthy and messy process. Disciples are made, not born. No Christian is given a pass on making disciples and no church exempt from this corporate mandate. Of this verse David Platt preached, "This is huge.

Biblically, to be a disciple is to make disciples. Scripture knows nothing of disciples who aren't making disciples."[12]

Jesus' earthly ministry took place in Israel. Now, his Bride is called to go outside Israel and disciple the whole world. The central focus for the disciples at the time Jesus spoke was to no longer focus only on Israel, but now, include the reaching of the Gentiles. This was a shift from Christ's previous instructions and would have been a great shock to his disciples. To the church today we are to disciple all people groups, all languages and all nations. No people group is to go undiscipled.

Washing and baptizing is a near constant theme throughout all of Scripture. The church in the wilderness was "baptized into Moses" (1Cor 10:2). The post-ascension disciples baptized as they went (Acts 2:38). Paul called for baptism in his epistles (Tit 3:4-7). Baptism is a rite of washing, in the name of the trinity and signifies and seals the covenant of grace. Baptism is the way a new disciple is called to publicly display his relationship with Christ.

Jesus commands the church to teach new disciples, "all that I have commanded." That is a staggering volume of information. While showing films, short-term mission trips and mercy ministry play a part in missions, the reality is teaching God's ways is a long, very labor intensive process. The missions ministries of church planting, discipling and theological education are where this aspect of the Great Commission is to be fulfilled. In relation to the significance this command carries, it is under represented in global outreach.

When should the church stop going to the nations and making disciples by teaching and baptizing them? Until the end of time, or as some have stated, until Jesus returns. Based on this, the Great Commission is something that should keep the church and its disciples busy for a very long time.

The Great Commission is given under the banner of the authority of Jesus Christ. Because Jesus' authority is universal the command must also be thought of as universal. All churches are to go to all people to teach the whole gospel. Charles Spurgeon said of the Great Commission, "This is the perpetual commission of the Church of Christ; and the great seal of the kingdom attached to it, giving the power to execute it, and

---

[12] David Platt, "Commissioned by the King," in David Platt Sermon Archive (Birmingham, AL: David Platt, 2012), 3558.

guaranteeing its success, is the King's Assurance of his continual presence with his faithful followers."[13]

God's Great Commission should not be thought of as optional, but compulsory. Not every church is required to reach every nation, but every church must play a part in discipling the nations. The lost soul across the street will go to the same hell as the lost soul in the jungles of Africa.

The Great Commission is a mandate from a merciful God to his faithful church to disciple the lost by going into the world and baptizing and teaching them to obey his commands. Matthew 28:18-20 requires an obedient church with disciples who are willing to avail themselves for God's glory. The result is the compassion of God spread to the elect.

Luke 9:1-6 - Sending the Twelve

Jesus' twelve disciples had studied at the feet of the Master. They had followed and learned from him. The twelve were not always together at Jesus' side. Some tended to homes and families. In fact, Jesus would call the twelve together only on three occasions. But, on the rare occurrence of Luke 9:1-6 Jesus gathered them together. They had learned enough, it was now time for them to teach others and multiply the faith.

Jesus equipped the twelve to have power over demons and illness and he authorized them to teach in him name. The newly commissioned twelve Apostles would learn from experience how to combat physical, spiritual and emotional hardship. They would learn to trust in and have faith only in the provisions of God.

The calling and the sending of the twelve Apostles would usher in a new era for the young Christian faith. The Apostles served as a model for future evangelists and missionaries. The sending of the twelve Apostles was a pivotal point in Christianity. No longer were Christians focused only on serving, learning and sacrificing for Christ. From this point forward in the history of Christianity being a disciple meant adding a new component; multiplication.

The twelve Apostles did not provide an example for a select group of teachers, preachers or missionaries. The twelve Apostles provided a model for all Christ centered disciples that would be echoed in Matt 28:18-20 and Acts 1:8. The calling and sending of the twelve Apostles was the launch of the spread and the multiplication of Christianity.

---

[13] C. H. Spurgeon, The Gospel of the Kingdom: A Commentary on the Book of Matthew (London: Passmore and Alabaster, 1893), 258.

There were several purposes for the specific call given by Jesus to the twelve in Luke. They were being called in order to be instructed by Christ and learn the qualities needed to be founders of the church following Jesus' resurrection. The twelve Apostles not only performed these miracles during Jesus' life but also following his ascension. Herman Bavinck confirmed, "Accordingly, when he sent out his disciples, he not only charged them to preach the good news but, with equal firmness and emphasis, to cast out evil spirits and to heal every disease and sickness."[14]

This call to the twelve is geographically and ethnically limited to the Jews. Following Acts 1:8 the disciples of Christ were called to go beyond Israel and into the entire world. But, Luke 9:1-6 is the beginning of a new era for the followers of Christ. Christ is no longer seeking attentive students. This call ushers in a period of dynamic involvement. From this point forward Christian disciples are called to share their faith and participate in evangelism and missions to the lost.

The call itself must come from Christ or it carries no authority. When the call came from Jesus the twelve Apostles carried with them both the ability and right to perform their actions and declare Christ as the way.

Without the call originating from Jesus the Apostles are either liars or should be considered mad. No man on his own can perform miracles of healing and control over demons. Shy of a Christ given call the apostles are simply telling a fictional and rather cruel tail of salvation. R.C. Sproul said, "Here we see the apostolic mission sanctioned by Jesus. He called his twelve apostles together, to commission them and to endow them with power and authority to carry out a specific mission."[15]

The twelve disciples who were commissioned as the twelve Apostles were not the most learned, nor the most devout. There is little to indicate they stood out as superior in their faith. They were full of doubts and sins and misunderstanding. But they had everything they needed; they were called by Jesus.

Does the calling of the twelve Apostles simply speak to those twelve men in history or does the call apply to modern missionaries as well? It is indeed both. The twelve Apostles were given very explicit instructions, but modern missionaries have much to learn here as well. Modern missionaries are not called Apostles, but they too should go with a heart

---

[14] Herman Bavinck, John Bolt, and John Vriend, *Reformed Dogmatics: Holy Spirit, Church, and New Creation, vol. 4* (Grand Rapids, MI: Baker Academic, 2008), 428.
[15] R. C. Sproul, *A Walk with God: An Exposition of Luke* (Great Britain: Christian Focus Publications, 1999), 187–188.

dependent upon God and reliant upon his strength and not their own. Modern missionaries can certainly benefit from emulating the faith of the twelve Apostles.

Jesus originally limited the twelve Apostles to Israel. The first phase of his salvific plan would show that a transformed Israel would result in a transformed world. The twelve Apostles gained experience in evangelism and faith that would bear great fruit when they were unleashed upon the rest of the world (Mat 28:18-20; Acts 1:8).

The actions and faith of the twelve Apostles provides a resounding example for all Disciples of Christ to follow. Strong faith, reliance upon God and discipling and mentoring others are not actions for a select few Christians, but for all who proclaim Christ as Lord.

Luke 9:1-6 shows Jesus as a sovereign and compassionate Savior who wills to use common and sinful man as a vessel resulting in the salvation of the elect. There was nothing unique or noteworthy about the twelve Apostles, as there is nothing noteworthy of the disciples who follow Christ today. The twelve Apostles demonstrated a faith and reliance on the Lord that resulted in the conversion of other sinful men. All that is good comes from Christ and is poured out on the world by his obedient disciples.

Acts 1:8 - A Missions Movement

Acts 1:8 is both an outline and a summary of Acts. As John Piper preached, "If I had to pick one sentence out of the book of Acts that would state the theme of the book, I think it would be Acts 1:8." The geographical scope of Acts 1:8 provides a rough outline of the entire book: Jerusalem (1 - 7), Judea and Samaria (8 - 12), the ends of the earth (13 - 28). As such it can well be considered the 'theme' verse of Acts.

In the Gospel of Luke, the narrative points the disciples of Christ to Jerusalem, while Acts begins to point believers away from Jerusalem and out into the world. In Judaism everyone came to Jerusalem, now in Christianity we are being told to leave Jerusalem for the world. In verses 7-8 of Acts 1, Jesus shocks the disciples telling them it is NOT about Jerusalem. It's about the world.

The apostles were being sent out to gather nations. They were being called to bear witness to the saving grace of Jesus Christ. Jesus was instructing them to preach and teach and explain "the Way" to the world. The apostles were to teach the world about Christ, not his teachings or their application in their lives, but the saving Lord. Jesus was sending these men out to preach and was fortifying their knowledge and abilities with the power of the Holy Spirit.

John Calvin said, "We must always see to it that they be adequate and fit to bear the burden imposed upon them, that is, that they be instructed in those skills necessary for the discharge of their office. Thus Christ, when he was about to send out the apostles, equipped them with the arms and tools which they had to have."[16]

Verses 1:1 to 8:3 of Acts is dedicated to the spreading of the gospel within the holy city of Jerusalem. Jerusalem was significant in Jewish history as the unifying capital of the tribes of Israel. The Old Testament pointed to Jerusalem as the location from where the future truth would come. While many viewed this promised coming as a political restoral of Jerusalem, it was indeed the expansion of the witnessing of the gospel of grace.

Today, we are to look at our "Jerusalem" as those individuals living around us. Those souls in our home, our neighborhood, our city and our culture are our Jerusalem. Steve Hughey stated, "Like the early Christians, we should share the Gospel with people nearby who are like us, with friends, relatives and neighbors who live in our own 'Jerusalems.'"[17]

Acts 1:8 next instructs the disciples to witness in Judea and Samaria. Indeed 8:4 to 11:18 of Acts is dedicated to the spreading of the gospel in those regions surrounding Jerusalem.

In this segment of their witness the apostles needed a nudge. Following the martyrdom of Stephen there arose "a great persecution against the church in Jerusalem," and the apostles were, "scattered throughout the regions of Judea and Samaria" (8:1).

Today, we are to see "Judea" as those persons who are similar in culture to us and may include our county or state, while "Samaria" might be considered those of a different culture who live close to us.

Finally, Acts 1:8 instructs the disciples to witness to the "end of the earth." Indeed Acts 11:19 through 28:31 are dedicated to the spreading of the gospel to the rest of the world. The apostles are now called to go beyond known borders and into hostile and unfamiliar cultures. Paul and Barnabas especially encountered people groups with whom they were unfamiliar.

This type of cross-cultural mission work was not a onetime command for only the apostles to obey, but all disciples are called to play a part in being witnesses to foreign

---

[16] John Calvin, *Institutes of the Christian Religion 1 & 2*, ed. John T. McNeill, trans. Ford Lewis Battles, vol. 1, The Library of Christian Classics (Louisville, KY: Westminster John Knox Press, 2011), 1063.

[17] Steve B. Hughey, "Witnesses... Where? The Four Arenas of Mission Involvement." Missio Apostolica 7, no. 1: 49

lands and cultures. The spread of the gospel is to have no limits and leave no land untouched. God's calling for his disciples is to reach all lands and all peoples.

Today, we are to see "the end of the earth" as those persons who occupy different lands and possess different languages and cultures from ours. Modern disciples of Christ are to continue reaching out to the nations with the power of the Holy Spirit.

Luke's work in Acts is centered on receiving power from the Holy Spirit and then witnessing in Jerusalem, Judea, Samaria and to the end of the earth. This is not some fictional tale…this is our call.

These geographical designations must have been a shock to the disciples. Jerusalem? The Lord was crucified there. Judea? They had previously been rejected there. Samaria? Minister to those half-breeds? The ends of the earth? Gentiles too? The words were not only spiritually revolutionary, but socially and ethnically unheard of.

What could be more unnatural than the act of leaving your comfortable home to go to a place you've never been, to speak a language you don't know, to love a people you've never met. Acts 1:8 is not a story of super-disciples, but a story of a bunch of sinners, just like you and me, who through the power given to them by the Holy Spirit, did the unthinkable to glorify their Lord.

Romans 1 & 2 - Without Excuse

Paul, in the first two chapters of Romans, makes it abundantly clear there is a revelation in every man that originates from God. This knowledge of God penetrates our consciousness so suitably that we possess an understanding of the existence of God. God has made himself, his works and his goodness abundantly evident to all mankind. However, the knowledge that God makes accessible to all men does not spell out the Trinity or the saving grace of Jesus. For this saving knowledge we need the gospel.

Paul knew there was an urgent need to bring the gospel to Gentiles, Greeks and barbarians (Rom 1:13-15). He expressed great urgency to share with the wise and foolish. Paul was ordained as the apostle to the Gentiles and felt a special obligation to those who did not know of God. God does not care for class or culture. He desires his message to save his elect, be they outcast or elite, wise or ignorant, Greek or Jew.

Paul was not sharing simple knowledge or trivial information with the lost. Paul's message was bound for the lost and was backed by the power of the God of the Universe. Preaching and disciple making are how God has chosen to reach the world.

God's wrath was righteously shown (Rom 1:18-32) because sinful man suppressed the truth about God. Man embraced an idolatry that led to a moral disintegration of human society.

There exists in the world a moral law of which all men are aware. We are left to the consequences of our freely chosen path and deserve our eternal punishment for knowingly turning away from the Lord. Paul's purpose is to show the whole of humanity is completely and totally depraved and incapable of currying favor with God. Man knows of God, chooses sin and is in desperate need of the Lord's mercy and pardon.

Paul opens chapter two of his letter to the Romans by saying man has no excuses and each one of us will be judged (v. 1-3). Of these first three verses Ronald Blue says God, "does not send people to hell; He lets them go. The judgment of course is for God to make, not other men, no matter how righteous they may seem." It is our own hardened and impenitent hearts that brings upon us God's wrath (v. 5). God shows no partiality toward man, the obedient will be redeemed and the wicked will be punished (v. 6-11). The heart and the conscience of sinners bares testament to the truth of God and our lack of acknowledgement of this calls judgment upon all humans in existence (v. 12-16). Of these five verses in Romans Lewis Johnson stated, "What has been said of the revelation of God in nature may also be said of the second source of the knowledge of God, the revelation of God in conscience."[18]

What about the Sentinelese people of Eastern India, or the Pintupi of Australia, or the Mayoruna of Brazil? What about those who are so remote they have never met a missionary or heard a preacher or read the Bible? Perhaps a remote people group deep the rainforest did the best they could. They worshiped a statue or the sun or the earth. Aren't those things really God by another name? No, worshiping statues and celestial bodies is what we are at our core, idolaters. That is man worshiping the created instead of the Creator.

What happens to the innocent person in the middle of the African jungle who has never heard about Jesus Christ? The reality is the innocent person goes to heaven. Unfortunately, there are no innocent people in the world, and there has never been one, save Jesus. All man has rightfully earned an eternity in hell separated from the love of God. If there were innocent people in the jungles, they would have no need to hear the gospel. That, however, is why we must go to them, and share the good news.

---

[18] S. Lewis Johnson, Jr., "Paul and the Knowledge of God," Bibliotheca Sacra, 129:513 (January 1972): 73.

Disciples of Christ must continue to be mobilized by local churches and ordained by the Lord to enter the frontiers that stand as barriers to complete gospel penetration into the entire world. God has so willed man's active participation in spreading his merciful call to the lost.

Charles Spurgeon was posed the question regarding the unreached heathen. "Someone asked, 'Will the heathen who have never heard the Gospel be saved?' Spurgeon responded, 'It is more a question with me whether we who have the Gospel and fail to give it to those who have not can be saved.'"[19] It is not possible to avoid an eternity in hell apart from embracing Jesus. This fact should stir us to action for the lost of the world.

Will those who have never heard the gospel be lost? Indeed, they will. Their separation from God throughout eternity will have been caused by the fact that they have sinned against God and they had not been taught of his grace. Because they were not taught they were unable to benefit from Christ's plan for salvation. All mankind was offered the free gift of God to reconcile them in a covenant relationship with the Creator. For those of us who embrace the gospel, the burden falls on us to share the truth with those who do not know.

Corinth - Instruction on Missions

In Paul's letters to the Corinthian church he desired the believers to be enthusiastic about the expansion of the gospel. In Paul's time, Corinth was located in an ideal geographic location to spread the new faith. A vibrant and mission minded church located in Corinth could easily use the heavily traveled trade route to speed the gospel throughout the world.

Paul's letters to the church in Corinth provided a clear missions parameter for both the young church and believers today. Paul called the Corinthians to send, train and provide for missionaries so they could spread the fragrance of the knowledge of God everywhere (2 Cor 2:14).

The call to be a fulltime servant and preacher of the gospel was not to be taken lightly. Paul told the Corinthians as Christ called them to share his wisdom to other lands, the Holy Spirit would empower them with the strength of the message itself.

The members of the young Corinthian church were concerned. How could these novices of the faith share such a significant message? Paul assured the Corinthians with

---

[19] T.W. Essex, *Obeying the Great Commission* (Bloomington, IN: CrossBooks, 2011), 25.

the example of himself. He instructed the new believers they should imitate him as he imitated Christ (1 Cor 4:16-17, 11:1-2).

Paul showed the Corinthians how God desired to work through their weakness for his own glory. Could God be glorified by the labors of the fractured church in Corinth? If God could use Paul and Apollos to work in conjunction to advance the gospel (1 Cor 3:5-15) he could certainly use the Corinthian church. As servants of Christ we are to go as we are called and proclaim God's victory over darkness.

The message the followers of Christ are to deliver is simple. It is outlined in scripture and is a perfect message prepared by God. Deliverers of the true gospel will lack in nothing they need to convey the message of salvation (1 Cor 1:7). Paul outlined to the church in Corinth the message is far more important than the messenger. The messengers may need to bend like a reed in the wind, but the truth must take precedence (1 Cor 9:19-23).

The gospel message is perfect and needs no help from us. The missionary should never preach more than what is written (1 Cor 4:6). In the first three chapters of his first letter to the Corinthians, Paul focused greatly on the point of the sufficiency of scripture. He warned the message barer to rely only on the message and not to become puffed up or conceited by their own abilities. It is a central point in preaching and teaching for us to recall we are only messengers and we should only focus on the humble deliverance of God's perfect Word.

The fulltime minister of the gospel has given himself for the advancement and glory of Jesus Christ. It falls upon his brothers in the faith to care for and facilitate his service. A cheerful servant brings great glory to Christ as he serves without grumbling. So too, the brothers in the faith bring great glory to Christ as they give sacrificially to make possible that fulltime service. While a laboring Ox should be fed and a temple servant should be cared for from the temple, so too a missionary should be aided by his brothers in the faith (1 Cor 9:8-14).

In Paul's second letter to the church at Corinth he became more insistent on sacrificial giving to support others in need and others busy in fulltime service of God's work. Paul told the Corinthians how their generosity to the believers in Jerusalem multiplied the grace of God in their lives. To the great glory of God, Paul also praised the generous giving of the Macedonian brothers (2 Cor 8:1-15).

Paul told the Corinthians they were not only to give financially in support of fulltime ministers of the gospel, but they were to help through prayer. Paul desired to have many brothers praying for missions work (2 Cor 1:11). Praying in the name of God that missionaries would have all they need to glorify God greatly honors our Father.

The Corinthians were also instructed by Paul to rejoice in the coming of future servants of Christ and to give recognition to such men (1 Cor 16:17-18). This seemingly odd command is echoed in other writings of Paul (1 Thes 5:12-13 and Phil 2:29). Indeed, the fulltime servants of the gospel are worthy of our gratitude.

Paul's letters to the church in Corinth provided plain instruction for the young church and also for believers today. Paul called the Corinthians to send, train and provide for the needs of missionaries, preachers and other fulltime servants for the Lord. When William Carey, famed 19th century missionary, volunteered to serve in India, he implored those who sent him, "but remember that you must hold the ropes." Paul calls missionaries to go, but he implored both the Corinthian church and modern Christian churches to hold the rope and support fulltime servants of the gospel of Jesus Christ.

Revelation - Missiological Imperative

Reaching the nations with the salvific gospel of Jesus Christ is at the heart of Scripture. Our Messiah came to earth not simply to save the lost, but to crush the enemy and march his disciples toward a glorious homecoming and resounding triumph.

It is clear how the story ends. God reigns forever and ever in the new heaven and new earth. Revelation pulls back the curtain and allows all to see the spiritual battle ragging all around us. As the warfare continues, people from every nation must participate before the glorious conclusion takes place. The great deceiver of nations will ultimately be bound. But, first the church must reach and convert people from all nations until the earth is filled with the knowledge of the glory of the Lord (Hab 2:14).

The word "nations" appears 23 times in the 22 chapters of the Book of Revelation, more than any other book in the New Testament. Revelation also has much to say about people, languages and tribes. By God's great design he has called his disciples to go into all the nations (Acts 1:8) and make disciples and teach his way (Mat 28:18-20). There is still much work to be done.

Revelation makes clear God's passion for all the nations and the lengths to which he will go to ensure people from all tongues and cultures will worship him. Christ has authority over the nations (2:26, 13:7) and died for all the nations (5:9). Revelation informs us Christ will rule over the nations (12:5, 19:15) and he is the king of all the nations (15:3). God has a great plan to protect all the nations (20:3).

Our Father is an equal opportunity lover of sinners. He does not favor any one tongue or geography, but loves his elect who come from all races, cultures and tribes. Our Creator desires to be worshiped and will succeed in having himself glorified in prayer and song from around the globe.

The beautiful thing about reading Revelation is we know how the story ends. God's disciples are victorious. Scripture leaves no doubt. People from every nation will be present at the end (7:9). The gospel will be proclaimed to all the nations (14:6) and all nations will worship (15:4) our Father. All cultures have sinned and are in need of Christ (18:3). Satan, the deceiver of the nations (20:8), has succeeded in turning man toward the things of the world. But, soon, the trappings of the world will no longer deceive all nations (18:23). The nations will be guided (21:24), and the nations will be healed (22:2).

All the cultures of the world will believe, but they must first hear and in order to hear someone must be sent to preach (Rom 10:14-15). The victory march to our real home must first begin with missionaries marching away from their earthly homes. Indeed, our side wins in the end. But, the same book which informs us of our victory also tells us that victory is not secured until every nation is reached and representatives from every nation are worshiping Christ. As we move closer to the conclusion of the Book of Revelation, what we know for certain is our churches still have much work to do.

God's Great Commission is not over. There are still many nations to be reached. Christian missionaries have not been sent into the world to serve as an occupying force, but a divinely commissioned army (Joel 2:11) sent to liberate those imprisoned by Satan. Until all God's elect have been freed, the church's Special Forces must continue to be trained, dispatched and their ranks replenished.

Today, over 6,000 of the world's 16,000 known people groups are still considered unreached. Over 40% of the seven billion people living today are unreached. The Bible has only been translated into 550 languages, yet there are over 4,500 known language which have more than 1,000 speakers. An estimated three billion people have never heard the gospel of Christ. And, over 80% of non-Christians in the world say they do not personally know a Christian.

If Revelation is so very clear the victory will come only when all nations are worshiping our Lord, and there are still so many people who do not even know his name, the Bride of Christ must act with greater urgency. Jesus does not need his disciples to reach the unreached, but in his great wisdom and for his great glory he has chosen to use our sinful vessels as a means to take his name to every tribe and every tongue.

The Book of Revelation is about a ragging battle and a resounding victory. God's triumph and our joy are inevitable. Revelation reminds the corporate body of Christ we still have much work ahead of us. Christ has called his churches to reach out to the nations and has promised us this broken world will continue until we have brought him greater glory by reaching the nations with his perfect word.

Chapter Two

Missions in your Home Church

The Christian church was always intended to be the mechanism by which God would call the lost to himself. The church, as the Bride of Christ, is perfect. The sinner which make her up are not. For some odd reason beyond reckoning God chose to use saved sinners to spread his salvific gospel to the lost. It frequently seems the rocks and trees could do a better job than we do, yet, God loves to use his imperfect disciples to take his name to the nations.

The modern Christian church was founded, only to sanctify existing Christian, but to train those Christians to go out into the streets and across the globe to find and disciple the lost. Through the ages, the occupants of God's church have become more focused on self-improvement and less focused on our mandate to reach the world for God's glory.

The church of Christ must return to its origins and send its congregants out into the messy world to reach the lost in the name of Christ. Too few Christians have the training or inclination to obey God's command to disciple the lost. Evangelism, missions, and outreach are viewed as tasks for specially gifted Christians, not mandates for all Christians. The Christian church must take center stage in training and sending the elect to glorify God by reaching the lost.

Launching a Missions Movement in Your Church

Many churches have, what they view as, great excuses for not being involved in global outreach and missions. Our church is too old, too young, too poor, too new, spread too thin, or just not ready. Another common reason churches are not involved in missions is failing to understand that involvement in missions is a biblical imperative. Scripture mandates local churches and their members to glorify the Lord by sharing his grace, mercy and truth with the lost across the street and around the world.

Acts 1:8 tells us we must share the gospel in our town and around the world. Matthew 28:18-20 commands us to go to all nations and make disciples. Jeremiah 22:3

tells us to show justice to the orphan and the widow. Isaiah 58:10 says we are to feed the hungry. Missions is important for the spiritual growth of Christian disciples and for the expansion of the kingdom.

If your church is one of the many that is not involved in global outreach here are a few ideas for you and your church leadership to prayerfully consider:

From the pulpit and in all your Sunday school classes begin teaching about what Scripture says about missions and serving the poor. Allow your congregation to be educated on the importance of glorifying the Lord through service. Many churches sacrifice teaching on the eternal wellbeing of others to make room for teaching that emphasizes temporary personal joy. Lesslie Newbigin said, "Mission is an acted out doxology. That is its deepest secret. Its purpose is that God may be glorified."[20] The church is a place to educate, instruct, and prepare its members to impact the world and share God's love, mercy, and message. Our purpose in the church is to make disciples for Jesus Christ and teach them to make disciples.

During your weekly services begin to pray for the missionaries you know. Pray as a congregation for several missionaries by name. Include missions ministries in your prayer bulletin and during all prayer times. A.B Simpson said, "Prayer is the mighty engine that is to move the missionary work."[21] If you don't know the names of missionaries ask your denomination or neighboring churches.

Invite a missionary to come talk about their ministry at your church and host them for a lunch. Allow Sunday school classes to ask questions of the missionary. Invite a missionary to preach on missions. When missionaries come visit your church thank them and honor them in front of the congregation. Charles Spurgeon said, "If God has fit you to be a missionary, I would not have you shrivel down to be a king." Cover the cost the missionary incurs visiting you. Plan a missions conference and invite several missionaries.

Get out in your community and have your church serve the poor where you live. Organize volunteer efforts for your church at senior centers, food closets, AIDS projects, or women's shelters. If your church isn't spreading the Gospel to the lost across the street and around the world, your church doesn't understand the Gospel. George Miley said, "Let's take God's global mission and put it right in the middle of the local church!" The lost seldom stumble into our churches on their own. Christians are mandated to enter the world and visit the lost where they live.

---

[20] Lesslie Newbigin, *The Gospel in a Pluralistic Society* (Grand Rapids: Eerdmans, 1989), 116, 127.
[21] Daniel L. Akin and Bruce Riley Ashford, *I Am Going* (Nashville, TN: B&H Publishing Group, 2016), 73.

Begin to financially support missionaries and missions organizations. Provide your congregation with opportunities to sew, collect baby clothes, donate food, or financially support a missionary on their own. John Piper said, "All the money needed to send and support an army of self-sacrificing, joy-spreading ambassadors is already in the church." Did God make U.S. churches the richest in history so they could buy new cushions for their pews or to spread the gospel around the world?

Contact your denomination or a non-denominational Christian missions agency and inquire about opportunities to send a short-term mission team next summer. Collect information on how high school and college students can be missions interns. F.B. Meyrer said, "The church which is not a missionary church will be a missing church when Jesus comes."[22] Organize several annual missions trips and make them regular events at your church.

Ask your congregants to prayerfully consider moving on the mission field. Encourage them to dramatically alter their lives and serve Christ in the world. Mike Stachura said, "The mark of a great church is not its seating capacity, but its sending capacity." Challenge your church to take a drastic step of faith to glorify God. The church is in greater danger by being safe than it is in taking risks to evangelize the lost.

Missions and global outreach can be hard for individuals and congregations to understand. Began to transform the DNA of your church and facilitate their growth. Foster a radical heart for the world in your congregation. The gospel doesn't teach us how to better love ourselves, we do that just fine. Instead, the gospel teaches us how to better love the world.

Preaching and Teaching Missions in our Churches

Missions are the bedrock of the Scriptures. It is hard to open a Bible and not land on a page with missionaries. Abram, Esther, Daniel, John the Baptist, Jesus, Philip, Paul, Aquila and Priscilla, and Apollos all provide examples of obedient servants who took the grace and mercy of God to other cultures. Sharing the gospel with the world and serving the poor are two of the most common themes in the Bible. They must be important to God. Therefore, they should be important to us. Ralph Winter, late missiologist and

---

[22] Paul Lee Tan, *Encyclopedia of 7700 Illustrations: Signs of the Times* (Garland, TX: Bible Communications, Inc., 1996), 813.

missionary said, "The Bible is not the basis of missions; missions is the basis of the Bible."[23]

In many churches missions is not being proclaimed with great frequency or intensity. While the Bible is full of God's passion for the nations, many of our Sunday school classes and pulpits don't share God's enthusiasm for global outreach. The church is charged with providing us God's truths by the reading of Scripture (Acts 15:21, Rev 1:3) and sound preaching (2Ti 4:2) from the pulpit. And, it is the church that is charged with teaching (Acts 1:41-42, Mat 28:18-20) its congregants God's Word.

The church is a place to educate, prepare, and instruct its members how to share God's love, mercy, and message. Canadian Pastor Oswald Smith said, "The supreme task of the Church is the evangelization of the world."[24] But, if the congregants in many of our churches seldom hear this, how are they to fulfill God's calling.

If the Bible is full of missions and our churches are instructed to teach the Bible, why is there so little discussion of missions in our churches? Our home churches must teach our brothers and sisters the vital importance of a global-centered gospel. Evangelical churches must have a passion for training and sending their people around the world. Our purpose in the church is to make disciples for Jesus Christ and teach them to make disciples.

Too often pastors and church leaderships focus on the number of people in their pews at the peril of educating and sending congregants out. If your church isn't spreading the Gospel to the lost across the street and around the world, your church doesn't understand the Gospel. The lost seldom stumble into our churches on their own. Christians are mandated to enter the world and visit the lost where they live. The purpose of the local church is to prepare their congregants to go out into the world and share the perfect message of Christ.

The church is in greater danger by being safe than it is in taking risks to evangelize the lost. It is sad how in recent years the words sacrifice, martyr and submission have become less popular and considered more extreme in our churches. Did God make U.S. churches the richest in history so they could buy new cushions for their pews or to spread the gospel around the world? God has called our churches to send their well-trained members into harms way. Too few disciples of Christ have been trained with a heart that is willing to sacrifice all for the Lord. John Mott, author of The Evangelization of the

---

[23] Lars Kirkhusmo Pharo, *Concepts of Conversion* (Berlin: De Gruyter, 2018), 9.
[24] David Shibley, *Great for God* (Green Forest, AR: New Leaf Press, 2012), 91.

World in this Generation said, "The greatest hindrances to the evangelization of the world are those within the church."[25]

In order to embrace our calling many of our modern churches need to reform their teaching and involvement with missions. Our churches must expand their enthusiasm for God's Great Commission.

Let's begin to teach about global evangelism in our churches. Make it a priority in the pulpit. Forget relegating missions to one weekend a year. If we teach and preach exegetically through the Bible, missions will become a weekly topic in our sermons and Sunday school classes.

Churches need to challenge their congregants out of their comfort zone. Let your people know that you want to train up and send their children around the world and into harms way. Encourage individuals to dedicate their lives to fulltime service. Mike Stachura said, "The mark of a great church is not its seating capacity, but its sending capacity."[26]

Send your church into your own community and serve the elderly, homeless, AIDS patients, drug addicts and prostitutes. Train your congregation through short-term missions in the US and around the world. Get your hands dirty. We are called by Scripture to serve the poor and care for the needy.

Encourage your congregation to be different than the world. There is nothing logical, from an earthly perspective, about giving your time, money and life to a people group that cannot repay you. Christian disciples must learn from a young age we are called to show God's grace and mercy to the least deserving. Martyn Lloyd-Jones said, "The glory of the gospel is that when the church is absolutely different from the world, she invariably attracts it."[27]

As it was always intended, the local Christian church is a training ground for instructing and preparing followers of Christ to glorify their Father in the world. Be it across the street or around the globe churches should be sending their members into the world to reclaim the lost for Christ.

---

[25] John R. Mott, *The Evangelization of the World in This Generation* (New York, NY: Student Volunteer Movement For Foreign Missions, 1900), 49.

[26] Robert S. Miller, *Survival Handbook For Young Pastors* (Camarillo, CA: Xulon Press, 2009), 146.

[27] John R. W. Stott and John R. W. Stott, *The Message of the Sermon on the Mount* (Matthew 5-7): Christian Counter-Culture, The Bible Speaks Today (Leicester; Downers Grove, IL: InterVarsity Press, 1985), 60.

Toward a Missional Ecclesiology

Many in the modern Western church misconstrue missions and evangelism as simply another program in the church. The academic and secular worlds view missions as imperialistic and condemn missional activities as an imposition of religious beliefs and Western values. The discussion of missions must move away from both modern secular and Christian misconceptions and into the essential understanding that a missional church is at the core of Christian theology. A missional ecclesiology helps Christians understand what it means to be evangelical. Having a better grasp of Christ's mandate that his church is to be missional will help Christians comprehend the foundational purpose of the church.

God's inerrant Scriptures tell a story of how the Lord desired to set apart his early covenant people to make them holy examples of his love and justice. The Bible goes onto explain how God no longer desired to separate the elect from the world, but to send his church to the nations to share his grace and mercy with the lost through the gospel. The entirety of Scripture attests to a missional ecclesiology.

The covenant of works was ushered in under Adam and outlined in the Pentateuch. Abraham was sent out (Gen 12) into the world to raise up a nation. As that nation was born and then fled Egypt God focused on strengthening his elect and making them holy. The Law was clearly designed to set Israel apart and draw the world to them instead of sending them into the world (see food law Lev. 11). As God's people grew in faith and prospered the Lord sent them to neighboring nations to show God's majesty and share his name with other cultures (Ps 67; Jonah). Still, Israel was kept separate from the world.

Jesus removed the aspects of the Law that had isolated Israel and provided instruction for God's people. Jesus selected, trained and sent out the 12 Apostles (Luk 9:1-6) to tell of the gospel of Christ. Jesus then mandated his church to go into the world (Mat 28:18-20) to disciple, baptize and teach the lost. Charles Spurgeon said of this passage, "This is the perpetual commission of the Church of Christ; and the great seal of the kingdom attached to it, giving the power to execute it, and guaranteeing its success, is the King's Assurance of his continual presence with his faithful followers."[28]

Acts 1:8 is the turning point of covenant theology as before this verse all of God's people were called to Jerusalem, now God's disciples are mandated to leave Jerusalem and

---

[28] C. H. Spurgeon, "The Drawings of Love," in *The Metropolitan Tabernacle Pulpit Sermons, vol. 63* (London: Passmore & Alabaster, 1917), 204.

go into the world. Howard Marshal said, "Acts is a book about mission. It is not unfair to take 1:8 as a summary of its contents. The purpose of the Christian church was to bear witness to Jesus."[29] The rest of Acts and Paul's letters to the Corinthians sets up a mandate and outline for Christ's church to send disciple making disciples into the world and for the church to care for and encourage those laborers. Romans chapters 1 and 2 then highlight the urgency of a missional ecclesiology by explaining the lost will perish without receiving the gospel of Jesus Christ.

Understanding God's Scriptures means understanding the systematic approach God had in identifying his people, setting them apart, training them and then sending them out to disciple the lost. God's purpose for his church is missions.

As the Christian faith spread, in its early years, from the East to the West the focus of the church began to shift. Missions stopped being a priority of the church when Christianity went from being an outlaw faith to being allowed within Western culture.

The me-centered consumer culture of the modern West altered Christianity even further. The focus of the modern church in the West is now on the care and cultivation of its members. The church has fundamentally moved away from a body whose purpose is the reaching of the lost with the gospel, into an entity that is centered around the growth and experiences of the individual Christian.

In modern Western Christianity, we have lost sight of the purpose of the church as outlined in its history and Scriptures. Darrell Guder states, "A reductionist soteriology did generate a reductionist vision of mission and a highly compromised understanding of the purpose of the church."[30] The reason the Christian church exists is to reach the lost where they are, around the corner or across the globe. The motivation for the church is to spread God's glory.

The Christian church in the West has gone drastically off course and forgotten its true purpose. It is, however, not too late to correct course and regain the biblically faithful purpose of the church. It is up to pastors and church leaders to refocus their teaching on a missional ecclesiology and it is incumbent upon disciples of Christ to alter their hearts and live their lives as living sacrifices (Rom 12:1).

The modern evangelical church is the richest church in history. Today our Western congregations enjoy a flood of resources. Churches have theological training, talent and

---

[29] I. Howard Marshall, *Acts: An Introduction and Commentary, vol. 5*, Tyndale New Testament Commentaries (Downers Grove, IL: InterVarsity Press, 1980), 25.
[30] Darrell L. Guder, "The Church As Missional Community" *The Community of the Word, eds. Mark Husbands and Daniel Treier*, (Downers Grove, IL: InterVarsity Press, 2005), 120.

financial blessings never seen before. Our churches must not assume those resources have been given by God for our own safety and comfort, but to spread his gospel around the world and across the street. God outlined in Scripture a plan for his post-ascension church to exist for the purpose of multiplication and reaching the lost. The purpose of the evangelical church is to embrace a missional ecclesiology.

Should my Church Invest in a Missionary or a National Worker?

Today, evangelical churches in the United States are the wealthiest churches in the 2,000-year history of Christianity. No, disciples of God have ever been more blessed with resources. This does not mean these churches wish to waste that which God has called them to be stewards over.

God's mission for his church is for her to go into the world and multiply. Be it around the world or across the street, the church is to train its members and send them into the world to make disciples, baptize, and teach God's ways.

Many churches which are obedient to God's call to reach the nations want to also be good stewards of God's resources. Many churches grapple with the concept that it may be more cost effective to send money to support foreign pastors than to send western missionaries. Funding one foreign pastor is cheaper than sending one missionary, but is it more effective?

If a missionary is sent by a church or missions agency there will likely be western forms of accountability built into the relationship. Budgets, financial accounting, timely written updates, periodic verbal reports, leadership structure, and more. The missionary is held accountable to the senders and the senders are accountable to the missionary. Frequently, when funding a foreign partner, there are neither similar mechanisms nor expectations in place.

There are simply too many bad stories out there about how a national pastor used western resources differently than agreed upon. The rest of the world simply has a different perspective on money and relationships than do churches in the West. Our cultural biases cloud our understanding of the expectations of a financial agreement. Not every culture shares our institutional standards of checks and balances.

The western theological training is simply superior to that of many other countries. A church generally understands they are sending a biblical literate missionary when they send a missionary trained in a western seminary. Seminaries and theological resources simply don't exist in the rest of the world like the do in the West.

It has been said that there are 5 million pastors outside the United States. Only 15% whom have quality theological education. In the U.S., the ratio of trained pastors to people is 1:230. In the rest of the world the ratio of trained pastors to people is 1:450,000. The global church can greatly benefit from the West sending its theologically trained missionaries.

A trusting relationship is definitely possible without the common cultural norms of language, a shared history, and a similar world view. But, it is much easier to build an ongoing relationship with a missions partner who shares similar cultural understandings as those who sent him. Some expectations and nuances are understood by members of a similar culture, which may be lost on working with a foreigner.

National churches should be taught to be dependent on God, not foreign money. When a national pastor or worker is paid from western purses the national church is not learning the joy of sacrificial giving. Foreign money can create rivalry and unhealthy competition among foreign churches. Sending money is an example foreign churches can't replicate. Our western churches should strive to develop fraternal relationships where we are equal partners with national churches, not situations where our churches are the patriarchs.

Scripture is clear that the Christian church should be a sending church. Simply sending money robs the sending church of the joy of sending from their own ranks. A missionary going from a local congregation is a blessing to those who send him. Sending churches learn to be part of God's call to evangelize by watching the obedience of one of their own. The local church must realize that simply sending money is not a complete fulfillment of God's Great Commission to go, make disciples, baptize, and teach.

One of the key callings of any missionary should be to train national partners to do their job. A missionary is in a great position to train numerous nationals to do their work. A single western missionary has the resources and the education to train and disciple dozens of national partners to serve their own culture. Western missionaries can greatly benefit foreign churches by teaching their pastors and church leaders. This is not only a wise use of resources, but enables the nationals with the skills they need to glorify God.

If a missionary from the West has prayed, sought counsel, and concluded they are called to serve in another culture, their calling should be honored. Certainly, that does not mandate all Christians are obligated to support them. It does mean they should be encouraged and prayed for. God continues to call missionaries from the West. That means God is still calling churches from the West to support those missionaries through prayer and financial support.

This polemic should not be perceived as a call for western evangelical churches to only support missionaries and not nationals. There can be a healthy blending of supporting our own missionaries and national pastors. At this time in Christian history God has seen fit to provide western churches with an abundance of resources and biblically trained men and women. It would be wise for our churches to share those resources and send our abled bodied missionaries to help train and prepare churches in other cultures to send out their own pastors, evangelists, and missionaries.

Missions: Churches Should Go Deeper Not Wider

Like many families, churches are trying to balance their monthly budgets and make those valuable dollars stretch in a way that best honors God. Churches that are involved in missions want to make a huge impact in global outreach and be good stewards of God's resources. As churches explore expanding their involvement in missions, the world map in the church lobby all too often becomes the benchmark for a successful missions ministry. Churches support missionaries so they can put pins in more countries or have a missionary on each continent.

Frequently you will see churches supporting ten, twenty or thirty missionaries at a small monthly amount. Missions involvement for most churches is a mile wide and an inch deep. Making a broad impact is nice, but making a deep impact would result in greater influence and bring greater glory to God. Churches that support 30 missionaries at a low level should prayerfully consider reducing their number of supported missionaries down to three to five and really dive deep into their ministries and lives.

When investing more substantively into fewer missionaries a church and its leadership will truly get to know their missionary partners. As that relationship and trust grow a church can care for the needs of the missionaries they support like they would care for their own congregants. Missionaries are more prone to be honest and forthright with supporters they genuinely know. The vast majority of missionaries are not cared for by a church family, not even their home church. They have few people to turn to when a missionary is in need. A church that has deeply invested in a missionary can share the grace and mercy of Christ with them.

Churches should continue to send short-term teams and interns, if that is what the ministry needs. In addition church leadership should consider visiting the missionaries on their turf for a "house call." Spend time doing neglected chores on the missionary's home, babysit the kids, do the grocery shopping and counsel the missionaries. Get to know your missionaries in their environment. Walk in their shoes for a few days or a week. Love your missionaries how they need to be loved.

As your church continues to visit the same ministry site, year after year, your congregation will get to know the national partners. By better understanding the culture and the people you will have a greater passion for them and their needs. It will benefit both your home church and the national church to view each other in a fraternal relationship instead a paternal one.

Over time and through regular contact you can have a more substantive impact on the ministry with which you partner. You honestly get to know the missionaries and ministries and can be viewed more like a partner and less like an ATM. If you go deeper you are creating a truly substantive, cross-cultural partnership. The depth benefits the missionary's ministry and the spiritual growth of your congregation. Everyone begins to understand what it means to be a global Christian.

If you spend time with your missionary partners once every few years, at furlough, or once a year, during short-term mission trips, a substantive relationship will not be created. Without substance your missionaries will not open up to you and you cannot help them with their spiritual health. Call your missionaries on their VOIP phone. Almost every missionary has one and it is not an international call for you. Send them an e-mail to let them know the church prayed for them today. Remember their birthdays and anniversaries with electronic gift cards. Help them fund a small vacation or new electronics. You can help your missionaries heal.

A larger financial contribution from your church to your missionaries will ensure two important things: 1) Their need to find fewer supporters meaning they travel less during furlough, and 2) If they have fewer supporters they may visit your church for a couple of weeks instead of just one Sunday every four years. Many missionaries have twenty or thirty supporting churches and dozens of supporting individuals. Nobody can keep in contact with that many ministry partners. A missionary with just a small number of large financial partners can invest more deeply in those relationships.

When churches support missionaries and international ministries by writing a small check once a month neither the church nor the missionaries truly receive a substantive benefit from that relationship. A generous investment of time, energy and finances into a missionary or global ministry helps the missionary feel connected and helps the church grow in their understanding of God's Great Commission.

As part of this increased investment churches must insist on reciprocation from the missionaries with whom they partner. No longer can churches tolerate missionaries who do not communicate and interact with church partners. Missionaries should communicate and churches should demand it. There is no excuse, in the 21st Century, for not receiving regular contact from your missionary partners.

When a more substantive relationship is formed the church, the missionaries and the nationals all benefit. Above all else, God receives greater glory from churches and missionaries who are connected and healthy.

Are your Congregants Ready for Missions?

Christian disciples have been unequivocally called to participate in global evangelism. God sent his son to pay the penalty for our disobedience. If that gift was for you and you name Jesus as your personal Savior you have been instructed to share that good news with others. The church has been instructed to prepare Christians, and send them across the street and around the world to disciple, teach and baptize the lost. How many Christian churches are avoiding this mandate and how many Christians have not been sufficiently instructed what is required of us all?

The Great Commission is not a call for every Christian to leave comfort and safety and travel to far off lands to disciple, teach and baptize. The call to make disciples is a corporate mandate in which your church must be involved. Is your church shirking its responsibilities? Are there people in your church who do not evangelize, pray for missionaries or support missions because they have not been properly trained and instructed? Many of our pastors and church leaders are ignoring Christ's final call to his disciples to the detriment of God's glory. The church has been instructed by Jesus to disciple the lost in their own cities, surrounding communities and around the world. Has your church told you about this obligation?

Indeed, God's Great Commission is a mandate given by Jesus to his church. Many Christian disciples use that fact to justify ignoring the lost. Let's make something clear, friendship evangelism is valid concept, but most people use it as an excuse to avoid sharing the gospel. The statement, "I share my faith through my life," would be wonderful if not for one, minor detail: you are a sinner. Nobody wants to see your life. Sinners need to see Jesus, not some sinner. Besides, I know what sins are in my own heart. I doubt my sins will drive many non-Christians to Christ.

Share the gospel of Jesus Christ. Not every Christian is called to travel to another culture, but every Christian is called to play an active part in taking the gospel to the lost.

If you are not actively discipling and teaching the lost, you must be fervently praying for and supporting those who are. In addition, what about the lost in your hometown? You don't need a passport to reach them.

Your pastor and church leadership should be explaining Scripture requires disciples of Christ to be involved in active Christian multiplication. When is the last time your pastor, Sunday school teacher, or small group taught about sharing the gospel with the lost? This is the purpose of the church. If your church has not been teaching you this imperative, you need to loving and respectfully have a private conversation with your church leadership. Too often churches feel their purpose is the care and nurturing of those already saved. The purpose of the church is multiplication. If your church is not teaching you the biblical mandate to multiply and not encouraging you to disciple and teach God's ways, they are not teaching the whole Bible.

Evangelism should not be thought of as a church growth exercise. Missions presentations need to happen more frequently than once every few years. The primary purpose of a pastor and church leaders is to train their congregants in Scripture and send them into the world. If your congregation isn't clamoring to become missionaries, evangelize their neighbors or share the gospel with their friends you are not teaching them all of Scripture.

Encourage, facilitate and pray those who sit under your teaching will leave the comfortable confines of your church and go out into the messy world and visit the lost where they live. Pray God will use your ministry to prepare missionaries, evangelists, and preachers who are willing to give their lives for the spreading of the gospel of Jesus Christ. If your congregants don't feel uncomfortable when hearing your preaching and teaching, you aren't doing it right. The gospel is offensive to the world and unpleasant for those not fully committed. God's vision for his church, the one with which he has entrusted you, is that it will produce disciples who ache to share the gospel with the unsaved.

If you are a pastor or church leader and you are still reading these words let me be the first to thank you, on behalf of your congregation. If these words are hard to read, it is likely because they are true of your ministry. I pray the sting is relieved by the liberation of praying God changes your ministry. If you are angry with your humble author, he is ok with that. I would rather know I shared God's truth and lost your approval, than remained silent and gained friends.

Training your congregants to love Jesus enough to leave the known for the unknown is not easy. Sending your best and brightest into the world is hard. It is my prayer you have the type of ministry where nobody is surprised to hear you stand up on Sunday and say, "Welcome to our church. We are glad to have you here. If you are a new we want to inform you, our primary purpose is to train your babies and send across the world, to some far-off land, so they can glorify Jesus in their life and death." May God be so glorified by your ministry.

A Ministry of Prayer for Missions

The most frequently told lie in the modern western church is, "I'll pray for you." Prayer has morphed from a powerful, God-honoring and intimate activity to a cliché Christians use when they don't know what else to say. Certainly there are Christians who really mean it and who really do pray. But, are we praying for our missionaries like we promised them we would or are we giving them lip service?

Christian churches and individual Christian disciples have partnered with brothers and sisters in Christ and promised to pray for them while they are advancing God's kingdom in other cultures. The Great Commission (Mat 28-18-20) is a corporate mandate and not an individual calling. Don't mistake a mandate for the church as permission to personally ignore your prayer for missions. The church sends missionaries, but while individual Christians are either goers or senders. If the missionary is holding up their end of the deal, it is incumbent on those you stay behind to dedicate themselves to prayer for missionaries. Frequent, informed, and passionate prayer brings glory to God, gets the person praying more involved in missions and benefits our missionary partners.

God calls his disciples to make our requests known to him in prayer (Phil 4:60). If we are seeking God's glory, God will provide us what we need (Ps 34:17; Mt 21:22; Mrk 11:24; Luk 11:9; Jhn 15:7; Jam 4:3). Disciples of Christ are to constantly be in prayer (Eph 6:18; 1 Thes 5:17). Even if we don't know for what to pray God will guide us (Rom 8:26). We are to ask for help (Jam 4:3), thank God for his provision (Col 4:2) and know our prayers bring glory to God (Jhn 14:13).

Prayer for the nations and for missionary workers exists throughout Scripture. Solomon prayed all nations would dedicate themselves to God (1 Kng 8:43). David prayed the nations would worship God (Ps 86:9). Isaiah prayed the whole earth would praise God (Isa 42:10-12). Luke said the church prayed for missionaries in distress (Acts 12:5). Paul asked churches to pray for the boldness (Eph 6:19) and opportunity (Col 4:3) in missions and regularly asked churches to pray for missionary work (Phil 1:19, 2; Cor 1:11; Rom 15:30; Phm 22).

In your church and in your family adopt a posture of prayer for missions. Schedule prayer and use frequent reminders to prompt you and others to pray. Don't be slavish or legalistic, but make your commitment to pray for missionaries as profound as the missionaries' call to go. Charles Spurgeon said, "I know of no better thermometer to your spiritual temperature than this, the measure of the intensity of your prayer."[31]

In your home, print out and post missionary prayer letters on the refrigerator. Involve the whole family in regular and frequent prayer for your missionary partners. Remember to pray for your missionary on holidays, birthdays, and anniversaries. Sometimes those are the hardest times for a missionary.

Make prayer for missions part of your church's DNA. Educate your congregation about the needs of the missionaries with whom you partner. From the pulpit, pray for the specific needs of your missionary partners by name. Post their prayer letters in a prominent place at church and e-mail them out to the congregation. Hold regular prayer marathons for your missionaries and correspond them with the start time of events on the mission field. Teach and preach frequently on missions and prayer.

If your missionaries don't send out regular prayer requests, insist on it. Don't be afraid to ask your missionaries for more detailed, more frequent and more honest prayer request. Report back to your missionaries that the were prayed for. Missionaries know they are being prayed for, but the sinful hearts of your missionaries love to be reminded they are not alone in their battles. Hudson Taylor said, "Pray for those you send, shield them by prayer."[32]

God called and ordained you to pray for and support missions in the same way he called the missionary to go. You are a team. Act like it. Pray for individual missionaries and missionary teams. Pray for specific people groups and for the mission agencies which serve missionaries. Pray for more supporters of missions and for future missionaries to be raised up. Pray your missionary partners have boldness, protection, good health, love for God, opportunities, grace, humbleness, mercy, wisdom, a healthy family, opportunities, joy, peace and resources.

Those who are called to pray provide the fuel on the bonfire that is lit by those who are called to go and make disciples. A lack of prayer for missions shows either of wavering belief in the sovereignty of God or lack of understanding of the importance

---

[31] C. H. Spurgeon, "Prayer, the Proof of Godliness," in *The Metropolitan Tabernacle Pulpit Sermons, vol. 41* (London: Passmore & Alabaster, 1895), 518.

[32] A.J. Broomhall. *Hudson Taylor and China's Open Century, Book Six: Assault on the Nine.* (London: Hodder and Stoughton and Overseas Missionary Fellowship, 1988), 294

God places on the Great Commission. Martyn Lloyd-Jones said, "Prayer, in many ways, is the supreme expression of our faith in God."[33] You may not be called to go, but you are certainly called to pray for or support God's Great Commission. Every Christian is a participant.

Tithing Church Members to Missions

The body of Christ must continue to reevaluate itself and adjust its actions as needed. When the church has fallen out of accord with Scripture and the will of Christ it must change course so as to better bring glory to God.

The purpose of man is to glorify God (Ps 86; Isa 60:21; Rom 11:36; 1 Cor 6:20, 10:31; Rev 4:11). The purpose of the church is to gather, educate and send Christ's disciples out into the world to bring more of God's elect into a saving relationship with Jesus (1 Cor 12:28; Eph 4:11-13; Mat 28:18-20; Isa 59:21). Based on these biblical definitions, and some reflective analyses, it may be time for a new reformation within the Protestant church.

The church is to both promote the gospel to its members and prepare them to proclaim it (1 Pet 3:15). The area in which Bible teaching churches can find room for improvement is the part of their directive which mandates them in the "proclaiming the gospel" and "sending out" their members. Reformed and covenantal churches need more active missionaries and evangelists. Presbyterian pastor and author Oswald Smith said, "Any church that is not seriously involved in helping fulfill the Great Commission has forfeited its biblical right to exist."[34]

The church exists to educate and train God's disciples in the way of the gospel and then to send them out into the world. This is not a debatable point. Somewhere in our recent history evangelicals turned the church into an entity whose purpose is to help Christians grow in Christ and have potlucks. The true purpose of the church is to train Christians to go into the world and to reclaim and disciple God's elect.

Certainly, the heart of the church is to build itself up in the faith (Eph 4:13-16), through teaching the gospel (2 Tim 2:2), in fellowship (Act 2:47), by maintaining ordinances (Luk 22:19), but then the church is mandated to communicate the gospel of Jesus Christ with the world (Mat 28:18-20; Mrk 16:15, 20; Luk 9:2, 6; Jhn 20:21; Act

---

[33] David Martyn Lloyd-Jones, *The Assurance of Our Salvation: Exploring the Depth of Jesus' Prayer for His Own: Studies in John 17* (Wheaton, IL: Crossway Books, 2000), 35.

[34] Raymond Culpepper, The Great Commission, The Solution. (Cleveland, TN: Pathway Press, 1988), 24

1:8; Rom 10:14-15). That final part is not optional and it is not for the super-Christian, it is for the obedient Christian.

There are not enough laborers currently tending to the harvest. If your church isn't spreading the gospel to the lost across the street and around the world, your church doesn't understand the gospel. Our purpose in the church is to make disciples for Jesus Christ and teach them to make disciples. The church is in greater danger by being safe than it is in taking risks to evangelize the lost. Only after the evangelical church fulfills its missionary obligation has it justified its existence. F.B. Meyer said, "The church which is not a missionary church will be a missing church when Jesus comes."[35]

In many of our churches there is too much introspection and playing at church and not enough sharing of the gospel. Scripture tells us the end comes only after disciples go into the whole world and proclaim the gospel (Mat 24:14; Mar 13:10). Scripture also tells us there are not enough laborers (Mat 9:37-38). Statistics bear this out. There are currently more than 2,500 people groups totaling nearly 200,000,000 people who have neither Scripture, the Jesus film, nor Christian recordings in their primary language. Ninety-one percent of all Christian outreach and evangelism does not target non-Christians, but targets other Christians. Despite Christ's command to evangelize, 67% of all humans from AD 30 to today have never heard the name of Jesus Christ.

The church is a place to educate, instruct, and prepare its members to impact the world and share God's love, mercy, and grace. The lost seldom stumble into our churches on their own. Christians are mandated to enter the world and visit the lost where they live.

What would happen if every Protestant church tithed 1% of their membership to cross-cultural missions? What would happen if pastors and church leaderships taught more on the biblical mandates for missions and told their congregation they wanted 1% of them to go onto the mission field?

Protestant churches in the U.S. currently have 48,000,000 frequent attenders. Those same churches currently send out 64,000 missionaries. Protestant churches are sending out missionaries equal to 0.13% of the people attending their services. If every Protestant church tithed just 1% of their membership to fulltime missions they would go from sending 64,000 missionaries to 480,000 missionaries, or an increase of 750%.

The evangelical church is spreading rapidly in Africa and Latin America. God is doing amazing things in the Middle East and Asia. Europe and North America are ready

---

[35] Paul Lee Tan, *Encyclopedia of 7700 Illustrations: Signs of the Times* (Garland, TX: Bible Communications, Inc., 1996), 813.

for a new reformation. The next step that is needed is a flood of theologically sound missionaries to crash the shores of the globe and spread God's mercy, grace and justice to the burgeoning and yet unformed Christian churches. Pastors and church leaders, continue to train your people well and start sending your best and brightest out into the world to reap God's harvest.

9 Steps for Planning a Mission Conference in your Church

Church organized missions conferences are a valuable tool in raising awareness of global evangelism and in helping Christ's disciples better understand the importance and urgency of reaching the lost. When done well a church-run mission conference can bring great glory to the Lord. When done poorly a missions conference can actually impede a church's impact in participating in God's Great Commission.

The concept of God's disciples living out the spread of his gospel is a foundational issue of the Christian faith. The local church is biblically how God intended to train, support and send missionaries. A well done mission conferences can be a major factor in this process.

There are, however, just as many examples of mission conferences done poorly as there are examples of them done well. If you are planning your church's first mission conference or you want to revitalize an ongoing conference, here are a few thoughts for you to prayerfully consider:

1. Prepare your Congregation

Pastors and church leaderships should begin preparing their congregations months in advance of a mission conference. In the time leading up to a mission conference a church should begin preaching and teaching on biblical examples of global evangelists. Abram, Paul, Acts and Jonah are great topics for instruction. The congregants should be given a passion and a basic biblical understanding of God's desire for his people to reach the nations.

2. Invite your Community

Leading up to your mission conference begin inviting churches near your community. Send postcards to the surrounding neighborhoods. Advertise on Christian radio. E-mail and mail your congregation. Encourage members of your church to invite co-workers and neighbors. Missions is a priority for God, make your missions conference important for your extended church community.

3. Cover Missionary Expenses

The missionaries who attend your mission conference are your valued guests. They are usually underfunded and overworked. Make sure you cover the cost of their air and ground travel, housing and food. Money they use on your mission conference is being taken from their ministry. Make sure you are blessing their ministries and not creating a financial burden for them.

4. Mix Mission Reports and Biblical Training

Use a balance of hearing from speakers who will teach on biblical examples of missions and of missionaries who are reporting on their labors. It is important for people to hear reports from real life laborers doing real work in the lives of real people. It is also valuable for the people to see the eternal connection found between God's examples in Scripture and flesh and blood missionaries. The theological and practical connection should be interwoven.

5. Include a Panel on Missionary Life

Ask your missionary speakers to sit on a panel and tell stories and entertain questions about day to day life. It is important to hear a school was built or a church was planted. It is also valuable for your congregation to make a connection that these blessings don't happen on their own. Fulltime missionaries are paying a personal cost. They struggle through culture, language and danger to glorify the Lord. Let your congregation ask questions of the missionaries about their personal lives. Most of our Western brothers and sisters have no understanding what it takes to live and serve in a foreign land. The possible lessons are mammoth.

6. Pray, a Lot

Make prayer the focus of your mission conference. Plan your conference with your congregation praying for missions and the speakers by name. During the conference make sure the missionaries and ministries are represented in corporate and small group prayer. Provide a way for the participants to continue to pray for these missionaries in the years to come.

7. Challenge the Audience

Let the participants of your mission conference know that missions doesn't just happen. Challenge your congregation to take short-term trips, become fulltime missionaries, pray for missionaries and financially support missionaries. Every disciple of

Christ is called to play a part in global evangelism. Make a commitment to missions a focal point of your mission conference.

8. Be Honest About Finances

A mission conference should not be centered on finances, but it should not be void of a serious financial component. Missionaries do not go on the field without money. God supplies the resources for missions, but he does so by calling local churches and individuals to financial support missionaries. Allow missionaries to make an appeal and prayerfully consider taking an offering for their projects.

9. Use Small Group Interaction

Schedule breakout sessions, meals and pray times to allow missionaries to share, interact and pray with smaller groups. Facilitate several opportunities where attendees can intermingle in intimate settings with missionaries. This will allow the participants to get to know several missionaries better and to ask burning questions they may not have been willing to ask in a larger setting.

A mission conference is more than throwing a few missionaries and a large group of Christians together with pizza. Missions is important to God and thus should be important to us. By prayerfully planning and facilitating a more intimate and real experience your congregation will better grasp the Great Commission, missionaries will feel they have experienced a time well spent and God will receive greater glory. Intentionally plan a missions conference, don't just slap one together.

How to Care for your Missionary on Furlough

You are a friend, family member, supporting church or prayer warrior for a missionary and they are about to come back to the US for furlough. To you it seems like they must be thrilled to be back "home" and their furlough is going to be one huge vacation. Now is the time for you to realize furlough is hard and you are indeed your brother's keeper.

Scripture tells us to bear each other's burdens (Gal 6:2), pray for each other (Jas 5:16), receive one another (Rom 15:7), serve each other (Gal 5:13), and be hospitable to each other (1Pet 4:8-10). We are to love one another. And, this is taught to us repeatedly throughout the Bible. Jesus commanded us to love each other (Jon 13:34-35). Paul taught it (Rom 13:8; 1Thes 4:9), Peter instructed it (1Pet 1:22) and John stressed it

(1Jon 3:11, 4:7). If you appreciate the sacrifices your missionary is making for the kingdom, love them while they are on furlough.

Many people act like missionaries are super-Christians. Most missionaries swallow their pain so supporters don't think they are a bad investment. But, your missionaries are struggling. Missions is hard and it takes a spiritual, emotional and physical toll on missionaries. Don't let their sinful pride tell you any different.

Encourage your missionaries to meet regularly with a pastor or counselor while they are on furlough. By them a dinner coupon and take their kids for the night so they can go out and repair their marriage. Set up play dates with their kids to help them be kids. Instead of expecting your missionaries to come to your house for dinner, realize they are doing that dozens of times on furlough and offer to bring pizza and a movie to them.

Start off with the understanding that your missionaries are in culture shock and they forgot how to live in the US. Think about what it takes to live in the US if you don't live there. Your missionaries don't have a place to live and hotels are expensive. They don't have a car and rental prices are outrageous. Their phone doesn't work in the US. Their clothes are out of date and they are embarrassed. If they have a temporary home it likely doesn't have internet, yet supporters still want updates.

What about when they come visit your church? Have one person volunteer to champion their visit. Without the missionary being forced to ask, organize a private place to stay, group meals, church activities, recreation and down time.

What about those long-term things nobody thinks about. Have a financial planner or attorney sit down and volunteer to help a missionary plan for the future. Ask them what they are doing for retirement, a will, kid's college funds, health insurance, voter registration. How are they managing paying taxes? Do they have a place to store family photos and legal documents? How are they schooling their kids and do they need help? These things are complicated if you live in the US, and are frequently neglected by missionaries who live thousands of miles away. A common result is that a missionary who comes off the field after serving for years finds their life in a mess. Don't let your missionaries be forced to suffer long after their service on the field is complete.

God wants us to rest. In fact, he commands us to rest (Jer 6:16; Mat 11:28-29; Heb 4:4; Rev 6:11). But, the reality is, furlough is far from restful for most missionaries. Often times furlough is just as stressful as on field ministry. Schedules, travel, presentations, training, support raising and reverse culture shock. Oh dear Lord, "Let my people go!" In times of candor you will hear many missionaries admit that they can't wait for their furlough to be over so they can get back on the field and relax.

Imagine being a missionary on furlough. It doesn't seem like a lot. All they do is show up in your church and preach and share and talk to 100 people and go out to lunch with the missions committee. Well, they also drove hours to get to your church and will drive hours to get back. And, there is the fact that their kids are tired of sleeping in a new bed every week, and strange food, and always being on their A-game. Well, then there is road weariness, and you don't see it, but they're fighting with their spouse, and money is low, and they forgot everyone's names. Oh, and they do that EVERY weekend in a new location, for their entire furlough.

Whether they admit it or not your missionaries need help resting. Ask them the hard questions about rest, vacation and spiritual health. Help them fund a vacation. Send them on a spiritual retreat. Buy tickets for them to attend a Christian conference. Help them to get out of their routine.

Furlough is an emotionally exhausting, painful, wonderful, whirlwind of joy and stress. Most missionaries do furlough wrong and they need your help to save them from themselves. It is important for you and your church to hear from your missionary and share in how God is being glorified in far off lands. It is also important for you to embrace your missionary partners and help them heal so they can live to serve another term.

Chapter Three

Before you Leave for the Mission Field

There is great romanticism in charging into battle or leaping without looking. However, there is great wisdom in a missionary preparing themselves for the hard times ahead. The more a missionary is trained and evaluated before they leave for the mission field the greater their chance of piloting a God-honoring ministry. Missionaries should trust God for his provision. In this case, God has provided missionaries with resources to groom his global servants.

Our modern Western churches are a global and historical anomaly in Christianity. No Christian church in the world or throughout history has is as blessed with resources as the Western church is today. There are so many ways for Western Christians to educate and prepare themselves for missions. It is a shame when it doesn't happen.

Missions is hard enough. Our missionaries do not need to handicap themselves. Gaining experience and honing our minds and hearts to serve in missions will bring greater glory to God and make the transition easier. Much prayer, training, and counsel should go into missions before a passport is ever stamped.

Justifications for Avoiding Missions

It is a well-documented that pastors and missionaries are super-Christians handpicked by God to administer his will and make other Christians feel guilty about their service to the kingdom. It has been my experience that the casual utterance of the phrase, "I am a missionary" has cosmic properties that cause the average Christian to spontaneously and uncontrollably erupt into unsolicited confessions as to why they don't financially support missionaries or haven't yet themselves embraced their call to missions.

I have heard dozens of excuses why Christians justify avoiding missions service. In fact, most of those excuses have been heard coming from my own mouth. Here are some of the more common excuses for avoiding missions:

As followers of Christ our lives were never intended to seek our own comfort, joy and entertainment. The purpose of our life is to seek God's glory throughout the world. We are all missionaries and every Christian is called to share the love of Christ. Without a clear calling to another ministry you are called to be involved in missions.

Missions is not something done by a select few individuals. Charles Spurgeon left little room for debate when he said, "Every Christian is either a missionary or an impostor."[36] Unless God makes it clear you are to stay home and support missionaries he wants you to be a missionary.

If you think you can't raise the money to go on the mission field you've already made your first mistake. God will raise the money, not you. Every dime that will be raised for your missions efforts comes from God and if he wants you on the mission field he will make it happen. God knows what you need before you do. Hudson Taylor, pioneering missionary to China said, "God's work done in God's way will never lack God's supplies."[37]

Way too many people have refused to let God show how big he is because they don't think he can succeed. Many Christians cut short their missions service, or simply don't go on the mission field, because they fear the funds can't be raised. Let God surprise you! Let God do amazing things! If God has ordained your ministry you will have no problem raising support for it. Why wouldn't God use his money to support his work?

Our life on this earth is only a blip in time. It should not be false safety and fabricated security we seek. If safety and security is what you pursue by not entering missions you are sacrificing eternal good for temporary comfort. We are called to make a sacrifice in our lives to facilitate the expansion of the gospel into the world. God is worthy of sacrifice and he is calling his people to give all they have, even to lay down their lives, so his gospel can reach the world.

The life Christ wants for us is full of risk, peril & requires reliance on him. C.S. Lewis stated, "God, who foresaw your tribulation, has specially armed you to go through it,

---

[36] Daniel Akin and Bruce Riley Ashford, *I Am Going* (Nashville, TN: B&H, 2016), 72.

[37] Mark Water, *The New Encyclopedia of Christian Quotations* (Alresford, Hampshire: John Hunt Publishers Ltd, 2000), 389.

not without pain but without stain."[38] When we can acknowledge our perceived security is false and safety is an illusion we can begin to risk everything and accomplish great things for God's glory.

There is still much work to be done. Nearly half of the world's 6.9 billion citizens belong to a people group that is unreached by the gospel. There are over 300 million people in the world today who don't have a Bible available in their own language. Over 1,000 people will die before you finish reading this article and most of them don't know Jesus. Matthew 24:14 tells us, "And this gospel of the kingdom will be proclaimed throughout the whole world as a testimony to all nations, and then the end will come." That time has not yet come.

Some have wondered, in this age of advanced technology why we can't simply fund Internet ministries and beam God's Word around the world with a single button push. The reality is a majority of the people in the world don't have access to Internet. In fact, less than 1% of the populations of North Korea, East Timor, Sierra Leone, and Burma have Internet. Those people must be evangelized the old-fashioned way: face-to-face.

No missionary has ever been sufficiently qualified to serve God, and every missionary I have ever met feels horribly unprepared to the task at hand. Your ability and skills are less important on the mission field than your willingness to serve others. You don't need training, certification or a job title to bring the gospel to the world. You only need an obedient heart inclined toward God.

Throughout Scripture God has used unqualified servants. Moses was a poor orator, Paul persecuted Christians and David couldn't keep his hands off his neighbors. God is glorified in our weakness. God knew your shortcomings before he called you to the mission field. Ephesians 2:10 tells us, "For we are his workmanship, created in Christ Jesus for good works, which God prepared beforehand, that we should walk in them."

Willing to make personal sacrifice is what being a disciple is all about. God calls us to be willing to give all we have. The Great Commission contains four directives: go, teach, baptize & make disciples. "Go" is the first and hardest to obey.

Commit the rest of your life to expanding the gospel. Don't be satisfied with the fleeting taste of a few weeks or months of service. If indeed God is calling you to the mission field he has prepared you. Allow God to use you for his glory.

---

[38] Mark Water, *The New Encyclopedia of Christian Quotations* (Alresford, Hampshire: John Hunt Publishers Ltd, 2000), 982.

Are you Called to Missions?

Much of our Western evangelical church views missions as simply another church program. Numerous churches communicate missions to their congregations as one of many ministry options to select from, like meals ministry, or producing the bulletin or putting out chairs. Oftentimes Christ's disciples see missions as something other Christians are called to. Congregants can frequently be heard saying, "missions is not what God has called me to." Seldom do we look at missions as a command intended for us.

The truth is, missions is not a calling. It is a command. Missions is not intended for a few, but for all Christians. John Piper says, "There are only three kinds of Christians when it comes to world missions: zealous goers, zealous senders, and disobedient."[39] There is nothing optional about disciples of Christ participating in missions. Our only task is to discern how we will participate.

Nothing about the grammar contained in Scripture makes missions sound optional. Throughout the Bible we are directed by God to participate in the global spread of his gospel. Look at the commands associated with missions texts: declare his glory among the nations (Ps 96:3), go and make disciples of all nations (Mat 28:19), you will be my witnesses to the end of the earth (Acts 1:8), go into the world and proclaim (Ma 16:15), say among the nations (Ps 96:10), go to the land I will show you (Acts 12:1) and go from your country (Gen 12:1). What part of those passages sounds optional? Might you be called to missions? No, you are commanded to participate in missions.

The shepherd's sheep have been scattered throughout the world. He has called us to find them and tell them it is time to come home. David Sitton stated, "Nowhere in Scripture is a 'mysterious (supernatural) call' a prerequisite before we can respond to the Great Commission."[40] Christians worship a God who requires unwavering obedience and calls us to participate in a mission that warrants extreme commitment.

Christ started his earthly ministry by calling his disciples to be fishers of men and ended with the instruction to go, and make disciples. Evangelism and global missions were never intended only for disciples who are seminary trained or exceptional orators. All disciples of Christ are called to make disciples for Christ who make disciples for Christ.

---

[39] John Piper, *Sermons from John Piper* (1990–1999) (Minneapolis, MN: Desiring God, 2007), November 3, 1996.

[40] David Sitton, "Don't Complicate the 'Missionary Call.'" DesiringGod. July 27, 2011. https://www.desiringgod.org/articles/don-t-complicate-the-missionary-call

Must then, all Christians sell all they own and move to a faraway land? No. Do not interpret this article as an attempt to guilt all Christian disciples onto the mission field. Missions is indeed a compulsory activity for all Christians, done out of a desire to glorify our Lord. How that is acted out in your life is between you and your Savior.

Are you called to go, send or pray? That is the question you must answer. Praying for missionaries, financially supporting missions or sharing the gospel cross-culturally, that is how we obey our Father. Across the street and around the world there are lost souls bound for hell. If we know the truth of salvation and do nothing with it, what does that say of our relationship with God.

You may not be called to go, but you are certainly called to pray for or support God's Great Commission. Every Christian is a participant. If God is not currently calling you to serve him as a cross-cultural missionary please pray fervently for those he has called. Those who are called to pray provide the fuel on the bonfire that is lit by those who are called to go.

Not every Christian is called to leave the country. There are poor, sick, and unsaved everywhere. Service is mandatory, location varies. The call to missions has more to do with the condition of our heart than it does the location of our feet.

Doctor, teacher and janitor is not your calling. Those are the means God has given to provide His mercy and love to others. That's your calling. Our talent is less relevant than how we use it when called upon by the one who gave it to us.

If you are sitting around and waiting for God's "call" to figure out how you were intended to serve the Lord, wait no longer. You have already been called, and commanded to aide in the spread of God's eternal truth to all nations. Read your Bible and obey that which God has already commanded.

Every person who calls themselves a disciple of Christ is commanded to participate in God's mission to call the nations to himself. Our objective in the church is to make disciples for Jesus Christ and teach them to make disciples. This is our purpose and our privilege.

Too frequently we give Jesus our unenthusiastic affiliation and token obedience. It is our absolute devotion and complete sacrifice he merits. God is worthy of sacrifice and he is calling his people to give all they have, even lay down their lives, so his gospel can reach the world.

Learn to Serve on the Mission Field by First Serving at Home

A heart for missions is not something which starts when you receive your new passport. A heart for missions is given to you by God and it is evident by the way you live your life. If you are not serving the needy now, if you are not loving the unlovable in your hometown, if your life is void of God's grace and mercy for others, you will not miraculously gain that ability by becoming a missionary. The desire to serve others is not a switch which is turned on when you arrive on the mission field. If you are not loving the lost in your own culture you will have difficulty learning to love them in a new culture.

The key to having a heart for serving others is not about having a heart for your fellow man, but having a heart for Jesus. We serve others, not because we love them. We serve others because we love Christ. Our service to other people stems from a desire to bring glory to God and to share his grace and mercy with the world.

The best way to strengthen your desire to serve on the mission field is by first serving in your own community. Love the lost where you live before you try to love the lost around the globe. Learn to love and serve in your home culture.

The best way to strengthen a muscle is to use it. Serve others, evangelize the lost and share Christ's mercy in your own town. By loving and serving others at home you will gain wisdom and passion to continue serving. The more you serve the more you want to serve. The best way to develop your servant's heart is on the job training.

Consult the leadership of your home church. Find out what service and mercy ministries they recommend. How do your strengths and your community's needs correspond? If no such ministries exist in your church ask your church leadership if they will provide permission for you to start such a ministry in your own church. Serve under the guidance and wisdom of your church leadership. Invite others from your church to serve with you. The experience you gain serving at home will teach you much about those in need and yourself. God will be glorified by your labors at home and you will learn more about your own heart.

Having a desire to serve others in the name of Christ can be one of the most addicting drugs you'll ever find. Knowing your Father's name is being magnified in the lives of those in need is a glorious experience. The more you serve others, the more you feel a need to serve others. Even though serving others can sometimes be filled with pain and tears, the praise your actions bring to God's name is rejuvenating.

The experience you gain in serving in your own culture will benefit your ministry on the mission field. Indeed, sinners, cultures and situations are different throughout the globe. However, the joys and the pain you experience will develop a heart and knowledge of service which will benefit your foreign ministry. God has a way of giving you new challenges which will stretch you, but having walked a mile in the shoes of s servant will pay dividends for future ministry.

Serving the less fortunate is important to God, therefore it must be important to us. Christ has called all his disciples to serve others in his name, with his power, and for his glory. The call to serve others is not a slavish directive centered on works based theology. We are not earning our salvation. A disciple of the Lord serves others as a way of demonstrating our love for Jesus. Our works are not done out of obligatory obedience to God. Our works are evidence of our love.

Attend to the poor, the widow, the orphan, the sick, the homeless, the aged in your town. Do it because you want to show your love for Christ by giving his grace and mercy to the broken. There are thousands of needy people within a few miles of your current home who are literally dying to receive the love of Jesus Christ. Be his standard bearer in your home town. Don't imagine a heart full of love and justice will magically appear in your chest once you receive your passport stamp to your new home.

Serving in a new country, using a new language, under new government regulations simply makes things harder and does much to diminish your desire to serve. Trying to understand your submission to our Father's call for service and your desire to pour out his love for those around you must not be something you try to invent or conjure up in a new culture and a new home. First serve in your own culture to help train you to serve better on the mission field.

Missions Training and Evaluation Before you Go

Missionaries who have it set in their heart they are going to the mission field are very anxious and can't wait to get started. The excitement and willingness to serve is a good thing. Too often, this desire to get on the field quickly supersedes the wisdom of being properly prepared before a missionary leaves their home country.

A missionary should invest time and resources into training and evaluation before they start their missions service. The more a missionary knows about missions and the more he knows about himself the higher the probability for success.

Christian disciples are instructed in Scripture to self-evaluate their Christian journey and spiritual maturity. Scripture also teaches Christians to submit to evaluation by others (Lam 3:40; Ps 26:2, 139:23-24; Job 13:23). Frequently, others have a clearer, and unbiased assessment of us, than we do of ourselves. It is always healthy to invite fellow believers to speak into our life and tell us how they view our character and faith. Having an experienced missionary provide that input is even more valuable. Evaluation can be temporarily painful, but the maturing and sanctifying aspect of honest assessment holds many long-term benefits.

Some missionaries are sent from big mission sending agencies, while others are sent independently from their home church. Not every missionary has evaluative tools readily at their disposal, but there are plenty of independent Christian agencies out there which specialize in pre-field missionary evaluation.

There is an abundance of tools that can be used in the assessment of a missionary's readiness for missions service. There are useful personality tests, theological and Bible exams, psychological evaluations, character assessments, and more. Trained and professional evaluators are worth the time and money needed to provide an honest, unbiased evaluation of how they see a missionary.

The ability to understand where we have deficiencies is a valuable tool. Doing it before a missionary is in the fishbowl of missions is imperative. Frequently we see ourselves differently than others see us. Being able to round the edges of our personality or work on change will reduce the probability of problems and increases our chance of success. Knowing our weak points before we jump into the pressure cooker of missions is a gift from God.

Christians are instructed by Scripture to joyfully receive training and instruction (Rom 15:4; 1 Tim 4:7-8; 2 Tim 3:16-17; Heb 5:11-14). The purpose of this training is to make us strong in the faith and to prepare us for the trials ahead. How much more valuable it is for a missionary to be trained properly before they depart to serve in a new culture, country, and language. The more a missionary prepares before they arrive on the mission field the better off they will be. No missionary has ever said, after arriving into to fulltime ministry, "I wish I hadn't trained and prepared so much before I went into missions."

Learning the language, culture, and history of your adopted culture is a must. Take formal language lessons before you arrive on your ministry sight and take more language lessons than you think you need. Learning about culture, traditions, and food before you arrive can help smooth out your learning curve and reduce many embarrassing moments. Showing your adopted culture, you love them enough to learn about their ways will say much about you.

Studying Scripture and reading classic missions biographies should be the cornerstone of any would-be missionary. Better learning the foundations of our faith can never steer a missionary wrong and should be paramount to other training. Learning how our missionary forefathers succeeded and failed is invaluable. Never discount the learning that comes from studying biblical and historical missionaries.

Before you leave for the mission field take courses on conflict resolution, leadership, counseling, basic medicine, cultural acquisition, church planting, and more. It is likely your adopted culture will not provide you as easy access to education, conferences, and training like you will find at home. Take advantage of the abundance of opportunities to better prepare yourself before you leave. Education and training that better prepares you for your ministry is time and money well spent.

Delaying your departure to the mission field to be better evaluated and trained for your ministry is smart. It is understandable and admirable to desire to rush into to missions. Before you leave, you are excited to serve God and get started on the new chapter of your life. There is no such thing as being too prepared to change cultures and become a missionary. Most missionaries overestimate their readiness for missions and get frustrated by the perceived bureaucratic delays of pre-field evaluation and training.

Absorb the wisdom of experienced and Godly evaluators and teachers and change your heart toward pre-field preparation. The investment of resources into preparation will better prepare a missionary for success and reduce the probability of major on-field problems. If God has called you to serve him in another culture devote yourself to being as ready as possible before you go. Trust in God and give yourself a better chance at bringing him glory on the mission field by participating in evaluation and training before you go.

Language Learning is Not Optional in Missions

Language acquisition is a vital part of missions. Refusing to learn a language can dramatically limit the influence a missionary can have for the kingdom of God. Many missionaries use age, education or ability as an excuse for not learning a new language. However, even the poorest speaker of a foreign language can bring great glory to God. In reference to Numbers 22:21-39 where God put words in the mouth of a donkey to speak to Balaam, C.S. Lewis once said, "One must take comfort in remembering that God used an ass to convert the prophet. Perhaps, if we do our poor best, we shall be allowed a stall near it in the celestial stable."[41]

There are only six countries in the world where English is the primary language of a majority of the citizens (US, UK, Canada, Australia, Ireland and New Zealand). Even in

---

[41] C.S. Lewis, *Letters of C.S. Lewis* (London: Harcourt, Inc, 2000), 359-360.

those countries, learning another language can be greatly advantageous. In the U.S., for example, there are 31 million people who don't speak English.

Of the 7.1 billion people on the planet only 340 million speak English as their primary language. Only 840 million people in the world speak English at all. That means 88% of the people on earth, or 6.2 billion humans, do not speak English.

English is spoken all over the world, but outside of the West most English speakers are found among business people and university students. Indeed, those people also need the gospel, but without learning language missionaries are very limited as to where and to whom they can minister.

Language is important to God. He created humans in his image with the ability to understand language (Gen 1:27-28, 2:19). We know that language is hard for some (Ezek 3:5-6), but if we are not clear in our speech our efforts are useless (1 Cor 14:9). God can be glorified if we speak clearly (Ps 19) and Jesus showed us that speaking in foreign languages can help understanding (Mar 5:41). Christ's sacrifice was for people from every language (Rev 5:9) and Paul used multiple languages to bring God glory (Acts 5-6).

A missionary is called, first and foremost, to make disciples and teach them God's way (Mat 28:18-20). How on earth can we expect to make disciples and teach if we can't communicate? A willingness to learn and be changed is imperative to having the heart of a missionary. A missionary who is not willing to struggle and look foolish is already starting off poorly. Part of being a missionary is learning and embracing the culture. That is a near impossibility without being able to communicate.

Living in another culture you learn the value of worshiping in your heart language. We are sinners and we like to worship God how we originally learned to worship. In the same context, speakers of other languages want to learn about the saving blood of Christ in their heart language. We cannot deprive them of that.

Learning a language can be a humbling experience. It is hard for a person who is successful, educated and articulate in English to be relegated to communicating like a four-year-old. The process of language learning provides an opportunity for us to depend more on Christ and his mercies.

Some people are naturals at acquiring languages. Linguists, like Bible translators, are worthy of praise. But, for many of us, language learning does not come natural and is a struggle. Your attempt to learn a new language is a testament to the nationals as to how much you love them and esteem Christ.

On numerous occasions I have heard nationals say versions of the following, "Yes, missionary X struggles with our language, but he tries. Missionary Y hasn't even bothered to learn our language. I respect missionary X for his dedication and will work with him." That sounds petty and heartless. But, how many times have you heard someone in the U.S. say, "This is America. We speak English here. If you want to come to America, you should learn to speak English." It is not so farfetched to assume others around the world feel similar about their country and language.

Language acquisition opens so many doors for missionaries. Being able to communicate well provides access to a depth of culture that could not otherwise be obtained. The richness and gained experience of communication helps a missionary to better relate to those they have been sent to disciple.

Many missionaries are needed to serve in English speaking regions around the globe. Many missionaries do a wonderful job ministering only in English. God can be greatly glorified using English. The purpose here is not to criticize those who minister in English. If you have been called to minister in English, thank you for your service.

If you are going to serve where God has called you and that is not an English speaking culture, know that you can bring greater glory to God by learning the local language. It is hard and frustrating. But, you will bring great glory to God by depending on him and you will make deeper relationships with those whom God has called you to serve.

9 Practical Ways to Prepare for Missions

Not every disciple of Christ is called to be a missionary. But, maybe you know you have been called to be a fulltime missionary. However, you know you aren't leaving for the mission field right away. School, training, debt, acceptance to a missions agency or something else has delayed the start of your missions service.

Let's assume you are certain you have been called to serve as a missionary, but for whatever reason you have a few months or years before you depart for the mission field. While you are waiting you don't need to be idol. Take the time now to make some changes in your life and you can increase the probability of success as a future missionary. Here are nine ways to better prepare yourself for missions:

1. Get Cross-Cultural

Try international foods, listen to global music, watch programs about other countries. Expose yourself cultures that are different from yours. Become adventurous and learn to enjoy new experiences. Learn about other people and the way they do things. Learning to embrace different cultures will give you a head start to a perspective that will benefit you in missions.

2. Study Scripture

Be it dependence on Christ, missionary examples or sharing your faith, you can do no wrong diving into the Bible and memorizing God's inerrant Word. While on the mission field you will be forced to become more focused and dependent on the Lord. Begin focusing more on the Bible and begin living a life sold out for his glory.

3. Read Biographies

Spend quality time reading missionary biographies. You will soon learn that amazing missionaries are not necessarily amazing people. Instead, you will learn about how sinful missionaries who depend completely on the Lord bring him great glory. Read how the great missionaries struggled and failed, but continued to embrace the grace and mercy of Christ.

4. Learn Languages

Become a language learner. Even if you don't what country you will be called to serve, begin to expose yourself to new languages. By learning new languages you open yourself up to the concept of struggle and failure. Few things humble a missionary like communicating at the level of a child when they are speaking their new language. Getting used to that experience early will help you in the long run.

5. Evangelize

Learn to share your faith. Become accustomed to articulating the gospel and telling how Christ changed your life. Take formal evangelism training (Four Laws, EE, Bridge, etc.). Evangelism is like a muscle, the more you use it the stronger it gets. Only when you become experienced at evangelism will you truly embrace the concept that winning souls is God's job, not yours.

6. Be Uncomfortable

Get out of your comfort zone. Serve the poor, feed the hungry, build things with your hands. Learn to do new things that don't come natural to you. Most of your time on the mission field will be spent in unfamiliar situations. Get used to it. Learn to be comfortable as an adult learner. Learn to fail gracefully. Learn to depend on others and rely on Christ.

7. Live With Less

Begin to cut back on your lifestyle. Spend less. Become less dependent on technology. Experience life with fewer options and choices. No matter where you serve in the world you will not experience the same foods, entertainment and selection you have now. Don't let material goods rule your life so completely that they impact your missions experience.

8. Serve Others

Develop a spirit of service. Gain the experience of putting the wellbeing of others in front of your own joy. Volunteer at your church or in your community, or simply step forward and help others in your day-to-day life. Learn to serve others so Jesus receives the glory and not yourself. Service is at the heart of almost every missionary's daily experience.

9. Pray More

Develop a life dedicated to prayer. Make prayer an important, unwavering part of your daily life. Condition yourself to make prayer your first and last response to every situation. Prayer brings glory to God and takes the focus off of you. On the mission field you will discover you need prayer more than you ever did before. Condition yourself to the concept that you can't, but God can.

Missions is hard and many missionaries fail. According to Rober Coote, "up to half of all new missionaries do not last beyond their first term."[42] However, pre-field training and conditioning can increase the probability that a missionary will have a healthy and productive experience on the mission field. With a heart focused on Christ and with the proper resources and perspective a missionary improves the prospect he will have a long and healthy career in missions. Use the time in advance of your missions service to train yourself to be a more qualified and better prepared servant for God's glory.

Should all Missionaries Have Seminary Training?

Many Christian disciples use a lack of formal theological education and training as a reason to not serve on the mission field. Willing servants, all too often, walk away from serving in global evangelism due to a perception that only the best and brightest theologians should hold the title of missionary. The truth is missionaries do not need to

---

[42] Robert T. Coote, *Mission Handbook,* ed by Samuel Wilson and John Siewert, (Monrovia, CA: MARC Publications, 1986), 63.

be the most theologically astute, but instead, those who are willing to give all for God's glory.

Few people would argue formal seminary training is advantageous to nearly every Christ-centered ministry. If we are going to serve how Christ has called us and in a way that glorifies him, it is important to understand the Bible. If we are called to "make disciples" and teach "them to observe all that I have commanded" (Mat 28:19-20) it is certainly beneficial to have an intimate knowledge of Scripture.

The Bible emphasizes leadership training (2 Tim 2:2) and the training of elders (Tit 1:9). The Bible was clearly designed for instruction (Mrk 12:26; Luk 24:27; Jhn 5:39; Acts 1:16; Rom 15:4; 1 Cor 2:13; 2 Tim 3:16; 2 Pet 1:21). Bible-centered theological training is certainly Christ-honoring. Formal seminary training provides exposure to biblical languages, unique fellowship, experience with theological diversity, and learning new ministry methods. While Bible knowledge is an imperative for missions and seminary training makes Bible training easier, formal seminary training is not a mandate for fulltime missions. It is possible to be a Christ-honoring missionary with no formal seminary training.

Nothing in this article should be perceived as diminishing, belittling or deprioritizing seminary training. Seminary training is extremely valuable and God-honoring. Not having seminary trained missionaries involved in a ministry can certainly make aspects of that ministry more difficult. While most missions ministries can be made easier with formal seminary training, no potential missionary should feel unwelcomed on the mission field without seminary training.

There are 4.9 billion non-Christians in the world today and there are only 140,000 fulltime protestant missionaries. That means there are 35,000 unsaved people per every single protestant missionary on the planet. This describes an urgent crisis of manpower. The Christian church is not in a position where it can afford to mandate seminary training for all missionaries.

At the same time we must never tolerate the sending out of biblically illiterate missionaries. A biblically illiterate missionary will not adequately grasp their own kingdom purpose nor the Lord's biblical truths. A missionary can serve in mercy, construction, theological education or teaching. But, they must comprehend the Bible.

Jesus has shown he can use all kinds of missionaries. When Jesus sent out his 12 Apostles (Mat 10:5-15; Mrk 6:7-13; Luk 9:1-6) he did not send the best, brightest, or the most spiritual. Jesus sent out men who were obedient and had the faith to be completely reliant on Christ. The Apostles were sinful disciples who were willing to be used as vessels for God's glory. The fact that Judas Iscariot, the false apostle and traitor, was among the twelve whom our Lord sent out to preach and heal the sick should speak volumes to us. Judas being among the chosen twelve Apostles tells us that good work flows from Jesus and not man.

Never forget God used an ass to convert Balaam (Num 22:21-39). C.S. Lewis said of this passage, "One must take comfort in remembering that God used an ass to convert the prophet: perhaps if we do our poor best we shall be allowed a stall near it in the celestial stable!"[43] There are several instances of the Bible where seemingly unremarkable men were chosen as leaders. Old Testament prophets like David and Amos were called by God in spite of their simplicity (1 Sam 16:1-13; Amos 7:14-15). In the New Testament Christ called lowly fishermen and other common laborers to convert entire cultures. Roland Allen said, "Missionary zeal does not grow out of intellectual beliefs, nor out of theological arguments, but out of love."[44]

Both inside or outside of seminary, the simple reading of books alone does not fully prepare us for fulltime ministry. Ministry experience and a heart for service pay huge dividends. You don't need training, certification or a job title to bring the gospel to the world. You only need an obedient heart inclined toward God. Your ability, skills and training are less important on the mission field than your willingness to serve others.

The church is a place to educate, instruct, and prepare its members to impact the world and share God's love, mercy, and message. Few things can prepare a missionary for global service like first experiencing hands on ministry in the local church. Charles Spurgeon said, "If a student should learn a thousand things, and yet fail to preach the gospel acceptably, his College course will have missed its true design. Should the pursuit of literary prizes and the ambition for classical honors so occupy his mind as to divert his attention from his life work, they are perilous rather than beneficial." [45]

Formal seminary training is almost always preferable for missionaries but should never be considered mandatory. A heart inclined toward God's will and a life dedicated to his grace can lead any missionary to glory for Christ.

---

[43] C.S. Lewis, *Letters of C.S. Lewis* (London: Harcourt, Inc, 2000), 359-360.

[44] Roland Allen, *The Ministry of the Spirit* (Cambridge: The Lutterworth Press, 1960), 35.

[45] C. H. Spurgeon, *Lectures to My Students: A Selection from Addresses Delivered to the Students of the Pastors' College, Metropolitan Tabernacle., vol. 1* (London: Passmore and Alabaster, 1875), viii.

Do Missionaries Need Missions Agencies?

One of the more common questions I field from future missionaries, current missionaries and missionary supporters has to do with the need for missions sending agencies. Do missionaries really need missions agencies? Wouldn't it be better to eliminate the administrative fees and send more money directly to the missionary? Doesn't all the bureaucratic mandates of a missions agency rob valuable time away from doing ministry on the field?

Missions can be done without being part of a missions agency. But, most everything about missions is hard and requires learning and experience. A missions agency brings many valuable resources to the table that increases the probability of success among missionaries.

Missions agencies have lots of experience working with missionaries. Their experience helps them understand what type of characteristics, personality traits and life experiences increase the odds of a missionary being successful on the mission field. They have seen many missionaries succeed and many fail. Missions agencies can encourage a missionary to accentuate their positives and manage their negatives. They can point missionaries to books, courses, conferences, counselors and other resources that help increase the probability of a successful missions experience. Most missions agencies encourage ongoing training and development to ensure missionaries have the must update knowledge they need to be successful at the ministry.

Missions agencies should not be viewed as the arbiters of your fate. Missions agencies do not exist to approve the type of personalities they want and fail those people they dislike. The purpose of the relationship with a missions agency is to have an unbiased and experienced group of people that can help a fellow believer affirm if they are called to serve on the mission field. Sometimes people want to serve in countries or ministries they are not gifted to serve in. Not everybody is called to serve in every ministry. Receiving input from educated servants of the Lord can help a person determine how or if they are called to the mission field.

Frequently in missions a missionary is faced with learning a new job under the watchful eyes of both the US government and foreign governments. A missions agency will help a missionary stay in accordance the laws and tax systems they encounter. In addition, many missionaries handle money coming from and going to numerous sources. So the missionary can remain above reproach the missions agency will require a certain level of financial accounting that helps everyone to see the missionary is acting in accordance to the legal system and is handling resources appropriately. God has trusted us to be good stewards and sometimes it is beneficial to have help doing that.

One of the untold realities of missions is that it is hard. Missionaries fail and struggle and sin at a rate that would shock most casual onlookers. Missionary life is hard and missionaries are notorious for not caring for themselves spiritually, physically or emotionally. It is the same selfless, self-sacrificing heart that makes a good missionary that also results in missionary misery. Missions agencies provide physical, psychological and emotion care for their suffering servants. Also, in the mundane, many missions agencies facilitate missionary care most of us don't think about until it is too late; health insurance, academic assistance, retirement, evacuation insurance and life insurance. Missions agencies care for missionaries in ways they won't care for themselves.

Missions agencies regularly seek and offer prayer for their missionaries by name. They lift up their missionaries to a Lord who loves hearing prayers. Missions agencies pray for and support missionaries in many ways those missionaries will never understand this side of glory. Missions agencies help to aide missionaries through recruiting and raising resources. They provide valuable support to those men and women who feel alone.

It is not imperative or ungodly to serve as a missionary without going through a missions sending agency. But, missions is hard enough without help. Even without a small army of support staff providing for you, most missionaries struggle. Missions agencies are, like missionaries, a bunch of sinners trying to glorify the Lord. Mistakes and problems can be expected when working with a missions agency. MORE mistakes and problems can be expected when NOT working with a missions agency.

The purpose of a missions sending agency is to afford missionaries with a higher probability of success. They provide resources and a lifeline to missionaries who have been called by the Lord to fulfill his Great Commission. When William Carey volunteered to be a missionary, he implored those who sent him, "Remember that you must hold the rope."[46] Missionaries must go, and senders of missionaries must remember to hold the rope. Missionaries embrace the help and wisdom offered you by missions agencies. Missions sending agencies are there to hold the rope.

How to Not Mess Up a Missions Presentation

The missions presentation is a tradition in western Christianity by which the missionary presents her ministry in a home or church. When done well, a missionary

---

[46] William Carey, "Rev. William Carey." The Gospel in All Lands, January 11, 1883, 15.

presentation can multiply God's glory and casts a vision which increases interest in God's global work. When done poorly, a missions presentation can act as a sleep aide for the audience and an anxiety builder for the missionary.

Missions presentations don't need to be painful or burdensome for the presenters or the spectators. Sadly, many missions presentations are done badly and don't cast a vision for the amazing work God will be doing through the missionary and his partners in a foreign culture. Missions presentations are a way to share the infectious joy God has given the missionary with those privileged enough to be present. Missions presentations are not rocket science, just eternally imperative.

When you plan on attending a church or missions gathering make sure you ask if you can make a presentation. Make sure you inquire well ahead of your scheduled visit. Don't assume anything. Ask how long your presentation should be and what the leadership would like you to discuss. Inquire if you can have a table to display additional information, and ask how long you will be afforded to talk.

Be flexible. Don't be a slave to your technology. Be capable of giving a presentation without technology if something goes wrong and be prepared to change your presentation on a moment's notice. Practice your presentation ahead of time and ask for critique from trusted friends before you ever give a presentation. Have memorized several presentation ranging from two minutes to 30 minutes. Respect the ministries of others by sticking to your allotted time. If you are given five minutes to speak, save everything you have to say within five minutes.

Tell a story about a national impacted by your ministry. Use names of real people and don't bore your audience with too many statistics. Be honest and transparent and don't be embarrassed to express your real emotions. Your enthusiasm and your heart will be contagious. Distribute additional hardcopy information to allow people to walk away with information in their hands and provide a way for people to sign up to receive additional information. Make sure you ask people to pray for you and ask for financial support, don't assume they know you need finances

Avoid giving an academic PowerPoint presentation and simply reading your slides. Don't feel the need to provide excess backstory or details. The stories you tell should create an emotional mind picture that doesn't need an abundance of narrative. Don't bore your audience with a history or government lesson about the people you will serve.

Don't be afraid to talk about your fears and emotions, but don't feel the need to give your resume. Never use your presentation time as a soapbox. You have been given a forum to present God's ministry, not to air your grievances. Your children and spouse should not be excluded from your missions presentations, but you shouldn't make your presentation about showing off your cute kids.

Submit to the will of the Lord. Neither your ministry, nor your missions presentation are about you, it is all about Christ. People will partner with you through prayer and financial support only if they are led by the Holy Spirit to do so. Your efforts neither gain nor loose supporters. God controls every penny and when you will depart for the mission field if and when he wants you to. Very few people will make a decision to support your work based on how badly you bumbled your presentation or how polished you were. People will support your missions work because they experienced God's involvement in your presentation and felt the pull of his Spirit to partner with you.

Bathe your presentation and preparation is prayer. Make sure your stories, literature, and words are focused on God. Ensure God is glorified by your presentation regardless of whether you gain financial partners or not. If people see God being glorified in the nations, yet still don't support your ministry, that is a win for the kingdom.

A missions presentation is a missionary providing other people the opportunity to glorify God. The decision of the hearers to support or not support your ministry does not reflect on you. Clearly convey how a need exists in another culture and how God has selected you to fill that need so he can have greater glory among that people group. Paint a picture for people that you have been called by God to go and others have been called to stay and pray and support your work financially. Help people understand that both goers and senders have been ordained by God to accomplish his will, and you are gathering your team to bring God glory around the globe.

Missions and the Shocking Reality of Culture Shock

Missionaries read about it, study it and most have experienced it. But, when you arrive on the mission field few things are as surprising as culture shock. The intensity of your initial culture shock and its lengthy duration are startling to most missionaries.

When, how and how often culture shock hits is different for each missionary. Some missionaries are hit hard, right upon arrival, while others don't get hit with it for months or years. Culture shock is hard to describe, but it is generally thought of as being negatively impacted by an unfamiliar way of life. Sometimes it is little differences, while other times it is a cumulative effect. Some people respond with sadness while others manifest their culture shock with anger or frustration.

Merriam-Webster's says culture shock is, "a sense of confusion and uncertainty sometimes with feelings of anxiety that may affect people exposed to an alien culture or environment without adequate preparation." It is a human response to sin. Culture shock occurs because we covet what we know. Our sinful heart longs for the comfort of the familiar.

Understanding what culture shock is and experiencing other cultures can help lessen the intensity and duration of culture shock. Intellectually, it makes sense that all cultures are going to be different, and that those differences can weigh on a person. The more cultural diversity a missionary is exposed to before they arrive on the mission field the quicker they will adjust. Investing time in experiencing other cultures, even if it is not your new culture, will help prepare your brain, heart and soul for the shock of a new culture.

It sounds so basic, but by exposing yourself to other cultures you begin to grasp the idea the world is truly different than your home. Your culture is not what life is like in the rest of the world. Intellectually this makes sense. Which is why culture shock can be so, well, shocking.

Before you start to experience other cultures on the mission field, expose yourself to cultural diversity in your own city. Your exposure does not necessarily need to be similar to the place you will serve, just different than what you are used to.

Go to an ethnic neighborhood in your own city. Go clothes shopping, get a haircut, eat at a restaurant, read a community newspaper, go to a movie. Experience the differences. Once you have experienced things on the surface, go deeper. Volunteer in ethnic communities, attend church, teach English or help kids with homework, make some friends, get yourself invited into homes. This all sounds very awkward and uncomfortable. That is the point. Missions is about being awkward and uncomfortable all the time.

It doesn't matter that the sub-culture you are experiencing in your home city is different than your future ministry home. The point is to experience differences. Be present when a woman exposes herself to nurse a baby. Walk by an old woman who spits on the sidewalk. Experience loud, public verbal altercations. Watch a lady squat to urinate in the gutter. The idea is that you come to the reality that the world is huge and diverse and your exposure to it is limited. The faster you learn that things are just different outside your world the better you will be. Once you can look at other cultures and think to yourself, "Well, that was unexpected and different," and you can just move on the faster you will be able to adjust. Developing that valuable skill will benefit you no matter where you work or live or minister.

Many missionaries think they have culture shock licked before they ever leave their home. We try to intellectualize culture shock. We think, "Ok, I get it. There is going to be poverty, new food, new language and new customs. Great. Let's move on." The reality is culture shock is exhausting. You don't realize how much your senses are bombarded by new sounds, sights, tastes and experiences. It wears a person down to continually process the external stimulus.

Then add in experiences like not being able to communicate, or understand anything, moral dilemmas and always getting lost. There is nothing more humbling than to be pulled from your home culture, where you are relatively smart and can communicate, and being plopped into a situation where you sound like an uneducated three-year-old and nothing makes sense.

All missionaries struggle with culture shock. The question is not if, but how and when it will hit you. Some members of the same family are hit differently, at different times and with different manifestations. Give yourself and those around you plenty of grace.

Culture shock sanctifies us and makes us more open to flexibility in God's service. It is humbling, frustrating and in some cases emotionally crippling. You can't control it, but you can diminish the negative impact it will have on you.

Expect it and even embrace it. Like the Apostle Paul, thank God for the thorn he has given you. Don't ignore it or view it as a sign of weakness. Culture shock is a natural and common experience for almost all missionaries. When it does hit you, use it as yet another reason to lean into the mercy of Jesus Christ.

Chapter Four

Finances and Missions

Much of our sin life revolves around money. There is little evidence to demonstrate Christians are better any better at addressing finances than are non-Christians. At the heart of the problem sits the idea, we think we are responsible for earning our money. The "hard work ethic" has so saturated our culture, even Christians believe they earned their money. If we believe we earned ours through our own efforts, like the world, we are reticent to give that money to help others. We believe others who need resources should pull themselves up by their own bootstraps.

Often times this Western view of money is so pervasive, Christians can't escape it. However, the sovereignty of God tells us our Lord is the source of worldly resources. If we have resources, they have been given to us by God, not our hard work. Because, we are so hung up on money we find difficulty in attributing its existence in our lives to God.

Because we all believe the money is our, we have a hard time seeking it or spending it on ministries which bring glory to God. Missionaries would not be so scared to ask for money and others would not be hesitant to give money, if we all truly thought the money was God's. We are all called to be good stewards of what resources God has given us. And, we should all be eager to turn it back over to the kingdom when God desires it of us.

A Biblical View of Financing Missions

The concept of funding missions through the financial support of others is not a new concept. In fact, raising support for missions has a long and distinguished biblical history. Throughout the Bible God calls upon his people to give sacrificially so missionaries can travel the globe to bring him glory.

Christians should develop a war-time approach to sacrificial support of missions. During great wars those who stayed behind sacrificed their comfort to help do their part so the boys in the trenches could fight on. The spiritual warfare that is being waged in every corner of the globe is no less deserving of sacrificial support than the great wars of man.

God has blessed American Christians with the ability to fund the global missions battle raging around the world. American churches are the richest in history not so they can provide their congregants with softer cushions for their pews. American churches are the richest in history to finance global evangelism. We must not mistake God's financial blessings as a reward for our good service. We have been blessed to glorify God, not to create comfort and security for ourselves. Local churches should focus their time and talents on local evangelism and their treasure on global evangelism.

Shouldn't all those lazy, freeloading missionaries stop begging for money and start supporting themselves like the Apostle Paul did? Paul, who was a knowledgeable tent maker, did not encourage missionaries to earn their own way. In fact, quite the opposite. He taught churches they should financially support fulltime servants of the gospel. People erroneously make the assumption Paul always supported his ministry by making tents. That was not his preferred method. Paul began by making tents, but quit as soon as church support came in.

For Paul, the concept of financial independence and apostolic authority were interwoven. In Paul's quarrel with his detractors in Corinth (1 Cor 4:12, 9:1-18, 16:5-6; 2 Cor 2:17, 8:1-9:15) he argues in favor of the church supporting laborers of the gospel. The Corinthian church was in a season of plenty. He explains to them that their financial blessing is not meant for them, but to share with other Christian laborers in need.

Throughout his epistles, Paul clearly encourages the financial support of missionaries and pastors through the church. He instructs the Galatians (Gal 6:6) that the church body is to financially support the teachers of the faith. He quotes the gospels (Luk 10:7; Mat 10:10) when in 1 Timothy he tells the church to allow the servants to eat (1 Ti 5:18). Paul thanks the church at Philippi for supporting him (Phil 4:10-20).

Much of Paul's letter to the Romans focused on financial support of missions work. Paul asked the Roman church to financially support Phoebe and her work (Rom 16:1-2). Paul also sought the aide of the Roman church to fund his mission work in Spain (Rom 15:20-24). Indeed, D.A. Carson says of this passage, "According to some scholars, Paul's primary reason for writing this letter is to establish a relationship with the Roman Christians so that they would financially support his mission to plant new churches in Spain."

Much of Paul's writing was not focused on missionaries carrying for their own financial needs, but rather Paul's desire for the church to provide for missionaries.

Jesus came from a working-class carpenter's home. However, he chose a life where he and his fulltime followers were dependent upon the contribution of those who supported his mission (Mat 10:8–11; Luk 10:38–42).

Jesus' ministry was funded by those who received his teaching (Luk 8:1-3). The women portrayed in this passage were paying the expenses for Jesus to travel through the cities "bringing the glad tidings of the kingdom of God." Jesus depended on others for support.

Jesus instructed the disciples to rely on others while ministering (Mat 10:5-15). He repeated this in Luke 10:7 when he sent out the 70 believers. Those he sent were not to provide for themselves.

God wants us to depend on him. He wants us to come to him with our needs. As our faithful Father, he is eager to meet those needs (Mat 7:7-12). God's way of disseminating blessings to his fulltime laborers is by providing those blessings through his church.

The concept of the church financially supporting missionaries and pastors is not confined to the New Testament. David presented his vision for building a temple to God, to the people and they joyously responded with their time, talents and treasures (1 Chr 28:1-29:20). Nehemiah sought support for the reconstruction of the wall of Jerusalem (Neh 1:1-2:9). In fact, the entire Levitical system was based on God's people financially supporting fulltime ministers (Num 18: 21-24). God's workers have always received financial support from other disciples.

God's teaching is very explicit. There are many examples of this principle being practiced throughout the Scriptures. How should missionaries receive financial support? Biblically, there is only one answer. As the Lord has commanded, those who proclaim the gospel should get their living by the gospel (1 Cor 9:14). God's hardworking missionaries are to be financially supported by God's exceedingly blessed church. Churches support your missionaries and missionaries do not be intimidated to follow God's instructions.

How Missionaries Should Raise Money

Nearly every missionary who has to raise support to go on the mission field is horrified by the task before them. Most people have little experience asking for money or promoting a cause. Millions of inexperienced people have done it before you, so it must be possible. Raising support for missions doesn't need to be scary. In fact, it can be a very sanctifying process.

If you think you can't raise the money to go on the mission field you've already made your first mistake. God will raise the money, not you. Most missionaries, when faced with the task of raising the financial support, think way too little of God and way too highly of themselves. Even if we view support raising as a herculean task, we flatter ourselves by assuming we have anything to do with the process. Our health, money and clothes come from God, we know that. But, if we agonize over support raising we are implying that God has less than 100% control and we have more than 0%.

Every missionary must start by believing, not just saying, that every dollar on the planet belongs to God and if and when he wants you to get to the mission field he will make it happen. Two of the most discussed topics in Scripture are sin and money. It should come as no surprise that money is at the core of much of our sin. This is why we are afraid to ask people for money, because we think our asking and their answer have anything to do with raising funds. Do not begin your support raising process until you have truly grasped the fact that God is 100% in control of the finances to be raised. If God wants you on the mission field, get out of the way and let him do the work. If you prayerfully conclude that God has called you to serve his will, why do you not trust he will provide all the resources for the task?

Now that you have changed your view of the sovereignty of God, you must change your perspective of the people you will be asking to join you in supporting God's work. View churches and individuals as people who might be called by God to partner with you in missions. You are called to go and they are called to give. Supporters and missionaries are a partnership. When you are asking someone to financially support your missions efforts you must believe you are providing them with an opportunity to glorify the Lord. You want to bring God greater glory and you want others to join you. You must not view support raising for missions as a burden for you or an annoyance for those you ask to join you.

Start this process in prayer and cover it in prayer daily. Ask others to pray for you. Not simply that you raise all the money, but that you glorify God in the process. If you are not spending time in prayer you are not focused enough on God's involvement.

Compile a list of people you know. It is not relevant if they are Christian or not. You will contact everyone you ever met. You want their mailing address, phone number and e-mail address. People from your youth, neighborhood and business. What about the service industries you frequent? Over the years you have given small fortunes to your hair stylist, mechanic, dentist and veterinarian.

Design all your letters, e-mails, information packets and phone scripts before you contact people. These don't have to be slick and definitely shouldn't be lengthy. Everything you send out should include an "ask" and should contain your name, contact information and action item. You want visual and contextual continuity in everything you produce.

Be persistent about contacting people. Not calling you back is not a "no." You should contact people until they say "yes" or "no." You don't have the authority to decide to stop contacting people because you are bugging them. That is God's job. Contact your entire list each week. Mail the first week, e-mail the second, phone the third, mail the fourth, e-mail the fifth...and so on.

View your life as bulls eye. Contact those who are emotionally and geographically closest to you first. Move out from there.

If someone says "yes" follow up with them until they have returned the documentation. If someone says "no" ask them if they will pray for you and send them regular prayer updates.

Ask people if you can meet with them to share what you are going to do on the mission field.

No matter who you talk to, your missions efforts are not nearly as important to anyone as they are to you. Other peoples' lives move on. Well-intentioned people who want to support you need to be reminded because their busy life has moved forward.

Always send thank you cards letting people know you appreciate their partnership.

Seldom have I met a missionary who wasn't worried about raising support during the process. But, seldom have I met a missionary who didn't grow closer to God in the process. Move forward knowing the Lord controls all resources and he is giving you this opportunity to share his glory and surround yourself with a team of eager co-laborers.

Stop Saying Raising Finances for Missions is Hard

Money and the Christian faith has such a cloudy relationship in the minds of most Christians in the modern western church. Don't misunderstand what you just read. God and the Bible are very clear about finances. Throughout time and in the rest of the world, other Christians have had a healthy biblical understanding of finances. However, in the modern western church, we turned finances into a complicated topic.

Because money is such a powerful idol in the West, raising financial support for missions is such a murky topic in our churches. Contrary to popular misconception, it is God who controls all finances. Many Christians say God is sovereign and in control of everything, but their actions and attitudes toward money prove differently. Too often, missionaries, churches and congregants act like they have ultimate sway over who does and doesn't make it to the mission field by their actions surrounding money. God controls every dollar, pound, franc and peso. If this is true, why do missionaries view raising financial support as such a hard task?

A missionary is not a super-Christian, simply an obedient Christian. Because of this, many missionaries enter missions with the same sinful attitudes the rest of us share about God and money. Missionaries view raising financial support not as a God-centered activity, but as a man-centered venture. Missionaries think the burden is on them to sell themselves and their ministry to individuals and churches who may or may not deem them worthy.

If God wants you on the mission field he will provide the means when he deems it appropriate. We have such a sinful attitude toward money and raising support, that potential missionaries avoid missions once they learn they have to raise their own finances. Missionaries are scared to ask people for support and then feel too beholden to supporters when they receive it. We too seldom even bring God into the equation.

Do a web search for "God and finances" and the articles that pop up have titles like, "Trusting God With Your Finances," "God and Your Money," and "10 Ways God Works Through Our Finances." Dear gentle reader, let me be crass for a moment to provide a little clarity…YOU DON'T HAVE ANY MONEY! Our view of God and finances in the western world is unhealthy and unbiblical. We too often act like we earned our money and it is ours. God is the owner of all money and he has seen fit to make us temporary stewards over a small part of it.

Give wildly to God and his ministries. Go crazy with God's money. Spend the money you have, but spend it on God's glory, not your own comfort and security. Do not view God blessing you with money as some sort of reward for your loyalty to him or some kind of blessing to be lavished on yourself. God put you through school, provided your job and gave you opportunities so you could more easily fund his ministries in your town and around the world. When we give our wealth and financial blessing back to God we experience his glory. If we have a perspective that says, "I just can't afford to tithe or support missions," we have already placed our own comfort ahead of God's glory.

God has made the Christian church which exists in the western world today the richest most financially blessed church in the history of the world. He did not do that so we could have softer cushions on our pews, but so we could finance the global spread of his gospel. Do you believe your church needs a more expensive building, new carpet or another secretary while the missionaries you've partnered with are struggling to pay for new Bibles, translated books or shoes for their own kids?

God's Great Commission is a mandate given to the corporate church to spread his gospel around the world. Yes, you are called to reach the heathen in Iowa, or Tennessee, or Illinois. Yes, the people in your town will go to the same hell as the people in the jungles of Zimbabwe, Laos, and Colombia. However, the people in your town are not more deserving of the gospel than the people around the globe. Please continue to reach the people in the town you have been called to minister, but never forget God has mandated you to participate in his global march toward the end of days. The Great Commission is not optional.

When we act like man controls all the money, missions seems impossible. When we acknowledge God controls all the money, missions seems much easier. Too many missionaries act like raising support is a hard task, because too many Christian disciples take God out of finances. When God is in control of finances things like an economic downturn, a local factory shutting down or a rich family leaving a church are far less relevant. When Christian disciples are focused on God controlling all finances, God will receive greater glory, and no Christian will ever again say, "Raising finances for missions is hard."

Why Missionaries Can't Raise Money

That daunting task of raising the financial support needed to go on the mission field is overwhelming for most missionaries. Too many would-be global servants believe raising finances is the worst part about missions. Sure you can leave your home and learn a new language, but asking people for money? Most missionaries think they just can't do it.

If you think you can't raise the money to go on the mission field you've already made your first mistake. God will raise the money, not you. Too often missionaries toil and stress and fuss and fret over the difficulty they encounter in raising financial support to serve in missions. The problem occurs when missionaries put the burden on their own shoulders instead of God's.

Most every disciple of Christ will acknowledge all riches come from God and not from man. Many can even point you to supporting Scripture (Ps 127; Eph 1:3-14; Rom 1:7; Jas 1:17). But, living that truth is something altogether different. If your ministry is ordained by God you will have no problem raising support for it. Why wouldn't God use his money to support his work? Missionary Hudson Taylor said, "God's work done in God's way will never lack God's supplies."[47]

The problem doesn't begin with missions, it begins in the heart of a Christian. Many of us don't act like everything we have comes from God. And if pushed on the subject, frankly we don't believe it, not entirely. We still think we have something to do with our station in life. Christians are called to present our bodies as a living sacrifice (Rom 12:1). If we honestly viewed ourselves as a living sacrifice we wouldn't be preoccupied with figuring out the minimum amount we were required to give to God.

If our missionaries truly believed it was God who was providing them with 100% of the resources they needed, they wouldn't stress so much about asking friends for a couple hundred dollars. Missionaries, be confident in Christ. You are not some burden who must compete with the Girl Scouts, soccer team and movie theatre for a family's dwindling monthly paycheck. You are a servant of the Lord. If you are indeed doing God's will, he will send you. John Piper said, "All the money needed to send and support an army of self-sacrificing, joy-spreading ambassadors is already in the church."[48] When you ask people to financially support your missions work do so with the joy in your heart of knowing you are providing them an opportunity to glorify God.

Churches, if you are not encouraging your congregants to spread the gospel or support others who do, what are you doing? If we as disciples of Christ are not actively sharing the mercy of Christ or facilitating the work in others there is a danger we do not understand why God has us here. The idols we make of comfort, safety and money are keeping many Christians from fulfilling God's command of global evangelism.

Finances, good health, material blessings and strong relationships mean nothing if they are not used to expand God's gospel and glory. Did God make U.S. churches the richest in history so they could buy new cushions for their pews or to spread the gospel around the world? Leonard Ravenhill stated, "Today Christians spend more money on dog food than missions."[49]

As missionaries you are called by God to go, so too are supporters called to pray and write checks. God has called both sides to partner together for his glory. Both, parties deserve the respect and honor of being obedient servants to the Lord. Goers and senders should pour out the mercies you have been given on those who have not been blessed as much as you have. Playing a part in world evangelism, be it going, sending or praying, is

---

[47] Mark Water, *The Christian Book of Records* (Alresford, Hants, UK: John Hunt Pub., 2002), 66.

[48] John Piper, *Don't Waste Your Life* (Wheaton, IL: Crossway Books, 2003), 172.

[49] W.K. Volkmer, *These Things* (San Antonio, TX: The Passionate Few, 2016), 187.

not for the super Christian, it is for the obedient Christian. The poor, the orphan and the lost are God's gift to us so we have someplace to direct the abundant mercy he richly bestowed on us.

If God has called you to go to the nations be bold in that calling. You are beholden to no man, instead, you owe all you have to the Creator of the Universe. He has set you apart for his glorious purpose. Humble obedience and confidence are appropriate for all missionaries. God has declared of you, "How beautiful are the feet of those who preach the good news." (Rom 10:15) My missionary brethren, act like your feet are beautiful. Do not shrink at the small task of going out and finding the few coins God has hidden for you to fund the ministry to which he has called you.

Be the intrepid warrior God has prepared you to be. Support raising is not a popularity contest. A rebuking of your request for financial partnership is not a rejection of you. Nor is an affirmative response a reflection on you. The raising of financial support for your missions efforts is a confirmation by God that he has called you to serve him. Use your support raising process as another way joyfully bring glory to God.

We Have Been Blessed in Order to be a Blessing

God has provided enormous blessings to today's Christian church in the Western world. We enjoy amazing freedom, resources and opportunity. Yet, at the same time world poverty and Christian persecutions are soaring. Why has God blessed our churches in such times? God's call to Abraham gives us insight, "And I will make of you a great nation, and I will bless you and make your name great, so that you will be a blessing." (Gen 12:2)

Our country, our churches and our families have been blessed in order to be a blessing to the world. Are we utilizing those resources to bless the world or are we using them to bless ourselves? We appear to have lost our biblical perspective. Our Western brand of Christianity is out of touch with world Christianity and historical Christianity.

If you make $49,802 per year (average income in the U.S.) you earn more money than 99% of the world's population. If your family earns $23,050 per year (US poverty level for family of 4) you are in the top 19% of the world's richest people. More than one-half of the world's population lives below the internationally defined poverty line of less than $2 a day. We are the richest church in the history of the world for a reason. It has more to do with the sick & poor than our own recreation & indulgence.

The gifts we have been given were not intended to provide us comfort & security, but instead used to better serve those in need. Our Christian brothers and sisters are struggling. Every year over 100,000 Christians are killed for what they believe. Today 200 million Christians in 60 countries are denied basic human rights because of their faith. Today 300 million people don't have a Bible available in their own language. Tim Keller tells us, "Because Jesus served you in such a radical way, you have a joyful need to serve."

While we covet our latest gadgets and spend God's resources on ourselves there are countless unsaved dying of preventable diseases and starving around the globe. World Christians are risking their lives to find a Bible, attend church and evangelize the unsaved. God has blessed us in the Western church so that we can be a great blessing to the rest of the world for the kingdom. In his book Dangerous Calling Paul David Tripp writes, "Don't confuse God's blessing as his endorsement of the way you're living."

Paul told the Christians in Corinth, "You will be enriched in every way to be generous in every way, which through us will produce thanksgiving to God." (2 Cor 9:11) God does not need us to expand his kingdom, but he has blessed us with the extreme privilege of sharing his name with the world. Our goal, in everything we do, is to glorify God. We are to bless the world and expand the gospel. God did not give us good health and resources so we could spoil ourselves. Use all God has given you to expand his kingdom and share his gospel.

Doctor, teacher and janitor is not your calling. Those are the means God has given to provide His mercy and love to others. That's your calling. Our time, our resources and our heart should be diverted from seeking our own pleasure and comfort toward expanding God's kingdom and glory. Serving the poor is not about sympathy for their condition, it is sharing the gifts we were given when God had mercy for our condition.

In Scripture James wrote, "Religion that is pure and undefiled before God, the Father, is this: to visit orphans and widows in their affliction, and to keep oneself unstained from the world." (Jam 1:27) As Christians we are called to bring glory to God by serving those in need. Serving the needy around the world or on your block is the calling of every Christian. When God places a needy stranger in your path he is doing so to give you the opportunity to show that person the grace and mercy of Jesus. Giving a coat or a sandwich to the destitute is like giving a piece of the new heart you have been given from Christ.

God has richly blessed our Western churches and families. Nothing says we cannot enjoy those blessings as well. Augustine told us we can enjoy God's blessings, but we must share them in God's name, "Find out how much God has given you and from it take what you need; the remainder is needed by others." We must use God's resources for what they were intended: God's glory in the world. God's grace and mercy poured out on us should create Christians who are devoted to blessing the world in God's name.

Giving our leftovers was not the goal when God called for us to give our lives. Make a sacrifice in your life today to better enable the expansion of the gospel into the world. When you give dignity, mercy, love, justice, charity and respect to others you are letting them see Christ in your words and actions. We must not lose site of why it is that God has blessed us so richly. Paul reminds us, "who comforts us in all our affliction, so that we may be able to comfort those who are in any affliction, with the comfort with which we ourselves are comforted by God." (2 Cor 1:4)

The late Adrian Rogers said, "You cannot obey God without your obedience spilling out in a blessing to all those around you."[50] Let's strive to bless the world with the blessings God has given us.

9 Items that Should be in Every Missionary's Budget

If the Christian church assumes God commands us to send missionaries to the nations, we must also assume God does not want those missionaries to needlessly struggle or go without the tools that will help them do their ministry more effectively. While no missionary should go on the field to improve their lifestyle, there is nothing in the Bible that says they need to live a miserable existence while on the field. We must ask ourselves, should a missionary suffer in a way we wouldn't tolerate for ourselves or our children?

The rest of this article operates under the assumption that a missionary on the field is already paying a significant price by being on the mission field and that the Lord's suffering servants need not pay an additional cost. Here are a few things every church should demand their missionaries have in their budget in order to live an average life, but also to lead an exceptional ministry:

1. Computer Stipend

Technology is vital today and allows us to research and complete projects that would have been nearly impossible a few decades ago. The time saved and value added by computer technology is great stewardship of the Lord's resources. The extreme weather conditions and unreliable power systems in other countries frequently take their toll on electronics. Missionaries need to be able to replace computers and accessories more frequently.

---

[50] Mark Water, *Evangelical Sunday School Lesson Commentary* (Alresford, Hants, UK: John Hunt Pub., 2002), 50.

2. Retirement

When a missionary is asked to sacrifice his earning years without contributing to his retirement he is actually giving much more to the Great Commission. If a missionary has no retirement and is forced to return from the mission field, due to illness or ability, he has no way to provide for himself. If a missionary has retirement investments, it is possible to self-fund their missions work in later years. Retirement provides a missionary with more options to glorify the Lord in their non-earning years.

3. Continuing Education

Missions techniques, knowledge and theory are constantly evolving. It is advantageous for a long-term missionary to stay abreast of the evolving ministry practices. Conferences, books and advanced degrees make it possible for a missionary to evolve and become a better practitioner of disciple making.

4. Health Care

A missionary with no way to care for catastrophic health care coverage is at great risk of harming their family or halting their ministry in a medical emergency. It is a fact that preventative care and regular checkups save lives and cost less in the long run. A healthy missionary is apt to serve longer on the mission field.

5. Child Education Expenses

Children should not be made to permanently struggle because their parent is an obedient servant to the Lord. Frequently international education is sub-par and parents need to options to educate their children. If a missionary serves a lengthy period of time on the mission field they reduce their earning power and ability to help pay for their child's secondary education. Assisting a missionary alleviate part of the financial burden of education helps ensure retention of quality missionaries.

6. Communications Allowance

Missionaries are notoriously poor communicators. For whatever reason many missionaries do not communicate God's glory well to the world and their financial and prayer partners. Providing resources to help missionaries communicate better keeps those back home focused and prayerful for the ministry. Webpage maintenance, online thank you card services, video conferencing, prayer letter services, and software to help with editing videos and pictures are all resources that will help missionaries better connect with their supporters back home.

7. Life Insurance

It would be terrible to see a disciple who is martyred during missionary service enter the kingdom and leave behind medical and burial costs, debt and a grieving family unable to care for themselves. Providing for the survivors of a missionary is important to the grieving process and a way of thanking a missionary and his family for serving our Father.

8. Shipping and Mail

Frequently ministry supplies and resources are hard to find in foreign countries. Often times supporters are eager to accumulate supplies and ship them to the missionary. Sometimes receiving trade periodicals, legal correspondents or ministry support can be expensive. Sending support raising videos, letters or thank you gifts from a foreign country can be hard. Correspondence in some foreign countries is often cost prohibitive.

9. Cost of Living Adjustment

When the cost of milk, bread and bus fare go up, but a person's salary stays the same it is equivalent to receiving an annual pay reduction. Missionaries should receive regular cost of living increases corresponding with the rate of inflation in the country they serve. Missionaries should not be punished for longevity.

Missionaries do not get into missions because of the perks. A missionary is willing to make certain sacrifices to benefit the kingdom. However, if the Christian church were better providing for its missionaries we might attract more qualified servants and encourage them to serve longer. Providing a missionary with the resources, assistance and peace of mind the rest of us enjoy is a wise investment for global evangelism.

How an Average Church Can Fully Fund a Missionary

The Barna Group says the average size of a Protestant church in the U.S. includes 89 adults. The World Bank tells us the average income in the U.S. is $53,000 per year. If those 89 average adults tithed the biblical minimum of 10% per year to their typical church, that church would have an annual budget of $471,000. Wow. What kind of impact could that church have on the lost in the world?

If every evangelical Christian was dedicated to the biblical mandate of the tithe (Lv 27:30) and if every evangelical church was dedicated to the biblical mandate of missions (Ac 1:8) we could flood the globe with new missionaries. There are currently 140,000 protestant missionaries serving in the world. Imagine what God could do with double or triple that number of missionaries. This would be a reality if every American church endeavored to fully fund just one or two missionaries.

Imagine what a missionary could do if he was only responsible for communicating with and visiting one church instead of two or three dozen supporting churches. More time could be spent serving God and discipling the lost. More missionaries being supported by a single supporting church would mean greater accountability and better missionary care. Envision the involvement congregations would have with global evangelism if each typical congregation was engaged with a single missionary overseeing one church plant in one people group.

The reality is very different than this God honoring hypothetical. More money is embezzled ($50 billion) by church staff each year than is given to missions ($45 billion). The average American Christian gives only one penny a day to global missions. Some missionaries travel around for years trying to raise the funds needed to enter the mission field, and when they are on furlough many missionaries drive tens of thousands of miles visiting all of their supporting churches.

Many churches aren't focused on their purpose as outlined in Scripture. God provided a corporate mandate for his churches to go into the world and disciple the lost (Mat 28:18-20), but, while the harvest is plentiful the laborers are few (Mat 9:37).

The change must begin in our pulpits. Pastors and church leaders must preach and teach Scripture. Only then will the average Christian understand that without the gospel the world will perish (Rom 1, 2) and that is why God mandates his church to go into the world (Mar 16:15). Hearing biblical teaching the typical congregant will understand that God has blessed us so that we may bless others (1 Pet 2:12) and that Christians are to return a portion of God's blessing to his church (Mat 23:23). Many believers will hear for the first time that the purpose of each disciple is to glorify God (1 Cor 6:20) and we are to live our lives as a sacrifice to him (Rom 12:1). This is not being taught by many of God's churches today.

God instructs every church and every Christian to pray (Phil 4:6; Jon 15:7; Luk 11:9). Ask God to bless you more abundantly so you may better bless others (1 Chr 4:10; Ps 67). Ask God to give you a heart for the lost. Search God's wisdom as to how your family and your church can reprioritize discretionary spending so you can better fund global evangelism. God desires to be glorified by more souls worshiping him. He desires those souls to be reached through his church. Ask God to use you and your congregation to reach the lost across the street and around the globe and his response may surprise you.

Change the culture and priorities of your church. Is your congregation striving to be more comfortable while there are millions of people in the world who have still not heard the name of Jesus? Make some hard decisions to eliminate frivolous budgetary items and make God's global priority for the lost an urgency for your church. Restructure your missionary spending so your church is investing more time and resources into fewer missionaries. Make a major investment of your time, talents and treasures into one people group instead a tiny impact into 10 people groups. Remember that God made the modern American evangelical church the richest church in history for a reason, and that reason has nothing to do with our comfort or security.

Too many congregations are playing at church and allowing their congregants be too introspective. Our lives were given to us by God, not so we may enjoy this world, but so that we can bring him glory. Changing the missions mindset of a church is a hard task. Most of us are content with being casual Christians and praying somebody else worries about the lost.

Changing the DNA of your church so that it becomes more focused on God's glory in the world can be painful and slow. However, nothing but God's glory can come of it. The purpose of the church is to disciple the lost (Jon 20:21-23). The motive of the church is to bring God greater glory (Ps 86:12; Rom 15:6). God is glorified when his church sacrificially sends missionaries into the world to make new disciples to worship him. Can your church fully fund just one or two missionaries? Yes, indeed it can. Some hard changes may be ahead, but God's glory is worth it.

Investments in Technology that Benefit Missions

Purchasing technology for your missions work is an investment that has a high probability of paying dividends. Electronic gadgets are not the answer to every problem, but technology can advance your ministry and help a missionary more easily glorify God. Certainly, quality global discipleship work has been done and will continue to be done without out the aide of contraptions. But, used properly, technology can be a huge boon for missions.

Many missionaries find out the hard way that purchasing technology around the globe can be challenging. Certainly, many countries have at least as good a selection as the stores in the U.S. However, in the developing world missionaries frequently find higher prices, lesser quality, and fewer options for technological gadgets. Making an investment in technology can save time and money for your ministry in the long run.

Several schools of thought differ from this perspective. Some people simply feel creating a dependency on technology sets one up for failure. A missionary must never become so reliant on technology that its absence harms the ministry. There is also the Luddite crowd who rebel against technological advances. This group believes paper and pen and hardcopy books will never let us down. For whatever reason, many missionaries make conscious decisions to avoid technology in their ministry, and that is just fine. But, technology, if used correctly and with wisdom can be a blessing to foreign missions.

The smartphone is the Swiss army knife of technology. It has your camera, Bible, library, editing functions, calendar, and more all in one place. Some countries block some popular applications for varying reasons. The affordability of data and telephone plans varies widely around the globe. Much of the rest of the world uses chips that will work on your phone, but it must first be unlocked. Even without a phone or internet signal a smartphone can be very useful. Some phone brands work better in some countries than others. This valuable piece of technology requires lots of research before investing.

Internet telephony (Vonage, etc.), video conferencing (Zoom, etc.), or hybrid platforms (Skype, etc.) are only as good as the internet connection which carries them. Poor internet can make them useless. Most voice and video services can be used via smartphones or computers. Some countries block some of these services. These tools can be incredible and inexpensive ways to keep in touch with family, friends, and supporters. Raising support, videoing into a missions conference, medical consultations, and so much more can be accomplished with these services.

The popular brands (Kindle, Nook, etc.) are getting more book titles every day. Few new books are released these days without an electronic version. Books for theology, school, pleasure, and more are all available. Many foreign language books are available to help you learn language or do your ministry. Most e-books are less expensive than their hardcopy counterparts, and the delivery is quick and free. E-books have made reading around the world much less expensive than it used to be.

There are dozens of biblical research options that range from free to expensive. Most of the popular Bible software packages (Logos, Bibleworks, e-Sword, etc.) have online and offline options if you have limited internet. The concept of having tens of thousands of electronic theology books at your disposal was unheard of just a generation ago on the mission field. New releases are coming in Bible software format quicker each month. These useful tools can be used for Bible studies, sermons, research, or reading. Any ministry, which has a biblical component, is made easier with these gems.

There are many kinds of data storage devices (jump drives, external hard drives, cloud storage, etc.). For dependability, you may find low-tech is the best option here. With all the pictures, videos, documents, flyers, etc. missionaries produce a safe place to store them all is a good idea. It is surprising how invaluable these device become on the mission field.

Mini projectors, solar lights, rechargeable batteries, voltage regulators, internet TV, plug adapters, laptops, upgraded virus protection, and more, are all items which missionaries may find useful in in a foreign setting. E-gift cards (iTunes, Amazon, etc.) become great birthday and Christmas gifts when you are far away.

No gadget should be considered compulsory. If a missionary is going to invest in any technology for ministry it should be a well-prayed over decision. Before you spend your or your supporter's money do substantive research. How hard is it to repair or replace broken parts? What is the internet and electricity infrastructure like where you are going? How does the device do outside of climate controlled settings? When you invest in technology ask others who live in your host city what devices they find useful.

Technology, if used properly, can increase a missionary's efficiency, quality, and communication. If the right capital investment is made a missionary's time and sanity, two precious commodities on the mission field, can be saved. Don't become a slave to your technology or make idols of the items you purchase. But, frequently a smart investment in useful technology can be a great way to increase God's glory on the mission field.

To What Church Should a Missionary Tithe?

This is a confusing topic which most every missionary has contemplated and almost nobody has been prepared to address. In all my time being trained for the mission field, training other missionaries, serving on the mission field and studying missions I can safely say I have never heard this question properly addressed.

Biblically, a missionary is sent by his home church. Missionaries remain members of their sending church. While the missionary is on the field, the sending church continues to be responsible for the missionary's spiritual growth and wellbeing as well as responding to causes for discipline.

However, daily, the church the missionary spends the most time with is the one they are attending on the mission field. Regular worship, administering sacraments, and theological growth all occur within the context of the host church. This is the church the missionary may grow close to and spend most of their time.

The difficult question for the missionary is, who receives his tithes? Nothing in Scripture says a missionary should stop tithing. Should a missionary tithe to the home church or the host church?

All we have comes from God. The air in our lungs, our possessions, and our family are all gifts from God. We are only stewards of that which Christ has entrusted us. He asks us to avail all to him and be willing to surrender all. As a mere symbol and starting point he commands his disciples to freely return a tenth of all we have for his service (Gen 14:20; Lev 5:16, 27:30; Num 18:25-32; Deut 12:17, 14:22-29, 26:12; 1 Sam 8:15, 17; 2 Chro 31:5; Neh 11:1, 13:12; Ezra 2:68; Eze 20:37; Mal 3:6-12; Luk 11:42; Heb 7:4-10). This symbolic offering is asked of all Christian disciples no matter their vocation, geography or financial status. Missionaries are nowhere excluded from tithing.

Some have rationalized since a fulltime minister of the gospel (missionary, pastor, etc.) is giving so much of their time and earning power to the service of the Lord they are exempt from the tithe. Nothing in Scripture makes this point, nor supports this rational. A fulltime missionary is to tithe as is every Christian.

Many consider the sending church back in the home country as the appropriate entity which the foreign missionary should tithe. On returning to his sending church Paul gathered the church to report on how God had been glorified by their combined efforts of sending and going (Acts 14:27). Missionaries are sent by their home church (Acts 13) and are responsible to them. Every local church is responsible to care for all its members (Eze 34:1-16; Gal. 6:1-2; 1 Tim 5:17; 2 Tim 4:1-5) no matter how far away they may live. It then makes sense for a missionary to tithe to their home church.

On the other hand, the host church, in the missionary's country of service, is the body where he is spending most of his time. A missionary is actively serving and spiritually growing in the host church. The missionary is reaping the benefits of the labors of the local pastor and church members and is deeply invested in the local congregation. Local resources (paper, electricity, rent, etc.) are contributing toward the care and feeding of the missionary's soul. It is the people of the local congregation who are investing the most day-to-day sweat equity into the lives of the missionary and his family. It would not be inappropriate for a missionary to tithe to his host church.

Both churches are investing in the life of the missionary. The missionary should not ignore what either church does for his sanctification. Hopefully, both churches are praying for, spiritual feeding and carrying for the needs of the missionary. Both congregations, even though they may be on separate continents, are part of the same body of Christ and both require tithes to function. It appears to be a rational alternative for a missionary to divide his tithe between the two churches who are carrying for him.

Tithes are given to the church as a way of facilitating Christ's ongoing mercy and grace through the church. Not tithing to any church is hording for oneself that which Jesus freely gave to you. A disciple of Christ must be willing to joyfully give all back to the Lord. Not being willing to give even a fraction says something profound about a missionary's heart. This is not a biblical option and should not be considered. Even the Levites, who were supported by the tithes of the people, were instructed by God to give a "tithe of the tithe" (Num 18:26b).

The missionary must go before the Lord in prayer and seek his guidance. As long as a tithe is given by the missionary, a profound argument can be made to tithe to the home church, the host church or both churches. Consult your church leaderships for wisdom and guidance. The missionary is ultimately responsible to God and is called to avail all he has for the work of Christ's Bride. The church of Jesus is a huge, multi-ethnic and diverse entity. Prayer and Christian prudence will reveal the correct destination for a Missionary's tithe.

The Dilemma of House Help on the Mission Field

Frequently missionaries get to the field and have a dilemma about using hired help with childcare, cooking, or housekeeping around their home. Statistically the West uses house helpers less than in the rest of the world. In the West domestic help is often seen as a luxury available only to the upper classes.

Domestic helpers are more common in the rest of the world. Employing domestic help doesn't come with the same stigma in other cultures as it does in the West. There are many good reasons missionaries should consider hiring domestic help.

In the developing world, it is common to see families who have very little income, yet still are able to afford domestic help. Since unskilled laborers in most countries earn a legal minimum wage of $2 - $20 a day, it is financially feasible for even poor families to hire help.

Around the world domestic helpers suffer a disproportionate amount of financial and physical abuse at the hands of their employers. Often national laborers prefer working for westerners because they are treated fairly. Employing domestic help on the mission field can provide a national with a safe working environment and a steady income.

Hiring domestic workers in countries with depressed economies and high unemployment can help a worker provide for her family. Many poor and uneducated workers rely on manual labor jobs to provide for their families. In Latin America, as an example, over 10% of all employees work as domestic workers. Poor families and the local economy count on the existence of domestic labor.

In some cultures, hiring domestic help is a way of helping an oppressed class of people. In many cultures those who do domestic work come from a subjugated ethnicity, gender, or religion. In the Middle East, domestic work accounts for almost 1/3rd of all jobs held by women.

Many missionaries struggle with the idea of using house help on the mission field because of the fear they may be perceived as lazy or living too lavishly. Because we struggle with God's grace, many evangelicals (missionaries too) operate falsely under the assumption a missionary must suffer on the mission field in order to be truly serving Christ.

Since our works-oriented hearts erroneously feel the more a missionary suffers the more he is truly serving, often we view hiring domestic help as somehow less righteous. Because missionary service is perceived as hard, a missionary who is suffering less is too often perceived as a lesser class of missionary. Therefore, it can be perceived that hiring house help is a sign of a missionary who just can't handle the ministry. This is an unfortunate and dangerous mentality.

Living in another culture can be confusing and add lots of stress. Sometimes, the most frustrating thing about missions is the perceived lack of efficiency in non-western cultures. Simple activities like paying bills or buying groceries in a culture, which is not your own, can take what seems to be an unnecessary amount of time.

Having a domestic worker in your home who can help relieve some of your burden and help train a missionary how to live daily life more efficiently can be a great blessing. Relieving your household stress and freeing up your time is not only good for your family's mental health, but it is also being a good steward of your resources. If a national worker can make a few meals, watch the kids, or do the laundry, that gives the missionary more time to spend discipling or training people in their new culture.

Daily interaction with house help who are from your new culture will create opportunities to practice your new language and to learn about cultural differences. Since domestic employees come from your new culture, they can introduce you to other nationals or traditions you may not know. Having a worker in your home can help teach you intricacies of the culture which may take you years to discover on your own. Topics like food, music, and politics become open to a missionary when they have a domestic helper who also serves as a cultural tutor.

A missionary can learn much from a domestic helper who is willing to give cooking lessons and take him out on shopping excursions. These are cultural experiences, which cannot be duplicated in a book or gutting it out on your own.

Other missionaries and supporters need to be careful when passing judgment on a missionary who chooses to hire house help. The status we place on hired help in the West is not consistent with the reality in the rest of the world. In addition, hiring national workers to help around your house can be a quick and efficient way of acquiring new language and cultural skills, which will benefit the rest of your ministry. Providing an income for an otherwise unskilled laborer is a great way of benefiting the people you serve.

Having house help is a valid option for missionaries. It can open many avenues which may otherwise be inaccessible to a missionary. Prayerfully consider if hiring domestic help is something, which can free you up for ministry and teach you about the culture while providing a needed income for a national.

Chapter Five

Short-Term Missions

In modern history short-term missions trips are a relatively new ministry. They have exploded in popularity in recent decades. However, they have their roots in biblical history. Short-term mission efforts were in the gospels and foundational to the founding of the early Christian church. God can be and is glorified by many short duration mission trips.

Done properly an individual or team focused short-term mission trip can accomplish a lot. Done poorly, short-term missions can do an equal amount of harm. It is important for those coordinating short-term mission trips, as receivers or goers, to have strict boundaries and to honor the long-term ministries they serve.

For every Western church leader who sees the benefits of short-term missions there is another one who views them as a waste of time and harmful to global outreach. The success of short-term mission ventures has much to do with the condition of the hearts of those participating and those sending. Participants in short-term missions must always have submissive hearts and must be willing to be learners and servants and not leaders and teachers.

Do Short-Term Mission Trips Produce Long-Term Missionaries?

While the importance of the Great Commission to the evangelical church is inarguable, there are many methods and missions techniques that cause schisms amongst theologians and pew sitters alike. One of the most controversial topics in modern missions in the value of short-term mission trips. Some churches and pastors refuse to participate in short-term missions while others consider short-term missions a vital part of their corporate fulfillment of the Great Commission.

Advocates of modern short-term missions site numerous values to both the sending churches and the receiving ministries that participate in short-term trips. One of the most hotly contested topics surrounding short-term mission trips is, do participants in short-term mission trips result in experienced missionaries who are more inclined to participate in long-term missions?

David Platt once preached to his church, "We want to be a part of what God is doing in His church, not just here, but around the world, and we want to lock hands with our brothers and sisters around the world, and together, through short-term missions impact the world."[51]

There have not been sufficient large-scale studies done on determining if short-term mission trips result in more long-term missionaries. Much of the data results from small scale reviews and experienced observations.

Michael Anthony wrote, "Statistics vary, but many short-term missionaries become career missionaries. 'Testing the waters' is a common objective, particularly for college-age students who do short-term missions assignments. They often use the assignment to overcome cross-cultural apprehensions and to try out the missions career field without the pressure of a long-term commitment."[52]

One informal study completed within Mission To the Word (MTW), the mission sending agency of the Presbyterian Church in America, found that between 2010 and 2016 eighty-four percent of new long term missionaries indicated they had previously served on a one to two week mission trip prior to signing up for long-term missions service. In addition, 48% of those new missionaries stipulated they were now returning to serve long-term in the same country they had previously served on a short-term trip.

Latin American Missions reported in 2000 that, "almost 99% of our applicants today have had some sort of cross-cultural experience." The National Association of Evangelicals said, "Some studies have shown that short-term mission trips increase participants' financial giving and prayer for missions, as well as the likelihood that they will become career missionaries." The Iversons, MTW missionaries to Japan wrote, "Because of God's blessing through short-termers returning as career missionaries, our MTW Japan Mission is growing rapidly while most Japan mission groups are shrinking." Christian Medical Fellowship reported, "Many people have changed careers and become full-time medical missionaries after completing a short-term stint."

The limited missions experience of my family has seen this truth bare out. In the nearly nine years my family has been serving in fulltime missions, the vast majority of the

---

[51] David Platt, "Creating a Future at Brook Hills," in *David Platt Sermon Archive* (Birmingham, AL: David Platt, 2007), 1040.
[52] Michael J. Anthony et al., *Evangelical Dictionary of Christian Education*, Baker Reference Library (Grand Rapids, MI: Baker Academic, 2001), 632.

long-term missionaries we have met first got their exposure to missions on a short-term mission trip. In fact, 19 of the 20 long-term missionaries that served with us in Honduras were first exposed to missions during a short-term mission trip somewhere in the world. These days it is a common experience. More and more young adults want to experience missions by first serving alongside experienced fulltime missionaries. This is a safe way to gain experience and a heart for the Great Commission.

When Jesus gathered 12 of his disciples and sent them out he was giving his 12 Apostles a missions apprenticeship that would pay long-term dividends for the kingdom well after Christ's ascension. Dan Williams wrote, "Jesus knew that there was a time for the twelve disciples to be together in basic training (which, by the way, included short-term mission experiences for them) and a time for them to be propelled into full-blown mission."[53]

In referencing the city of Nineveh Philip Ryken said, "God's plan for saving the city began with recruiting Jonah to go on a short-term missions trip."[54] The short-term mission work of Jonah resulted in long-term glory for God. Scripture calls the disciples of Christ to commit their lives to expanding the gospel. We should not be satisfied with the fleeting taste of a few weeks of service.

When discussing short-term missions we frequently overlook the impact on our own heart. Often we approach short-term missions like we are spending the rest of the year preparing ourselves to glorify God during the one-week mission trip we take in another country. We miss that God is using short-term missions to reform our heart and help us to more focus on global evangelism. A missional heart is not switched on one weekend per month or one week per year. A missional heart sees every interaction as an opportunity.

The more we have churches participating in short-term missions and the more we send our congregations out on short-term mission trips, the more frequently we will be sending our congregants into long-term missions. As the DNA of our churches change and we focus on the Great Commission the more we will be sending missionaries from our own churches onto the mission field for lengthy periods.

God uses short-term missions to get individual disciples and entire congregations excited about selling out for long-term missions. Be it the heart of one believer or a body

---

[53] Dan Williams, *Seven Myths about Small Groups: How to Keep from Falling into Common Traps* (Downers Grove, IL: InterVarsity Press, 1991).
[54] Philip Graham Ryken, *Discovering God in Stories from the Bible* (Wheaton, Ill.: Crossway Books, 1999), 43.

of disciples, experience in short-term missions turns our heart toward glorifying the Lord in long-term missions work.

Send Me Your Short-Term Missionaries

From 2008 to 2013 our fulltime mission team in Honduras has hosted 50 short-term mission teams consisting of 500 short-term missionaries. Many people ask, "Wouldn't it just be better if all those people sent you money instead of wasting their resources and your time?" Our answer is an emphatic NO. Money cannot hug a fatherless child or fellowship with Christian brothers. Money cannot play soccer with drug dealers or wipe the tears from a hungry child. Christians we are called to serve the poor, sick, widows and orphans. Money can buy food for the poor and build houses for the homeless, but just as Christ touched the leper (Matt 8:3), the poor also desire the touch of a loving and merciful hand.

In 2005, 1.6 million US church members took a short-term mission trip. Increasingly church leadership and laypeople are questioning the wisdom of sending short-term mission teams. Some argue short-term missions cause more harm than good. Objections include increased dependency, lack of compassion for local cultures, incorrect motivation, circumvention of existing ministries, and excess costs.

As an experienced host of short-term mission teams I will be the first to admit there can be problems when hosting teams. However, those problems can be reduced if not eliminated with communication and altered attitudes.

To the short-term missionaries: Churches sending short-term missionaries must stress that participants are going to assist and serve the long-term ministry. They are to provide love, fellowship and resources to people who minister in that community. Short-term missionaries must leave their expectations and cultural biases at the airport and must trust the indigenous leaders or long-term missionaries. A mission trip should be approached with the desire to be a servant and not a burden.

To the long-term missionaries: Long-term missionaries and national partners who host short-term mission teams must establish guidelines before the short-term missionaries leave home and must enforce guidelines while they are on the field. The hosts must protect their ministry and advance God's plan for their calling. If a short-term missionary did something to harm a ministry it occurred because you let it happen.

The leadership in your home church would never allow a visitor to walk in the front door and demand your pastor preach a different text or the worship leader play a new style of music. Short-term missionaries should go on short-term mission trips with the perspective that they are in the new location to serve as the long-term ministers deem appropriate.

As an ex-leader in my home church and a current international missionary I see short-term missions as beneficial to both the home church and the receiving ministry. Here are a few reasons:

Christianity is a global fellowship. It unites people regardless of age, race, gender, ethnicity or socio-economic status. Frequently we tarnish Christianity by viewing it threw our cultural biases. Short-term missions allow those serving and those being served to see they have brothers throughout the globe.

Believers can give and receive love. I often tell short-term missionaries that I don't just need people to come to Honduras who have construction or language skills. I would welcome a team that is willing to sit on a soccer field and hug a child for a week. We work in a culture where few homes have a father and mom is off working. The kids in our community don't know unconditional love and seldom interact with adults. You can send a check, but I'd rather you brought a willingness to hug a skinny, dirty, snot-nosed kid.

Missions can be expanded in our home churches. Missions is at the heart of Christianity. Unfortunately, it is under taught and undervalued in our Western churches. Short-term missions can increase the understanding of the importance of missions in the sending church. If your church sends a short-term team it is reasonable to think your congregants are thinking and praying more about their role in the Great Commission.

Increased prayer and giving in Christ's name. If your church sends 10 people on a short-term mission trip the assumption is each of those missionaries asked 10 others to pray for them and asked 10 others to write checks supporting the mission trip. Realistically, your short-term mission trip results in 100 additional people praying in the name of Christ and for the advancement of God's Kingdome and 100 people writing checks to the glory of God.

Increased participation in long-term missions. Our mission team consists of nine fulltime, adult, missionaries. Each of them got their first taste of missions through a short-term mission experience. It is easy to say that most current missionaries under the age of 50 got their start in missions during a short-term experience. Not every short-term missionary is called to long-term service. But, increased exposure to missions result in increased prayer and financial support for missionaries.

The Apostle Paul was a long-term missionary who advanced Christianity through short-term missions. It is widely accepted that Paul seldom stayed longer than a few months or even weeks in a single location. What about Jonah, Jesus, the 12, the 70? We can say short-term mission principles were used throughout the bible to expand the early church.

With a Christ-centered, servant's heart short-term missions can be used to aide the needy, educate fellow believers and expand God's kingdom in all corners of the globe. Short-term missions has and will continue to have a healthy role in the advancement of Christianity.

How to Prepare for Your Short-Term Mission Trip

Over the years we have talked to many churches and learned how they prepare (or don't) their congregants for mission endeavors. Reading, in the Presbyterian and reformed world, is a typical way to prepare for...well...anything. Most churches that have their missionaries read before mission trips frequently have them read *When Helping Hurts* by Steve Corbett and Brian Fikkert. While many mission minded people support this book, we cannot recommend it. The book has more to do with assuaging anti-welfare guilt than it does with sharing the grace and mercy of Jesus Christ. To learn why we are not fans of the book read Mike's book review.

If you are a reader and want to prepare for short-term missions we would recommend the books The Whole In Our Gospel by Richard E. Stearns and Mack & Leeann's Guide to Short-Term Missions by Leeann and Mack Stiles. Also, you can read the articles "Short-Term Missions: Blessing or Bother?" by Dan and Carol Iverson, fellow MTW missionaries to Japan.

As you prepare for you mission trip you need to focus on four key things: prayer, service, flexibility and relationships.

Prayer – Pray in advance that the Lord would prepare your heart and the hearts of those you will serve. Pray you die to your pride, so when you struggle with culture, language or ministry you remain loving. Pray for your teammates, the long term missionaries and your family staying back home. Pray God will show you what he wants you to see and you don't force your own will into the mix.

Service – You are going on your mission trip to be a servant. You are there to serve how the long-term missionaries and the nationals want you to serve, not how you think is best. Have a servant's heart to all those around you, including your teammates. Serve as Christ served. Be humble and accept your role.

Flexibility – Never forget that Satan is involved. He will try to waylay your plans. In addition, other cultures do things differently than you do. Die to your schedules, plans and expectations and know God will have you do exactly what he wants you to do. Your plans will get changed…get over it. Instead of complaining about the changes or problems, understand that the missionaries you are serving deal with this kind of uncertainty daily.

Relationships – No matter what project you think you are there to do, understand you are there to show the love and mercy of Christ. Your plans, projects and schedules are secondary. You are there to show grace to others. You don't need to speak the local language to show love and compassion. Show the locals you love them so much that you came all that distance to see them. Focus on people and not projects.

Go with only the expectations that you are open to God's plan and you want to be used in any way he wants to use you. Go with the heart that you have been sent by God. Act like a diplomat of God's kingdom, because you are.

Short-Term Missions Should Support Long-Term Ministry

Short-term mission trips can add great value to long-term ministry. The energy, focus and resources provided by short-term missionaries can be a boost for any existing cross-cultural work. However, short-term missions done alone can be a disaster. When a short-term mission team ventures into the world, they should do so by coming alongside a long-term ministry which is sustained year-round by fulltime missionaries and/or national partners.

Too often short-term missionaries read a book, watch a film or hear a sermon and they feel they have imbibed everything needed to storm a new culture and make a massive impact in a week or two. Short-term missionaries are indeed very important and appreciated by many fulltime ministries, but they must do their work in support of and under the direction of those who live in the culture.

Imagine for a moment, a group of ten Peruvian Christians hop on an airplane and land in your city. Their plan is to save the lost in the United States. They are in your town for two-weeks and during that time they start building a Peruvian style home and come to your church to teach the gospel to your kids. During their time in your town they are condescending to your neighbors, they openly question your culture, they make faces at the food they are served and they want to do ministry their way. Absurd, right? That is exactly what a few short-term mission teams from the U.S. do every summer.

Imagine that same Peruvian team of short-term Christian missionaries being invited by your pastor to come serve your congregation and your surrounding community. While they are in the U.S. they are humble, obedient, take direction, and are gracious.

They have the hearts of true Christian servants and are simply thrilled to be able to minister however they are asked.

The first option is a nightmare. The second option is a blessing. Look at short-term missions from the perspective of the receiving culture. It may help you change your heart and actions next time you serve cross culturally.

The long-term missionaries who live and serve in the culture and the nationals who are from the country understand nuances of the culture you may never have thought of. They know intricacies about their neighbors and the people they serve more than you ever will. Living alongside the people you came to serve has given them insight you simply don't possess.

Trust they know what needs to be done and what should be avoided. The long-term missionaries and national partners are your teachers and guides. By trusting their experience a short-term mission team will serve Christ and the new culture more effectively. Their experience combined with your hard-working servants heart can make a big impact without all the cultural missteps. Have faith that God has called them and prepared them for their ministry and that God has called you to serve alongside them for a season. If you wouldn't tell a fireman or a professional quarterback how to do their job, be sparing of your criticism of those who serve Christ fulltime.

You don't need to reinvent the wheel. It is likely the long-term missionaries or national partners have tried ministering your way and it just didn't work. They have likely put years of work into to trying and failing and figuring out what works best in their ministry context. What worked for you in the U.S. may not work in a Kenyan or Mexican setting. Trust that before you arrived they toiled and labored and prayed over their ministry. You may have ideas that you think are more effective or efficient. Share those ideas in a private conversation and no matter the response don't forget you are there to serve.

The ministry you are doing during your short-term mission trip must remain sustainable after you return home. Sometimes a short-term mission team can provide a shot in the arm or can provide specialism the long-termers can't provide. If that is what the long-termers want, that is wonderful. In many cases if a short-term mission team provides a quick blessing, it may be expected by those receiving the service that the fulltime ministry continue providing that service and that just may not be possible. Sometimes the fulltime servants need to think about long-term sustainability versus short-term blessing. In some cases, your efforts may do long-term damage. Let the fulltime missionaries and national partners make that determination.

If a short-term missionary goes on a mission trip with the heart of an apprentice and a servant. They may learn something important about sustainable ministry in this new cultural context. Be willing to absorb from the wisdom and experience of those doing this work fulltime. This will teach you to be a better servant at home and on your next mission trip.

These words are not intended to be a rebuke of short-term missions, simply a guide to help you redirect your heart. Short-term missionaries are valuable and important to long-term Christian ministries. If you weren't valuable, you wouldn't be invited. Your Christ-like service is needed. Pack your willingness and learner's mentality in your suitcase, but leave your criticism and words of descent at home.

Being A Team Leader Of A Short-Term Mission Team

Short-term mission trips are a major part of the modern fulfillment of God's Great Commission. Done well, short-term missions can be a God glorifying event for the sending church and the receiving ministry. Done poorly, it can be a disaster for both. Fair or not, much of that burden falls on the shoulders of the local church's appointed leader of the short-term mission team.

The leader of the short-term mission team must be called by God, supported by church leadership, and have a heart to serve. The short-term missions team is called to be sent by the domestic congregation to bless the foreign culture and serve the long-term ministry. The leader of the short-term team has a labor-intensive job which starts long before boarding a plane and ends many weeks after return.

Your short-term missions trip should start and end with prayer. Months before you go, ask your church and the families of your participants to pray daily. Pray for your home church, your mission team, the ministry you will serve, and the nationals you will encounter. Pray regularly as a group.

Do your research. If possible, contact the fulltime ministry in advance. Ask them to share details about your accommodations, conditions, and ministry. Do research on the internet. If there is a sending agency, ask them questions. Get prepared and make sure the church and family staying behind has all the information. Mentally and spiritually prepare your team.

Ask the fulltime ministry you are serving if you can bring anything for the ministry or for their families. Check with the Center for Disease Control to find out about required and recommended vaccinations. See what type of travel advisories are put out by the U.S.

State Department. Make sure everyone has a passport and correct visa documentation. Study your Bible as a group and prepare your hearts to serve.

First and foremost, you are there to God and benefit the fulltime ministry. With the heart of a servant, avail you and your mission team to go above and beyond. Serve exactly as you are instructed, without challenging the fulltime missionaries or national leaders. Offer to serve those ministering fulltime in a personal way. Treat them to a nice meal. Offer to watch their kids, or clean their house.

Serve your short-term teammates. Many of your teammates may be struggling with homesickness, culture shock, or faith issues. Pray with and for them. Have a daily time to study the Scriptures and process together. Make sure they are drinking lots of water, sleeping, and eating. Many people who have never left their home country are shocked by what they see. Help them process and serve well while in the host country.

As technology and time allows the team leader should attempt to keep the home church and supporters informed of ministry activities. God has called you to go, but he has called them to pray and support your efforts. If your situation allows, keep a trip log on social media so your home church knows best how to pray. A picture and a few words on a blog, Facebook, or Twitter keeps people focused on glorifying God through prayer.

Once you are back from your short-term mission trip let your home church and supporters know how it went. Provide a short video. Write thank you letters. Make a brief missions presentation at church. Keep the missions high going both on your team and in your church. Use the experience to build on. Expand your church's global outreach with additional trips and by increasing service in your local community.

Pray for all those involved. Pray God would use the experience to raise up new short-term and long-term missionaries from your church. Pray the nationals you served saw Christ in your actions. Now that you have a taste of the ministry, pray for the fulltime missionaries and the ministry you served alongside. Pray God would continue to use you and others to glorify him by sending and going on mission.

Prayerfully consult your church leadership about returning to the same ministry with a mission team next year. Seek direction from God about going to the same location or serving in a new culture. Help young people in your church learn about missions internship. Attend missions conferences. Plan a missions conference or Sunday school class on missions at your own church. Provide missions books for your congregation to read. Learn how God wants you to promote missions further.

The team leader of a short-term mission team can let things happen or he can make things happen. Prayerfully seek God's guidance as to how God can be best glorified though your church's involvement in missions. Your church leadership and God's wisdom should be sought, but be willing to put in the time, prayer, and effort to make your church's missions experience a good one.

It all may seem like too much work and pressure. But, if a team leader has a heart sold out for God's glory in the world, he can help create a Great Commission culture in his church and on his short-term mission team. A short-term mission team led by a team leader seeking God's glory will find it at home and around the globe.

9 Ways to Raise Money for Short-Term Mission Trips

In Scripture God is clear how he wants us to view finances (Mat 6:3-4; Luk 3:11, 6:38; Pr 28:27). Jim Elliot, missionary to Ecuador and martyr for Christ said, "He is no fool who gives up what he cannot keep to gain that which he cannot lose."[55] British theologian and author, C.S. Lewis stated, "I do not believe one can settle how much we ought to give. I am afraid the only safe rule is to give more than we can spare."[56]

Yet, our sinful heart is fearful of asking others for money in God's name. If we truly viewed God as the originator and distributor of all resources we shouldn't be intimidated by asking for financial support. The fear of raising finances is a major reason why many Christians do not participate in missions. The reality is when we raise money for mission trips we are providing others who can't go, with the ability to glorify God by sending us.

The following ideas are a few practical ways to raise support for short-term missions. Before we begin let's review a few provisos: 1) Don't start this process unless you are covering every aspect in prayer. 2) Reading beyond this paragraph assumes you have received permission to raise support from your church leadership. 3) Every participant in the mission trip should be a participant in the raising of funds.

1. Letters

Each participant in the short-term mission trip should write a Christ-centered appeal letter to a few dozen friends and family members. Make the letters are short. Include a return envelope and a deadline. Describe the work you will be doing and how the giver's support will glorify God and impact the nations. Follow up to the recipients with e-mails and phone calls.

---

[55] Mark Water, *The Christian Book of Records* (Alresford, Hants, UK: John Hunt Pub., 2002), 157.
[56] Mark Water, *Hard Questions about Christianity Made Easy, The Made Easy Series* (Alresford, Hampshire: John Hunt Publishing, 2000), 59.

2. Yard Sale

Ask members of your church, friends and family to donate household items for a yard sale. Advertise in your church and community. Have all mission trip participants working at the yard sale. Promote the yard sale as a fundraiser for Christian missions. Donate all leftover items to another charity.

3. Three Servants Parable

Based on Matthew 25:14-30 take seed money and put it in a large number of envelopes. Place some money (roughly $20) in each envelope. Stand before your congregation and read the passage. Pass out an envelope to every adult. Place a box in the back of the church. Invite everyone to participate in whatever way the Lord leads them. They can anonymously place their money in the box, keep it for themselves, or use it to purchase supplies for their own fundraiser. Invite participants to organize their own car wash, bake sale or other event. Allow several weeks for participants to complete their effort and return their profit.

4. Car Wash

Host a car wash in front of a local business in your community. Use lots of signage and energetic participants. Instead of setting a price, allow car owners to give what they feel is appropriate. Sell advanced sale coupons in your church and to friends and family.

5. Rent-A-Missionary

Pick a weekend to rent out your short-term missionaries for yard work or babysitting. Allow the renters to pay as they feel led. Organize a parent's night out at a home or church. Allow parents to drop off their kids at one location and have the missionaries babysit. Create a spring-cleaning day and volunteer to take truckloads of trash to the dump.

6. Meal Tickets

Host a crab feed, spaghetti feed or bar-b-q after church. Get your food, plates, drinks donated or purchased at a discount. Sell advance tickets. Turn the event into a church social. Have the mission trip participants serve as wait staff, cooks and table bussers.

7. Bake Sale

Ask volunteers and mission trip participants to volunteer to bake cookies, cakes, pies and cupcakes. Sell them all to the highest bidders after church. This can easily be combined with another meal or fundraising event.

8. Restaurant Discounts

Many restaurants offer to help churches and philanthropic organizations raise money for special service events. Work with the restaurant on their method, but frequently restaurants offer a percentage of sales on a specific day or a percentage if your organization is mentioned at the register. Frequently restaurants offer advanced sale coupons where you get all the proceeds.

9. Crowd funding

There are dozens of websites (GoFundMe.com, GoGetFunding.com, etc.) that help you raise funds. The website hosts your page, receives the donations and takes a percentage. Crowdfunding support raisers work best when the URL of the fundraising site is shared via social media or e-mail. This is a near effortless way to raise support, you just have to get the word out.

Use your support raising opportunities as teaching moments for the mission trip participants and your church. Make sure everyone is regularly in prayer and seeking God's glory and provision. Help everyone see how God provides resources for those who seek to serve in his name. Turn support raising for your mission trip from an anxiety ridden, sinful venture into a way to bring glory to the Lord and teach about his sovereignty.

Taste and See that Missions is Good

The people of the world are changing and with it the Western Christian landscape is fluctuating. Church attendance, tithing and missions participation are declining in much of the American evangelical church. Reformed and Bible-believing Christian ministries are declining less dramatically and are seeing increased involvement in some areas.

Missions, God's mandate to reach the nations, should never slow because finances and interest are down. Now, when the world is moving away from Christ, his obedient disciples must strive to serve him even more. If the evangelical church is to recruit, fund and replenish the frontlines of the battlefield with the next generation of missionaries, the evangelical church may need to better understand those new recruits.

Most researchers assign the term millennials to those individuals born in the early 1980s to about 2000. Millennials are currently the largest generation and view many things differently than previous generations. In 2015, Mission to the World (MTW), the mission sending agency of the Presbyterian Church in America, completed in-depth research on how millennials perceive missions. In their findings MTW wrote, "Generally millennials want to make a difference, they desire to be mentored, and want to be trusted with leadership responsibilities." MTW's research found the millennial generation perceives international missions differently than generations before them. They do not define long-term commitment the same as others have. And, millennials prefer to learn about new experiences in person, in a hands-on setting.

No church or missions sending agency should change to an un-biblical methodology or place any group of sinners ahead of the glory of God. Can missions remain Christ-centered and gospel driven and bend to accommodate the next group of missionaries? Yes. While no facet of Scripture should ever be sacrificed, missions can evolve to better impact an ever-developing world. Expanding the existence of one to three year mentored missions experiences may be the motivation Christianity and millennials need to reunite.

Psalm 34 contains the passage, "Taste and see that the Lord is good." (Ps 34:8) That methodology is idyllic for the millennial generation which desires to experience new undertakings with their own hands and determine if those experiences are right for them. Far from being a psalm about lack of commitment and erratic faith, Psalm 34 is a thanksgiving to God for caring for those who love him. The psalm pleads with the reader to join in on blessing the Lord. The author says that when we have tasted with our own experiences and seen the love of God, we will know he is worthy and we will see the Lord cares for his disciples and answers their prayers.

The generations of man have changed and morphed, but our eternal Father remains forever perfect. Throughout Scripture God has described spiritual wanderers who finally find joy once they trust in what God showed them. It is glorious to find a child who commits his life to missions at an early age and then serves God their entire life in a far off land. That seldom happens. Are millennials and their taste and see mentality really that different from the generations of spiritual wanders before them?

Arguably the most impactful missionary is history was the apostle Paul. Certainly Paul was the most influential missionary who focused on shorter duration missions experiences. With fairly accurate certainty it can be estimated Paul spent the bulk of thirty year traveling, what is now called, the Mediterranean Basin. During those three decades Paul served as a missionary dozens of recorded times for durations ranging from a few days to several years.

Paul's first missionary journey (Acts 13-14) was thought to happen around A.D. 46-49. During that period Paul wrote that he visited 10 locations. Paul's second missionary journey (Acts 15:36-18:22) likely took place A.D. 50-52. In that time Paul claims he visited 13 locations. Paul's third missionary journey (Acts 18:23-21:15) was believed to have taken place A.D. 53-58. On that trip Paul visited 13 locations.

Paul, the model for missions in the modern evangelical church, certainly took many mission trips, but for how long did he serve? By juxtaposing history with Scripture we could easily assign accurate durations to most of Paul's missionary journeys. For the sake of this analysis we'll discuss only the four missionary journeys, which in Scripture, Paul assigned a duration. Paul said his first visit to Corinth lasted a year and a half (Acts 18:11). Paul went to Achaia where he stayed three months (Acts 20:2-3). Paul wrote that he stayed in Ephesus for three years (Acts 20:31). And, he spent seven days in Tyre (Acts 21:1–6). Paul greatly influenced the spread of Christianity by focusing on shorter-term missions experiences.

The next generation of missionaries is truly no different than the previous generations of sinners. Like Adam's descendants before them, millennials are concerned with their experiences and personal views. If Christians strive to put God's glory ahead of their happiness there is nothing wrong with tasting and seeing if missions is right for you.

As Psalm 34 promises, when millennials experience missions through one to three year mentored mission experiences, some will see that the Lord is good and commit to longer terms of service. Others will likely gain a heart to pray for and support other missionaries.

What a Good Short-Term Missionary Looks Like

Realistically, any Christian who decides they want to participate in cross-cultural missions can't be all that bad. By leaving their home and going to a foreign land they have shown a desire to be obedient to God's Great Commission. God doesn't require super stars, he only requires obedience. So, right off the bat let's take a moment to thank anyone who has ever been on or is planning on going on a short-term mission trip. Your efforts and your sacrifices are appreciated.

With that, let's now explore the shades of grey. If we assume the simple act of going on a mission trip is good, how do we turn obedient short-term missionaries into exceptional missionaries? What follows is an experienced look at the difference between a good, better, and great short-term missionary.

A good short-term missionary is on time for every briefing and departure. He respects the time and effort put into planning his trip by the nationals, long-term missionaries, and his short-term teammates. A good short-term missionary does everything asked of him. He is compliant, doesn't complain, and follows the rules established by his leaders and hosts. A good short-term missionary doesn't complain when unexpected changes occur. He eats all the strange foods put in front of him and avoids openly criticizing those things which are different. A good short-term missionary may not like the rules and guidelines established by those in charge, but he understands they were put in place by people with more experience and were intended to keep everyone healthy and productive.

A better short-term missionary is eager to learn and asks questions. She understands the long hours and hard work put into organizing the mission trip and does what she can to relieve the burden from the leaders, long-term missionaries, and nationals. A better short-term missionary anticipates what is needed next and asks if she can help or relieve others of their responsibilities. She is eager to understand the reasoning and history behind the activities and shows interest in the behind-the-scenes details. A better short-term missionary helps the sick, takes the burden from the tired, and comforts the hurting. She asks to try new foods, learn new language, and experience new customs, no matter how hard it is or how foolish she looks.

The great short-term missionary shows interest in the history and motivation of the long-term missionaries, nationals, and her short-term teammates. She is energized, punctual, and enthusiastic to work alongside others and learn from them. The great missionary desires to learn about the nationals, long-term missionaries, and her short-term teammates on an intimate level. She volunteers to pray with and for her fellow servants. Money, time, and effort are not deterrents for the great short-term missionary. She understands God is the giver of all gifts. She desires to serve others and wants Christ to be glorified in her actions. Before she left the great short-term missionary contacted the long-term missionaries and asked what they needed delivered from home. She arrived with personal and ministry gifts and when she leaves she gives her leftover spending money and clothes to the fulltime ministry. She understands the sacrifices of others and is willing to give of herself. Once she returns home, the great short-term missionary continues to pray for the long-term missionaries, nationals, and her short-term teammates. She explores how she can raise awareness of the fulltime ministry and how she can be more involved in planning the return trip next year.

It can all be boiled down to heart. Having a heart for service and a desire to glorify God is what it is all about. The more a short-term missionary desires to glorify God, the more he will want to serve others in the Lord's name. What separates a great short-term missionary from a good short-term missionary is understanding they can be the difference between a terrible and an amazing experience for everyone. A good missionary obeys all the rules and guidelines, while a great missionary sees those rules as a way of serving others.

A great missionary doesn't view the existing ministry or culture as bad. Instead a great missionary grasps the fact that he is a servant with very little knowledge or background, and all he wants to do is serve others. A single great missionary on a short-term mission team can turn around an event, make a bad day good, or make a hard situation memorable. Simply by having an open heart and a willingness to serve others a great short-term missionary can help everyone better glorify God. A great short-term missionary sees every adverse situation and every struggling individual as a way for God's grace and mercy to be shared.

Certainly, what needs to be understood here is God is pleased with everyone who serves in his name and the simple act of saying, "here I am Lord, send me" brings great glory to God. The guidelines provided here are surely subjective and will differ from case to case, and ministry to ministry. The valuable point, is to understand that the attitude, heart, and service of one short-term missionary can make the difference on a mission trip. Your servant's heart, flexibility, and desire to learn is contagious and can make more of a positive impact they you could ever imagine.

What a Bad Short-Term Missionary Looks Like

Any person who sacrifices their time, finances, and energy to glorify God around the globe is to be thanked for their sacrifice in participating in God's Great Commission. Scripture tells us God has a mission for the church to reach the lost. All Christian disciples are to play a part, be it goer, sender, or prayer.

Nothing in Scripture says only the best and the brightest can be sent to the nations. Missionaries should not be compared to one to another. The only desire is that every participant in missions gives a maximum effort from the ability they possess. If a group of young, unskilled Christians go on a short-term mission trip, they should not be expected to perform like a bunch of seasoned theologians and construction workers.

However, the sad reality is, not every short-term missionary is willing to give their personal best. That is when their efforts, or lack thereof, can be injurious to God's glory, place others in harm's way, and cause damage to the fulltime ministry they came to serve. A bad short-term missionary is not defined by their physical ability or biblical knowledge. Being a bad short-term missionary has more to do with the condition of that person's heart.

The bad short-term missionary quietly protests their temporary lot in the ministry. They dislike the culture, the food, the ministry, or their fellow missionaries. Maybe they romanticized what short-term missions was going to be like, or they were not properly informed ahead of time. The result is, they are unhappy and they going to rebel by not giving their best effort and plan to simply endure the mission trip instead of making the best of it.

They do not heed the safety warnings and put themselves and others at risk. They may feign illness or over-dramatize a minor injury to get out of service. The don't eat the food, don't interact with the nationals, and do no more than asked of them. Their body posture betrays their displeasure. They remove themselves from duty and simply try to survive their short-term missions experience.

Worse short-term missionary dislikes their conditions, the ministry, or the culture and they sow seeds of discontent among fulltime or other short-term missionaries. They gossip, and try to quietly win allies to their position. They make poor decisions which are contrary to the long-term ministry's standards or desires.

This missionary creates additional work for their fellow short-term missionaries and the long-term ministry. Instead, of doing a ministry as they are instructed, they do what they think is right. They believe their way is best and ignore the instructions given by those who live in the culture. They publicly challenge authority. They continue to go beyond the safety limits and ministry boundaries established. Their actions and attitude, at minimum, create an uncomfortable experience for others, and may do harm to the long-term ministry.

The worst is a short-term missionary whose words and actions undermine the fulltime ministry as they choose to do things their way. They were properly briefed and educated before they arrived and after they started their short-term mission trip. However, they believe their perspective is the right way and they continue to argue and debate their points. Even though their task has been made clear from the start, they never had any intention of doing things the way they were asked. They continue to challenge and change the schedule, the ministry, and their duties even though their purpose was clearly conveyed by the long-term ministry.

They criticize the culture, the schedule, and the long-term ministry. Because this short-term missionary did things their way the long-term ministry must spend valuable time and finances to repair their mistakes after they have gone. They have damaged the ministry and created additional work. In the short-time they were in the country they created harm to relationships with nationals which may have taken years to establish, and will now take more time to fix. Their arrogant approach to believing they know best has added to the cultures already tenuous view of North Americans and other missionaries' negative view of short-term missions.

The problem with a bad short-term missionary has next to nothing to do with their ability or their service. The damage is done by a bad short-term missionary through the condition of their heart. They have ignored one of the primary requirements for all Christians: a heart inclined to serve others. A missionary who has the heart of a servant, is worth her weight in gold. A missionary who has a discontented heart will not only damage a long-term ministry, but their actions may do damage to God's glory as well as the word's view of missions. It is the heart of the bad short-term missionary which causes the greatest damage.

It doesn't take much to slip from being a good short-term missionary to a bad short-term missionary. The slippage of the heart, from that of service to selfishness is all it takes. However, to fall from bad to "don't call us, we won't call you" takes a calculated effort. If a short-term missionary simply keeps tabs on his heart he can glorify God, and benefit his global ministry.

You are Back From a Short-Term Mission Trip, Now What?

The summer mission season is over and you just came back for your first (or 21st) mission trip. You are on a huge post-mission trip high. Your closeness to God, your focus on the Great Commission and your dedication to sharing God's mercy are at an elevated level. Now what? Most short-term mission trips result in an elevated enthusiasm for missions, but then life happens. Day-to-day life again becomes your reality and before you know it, you've stopped thinking about missions.

This is an all too common post-missions experience. One of the great benefits of short-term mission trips is the heightened focus on global evangelism that occurs in you, your peers and your church. Don't let that slip away. Take advantage of your immediate passion to make missions a fixture in your life and the life of your church.

Here are a few recommendations how you can turn that temporary post-mission trip high into a life altering, God honoring experience:

Take the ministry you just served before the Lord, daily. Keep the fulltime missionaries and nationals you met in your prayers. Pray for the people who joined you from your church and ask God to create a greater passion for missions in them. Ask God to keep your heart focused on missions and seek his will for your next step.

Tell your friends about your experience. Get others in your church and your social circle excited about missions. Post pictures, videos and blogs on social media. Let others know how you saw God working. Share amazing experience of how you learned God is being glorified in other cultures. Ask your church leadership if you can make a post-mission trip presentation in front of the congregation.

Care for missionaries. These obedient servants are some of the most silent suffering Christians in existence. Serve the missionaries you appreciate. E-mail or call them periodically. Drop them a quick note letting them know your church prayed for them today. Remember their anniversaries and kids' birthdays. Send them e-books or electronic gift cards from Amazon or ITunes. Ask them how you can serve and care for their personal needs.

Contribute sacrificially to a missionary or ministry. Missions doesn't happen without money. Finances are needed to make missions work happen. Become a monthly supporter of missionaries doing ministry you support or in places you are impassioned about. God has called some to go and some to support, but he has called all of us to participate in missions. Maybe you have learned that going on mission trips is not for you. If you are not a goer, then become a sender.

There are thousands of books on missions. Consult your pastor or the missionaries you just served with about what missions biographies or missions theology books you should read. Learn about what Scripture says about missions. Read about missionary heroes from the past and learn about their obedience, struggles and service. Dive into modern missions blogs maintained by missionaries currently on the field. Learn what it really takes to be a fulltime, cross-cultural servant.

Today, most missionaries utilize blogs, Facebook, Twitter, Tumbler, YouTube or other forms of electronic media. It is easier than ever to follow the regular activity of your new missions friends or the ministry you just served. Sign up to receive missionary prayer letters via e-mail. Many missionaries write about both the amazing and mundane. They post about the joys and struggles. Social media has been an incredible benefit to missions in the past ten years. Almost everywhere in the world missionaries have access to the Internet and are daily sharing their experiences to bring greater glory to the Lord.

Plan your next short-term mission trip. If you go to the same ministry or to another country, just go. Sign up for your next mission trip right away. Put it on your calendar. Make annual mission trips a priority for your family and your church. The more direct exposure you have to missions the better your understanding will be about God's passion for the lost. Now that you are experienced in missions ask your church leadership if you can organize and lead the next mission trip.

Prayerfully discern if God is calling you to a longer-term commitment to the mission field. Most fulltime missionaries I know received their initial heart for missions on a short-term mission trip. You may have just met your first missionaries. You now know that missionaries are not super Christians, they are simply those willing to accept the call. Does God want you to take more short-term mission trips, support missionaries or move to the mission field? Ask him to make the answer clear to you.

Not every church is involved in missions and very few Christians have ever participated in or supported missions. If you have just returned from a short-term mission trip, you have more experience in missions than most people in your life. Use your experience and your newfound passion for God's Great Commission to expand missions involvement in your family and church. Become zealous about reaching the lost through missions, because God is zealous about reaching the lost through missions.

Chapter Six

Ministry on the Mission Field

Theoretical missions is often times much different than missions in practice. Many well-intentioned people have many opinions as to how missions should be done, and which ministries are best. The only foolproof place to turn when determining what ministries are best is Scripture. Scripture certainly places a premium on theological education and discipleship. That is not to say, the Bible frowns upon other missions ministries. While mentoring and Bible instruction are clearly outlined as central ministries in global outreach, other ministries can be just as God honoring.

The major caveat is, all ministries must draw the world closer to Christ. That is the purpose of global outreach. Mercy, construction, medical, trade, and other ministries have great value. However, they must all bring God glory and be focused on draw the lost into a biblical discipling and mentoring relationship. Medicine, mercy, and education may be the draw of missions ministries, but churches, biblical instruction, and mentoring relationships should be the purpose.

With that in mind, missionaries and churches should be wary of any group or movement which proclaims missions should only be done in a specific geography, to a precise people group, and in a explicit manner. If a missionary seeks informed counsel and prays to God for guidance and concludes God would be best glorified if the missionary serves in location doing a certain ministry, who are the rest of us to question God's direction. Many missions fads, and those who support them have done much to discourage missionaries and dampened a desire to serve.

The Importance of Discipleship to Missions

The Great Commission (Mat 28:18-20) is Christ's charge to his followers found at the end of his earthly ministry. It provides God's command and authority for Christians to participate in global missions. The Great Commission is straightforward and clear. Unfortunately, it is misunderstood by some missionaries and disobeyed by others.

Jesus begins his command by affirming that all authority has been given to him. This provides him the sole right to say what comes next. The first action word in the English translation is "go." Going has become the fulfillment of the Great Commission in the minds of many modern missionaries. However, the focus of the original text is not the going part, but the making disciple part. The Greek (mathēteuō) is translated as "'to make disciples" or "be discipled." The original word for "make disciples" is used only three times in the gospels, all three in Matthew. Its rare usage adds to its significance. Followers of Christ are commanded to go to all nations. This stands in stark contrast with Christ's earlier instruction to his disciples to limit their mission to Israel (Mat 10:5-6, 15:24). The other portions of the Great Commission (go, baptize and teach) are all supportive of the focal point, to make disciples. Being a missionary, fulfilling the Great Commission, is done in the making of disciples. The commission concludes with Jesus assuring his followers that he is with them as they fulfill his commands.

Christ's focus on making disciples is the heart of his Great Commission. But, more and more missionaries are viewing the process of going or the act of evangelizing as the heart of missions. Unless missionaries are making disciples the Great Commission is not being fulfilled.

The acts of going, baptizing and teaching explain how the making of disciples is done. Going can be fulfilled in a few days, but to make a disciple takes a much more substantive investment of time and effort. Christ says that making disciples is done when we teach them, "all that I have commanded." That is a lot and is extremely complex. As pastor David Platt preached, we are making disciples when we are, "sharing, showing, teaching the Word."[57] Missionaries should either be accomplishing this or helping others accomplish it.

Too many missionaries are conceding the primary point of the Great Commission. Many times it seems as if missionaries are doing everything except making disciples. Christ never said to go and build a medical clinic or a high school or an orphanage. The Great Commission does not tell us to go unto the nations and teach English, show a movie and play soccer with kids.

Sharing God's grace and mercy, healing the sick, feeding the hungry, serving orphans and widows are all biblical and God honoring. They are not what we are called to do in the Great Commission. These other ministries should be used as ways draw disciples in so they can be baptized and taught to observe God's commands. An orphan comes off the

---

[57] David Platt, "Brook Hills: Vision, Mission, and Goal," in *David Platt Sermon Archive* (Birmingham, AL: David Platt, 2011), 3229.

streets for food, but truly he comes to be baptized. A widow goes to a clinic to be healed, but truly she is coming to be taught God's ways. A child comes to a church to learn English, but truly he is coming to become a disciple of Christ. All other ministries are superfluous unless they are leading people to be discipled, baptized, taught the instructions of Christ.

If missions were simply programs and events, it would be much easier. If read properly the Great Commission is in fact a hard command to follow. Conversion and baptism are required and then begins the arduous task of the ongoing teaching of what Christ taught us. Discipling, mentoring and counseling new converts, these added complications, are why it is important to know we labor under Christ's authority and that he is with us always. Without Jesus the process of discipleship would be impossible. Of the Great Commission Charles Spurgeon said, "From it we learn that our first business is to make disciples of all nations, and we can only do that by teaching them the truth as it is revealed in the Scriptures and seeking the power of the Holy Spirit to make our teaching effective in those we try to instruct in divine things."[58]

Making disciples is not easy, because being a disciple is not easy (Luk 14:27). Believers are called to pray earnestly for workers to labor in the harvest (Mat 9:38), not because making disciples is easy, because it is hard.

When Jesus began his ministry and called his disciples the first thing he said to them is, "Follow me, and I will make you fishers of men." (Mat 4:19) That is how being a disciple of Christ begins and it ends by making other disciples. When we follow Christ, we become fishers of men. Instead of drawing fish into a net our job is to draw people to the kingdom and disciple, baptize and teach them. Missions is about making disciples. Making disciples is about multiplying. This is so important it is the first thing and the last thing Christ said to his followers in Matthew.

Missions Without Discipleship is Tourism

Few in our modern churches have not heard of Jesus' Great Commission which is found in Matthew 28:18-20. When we read it, many of us hone in on the first word found in verse 19; "Go." However, the imperative of the Great Commission is, in fact, "make disciples." This imperative explains the primary purpose, while the participles (go, baptizing, and teaching) explain parts of that process.

---

[58] C. H. Spurgeon, *The Gospel of the Kingdom: A Commentary on the Book of Matthew* (London: Passmore and Alabaster, 1893), 258.

In an effort to energize and mobilize missionaries our modern missions movement has focused almost exclusively on the word "go" in the Great Commission. Certainly, the Great Commission cannot be fulfilled without obedient goers. But simply going can be fulfilled by taking a vacation to a resort town. Making disciples must remain at the center of our efforts in obedience to God's Great Commission.

The purpose of this article is not to disparage short-term missions, practitioners of mercy ministries, financial supporters of missions or any other non-disciple making ministries. The purpose of this article is re-focus our modern church on the disciple making found in he Great Commission. Just like a good military force needs truck drivers, doctors, and supply lines, missions also needs those who make the battle possible.

In missions, the short-term teams, mercy ministries and missions supporters must always help to refocus our missions efforts so the lost are directed into the disciple making process. These other aspects of missions are valuable in demonstrating God's grace and mercy to the lost. Frequently the lost can be directed to Christ through short-term or mercy ministry work. But, the long, arduous fight to teach and train believers occurs in the one-on-one or small group settings of discipleship.

Missionaries should not simply seek a confession of faith, but the making of a disciple for Christ. New converts should be connected to fulltime missionaries or national pastors who can facilitate a discipling relationship. Making a disciple who doesn't yearn to share the gospel is like making a Ferrari that doesn't ache for the open road. Christ started his earthly ministry by calling his disciples to be fishers of men and ended with the instruction to go, and make disciples. Clearly, discipleship is important to Jesus. Dietrich Bonhoeffer told us, "Christianity without discipleship is always Christianity without Christ."[59]

Evangelism, the sharing of God's grace and mercy through word and deed, plays a very important role in the expansion of God's kingdom and the winning of souls. Discipleship, on the other hand, is the arduous task of training a new believer how to follow Christ. Discipleship is how Christianity becomes the foundation of a new believer's life. Today, evangelism is eclipsing discipleship because of fear and the self-centeredness of some Christians. Discipleship can be painful, messy and laborious. Discipleship takes effort and time. The hard work of discipleship must remain at the center of missions efforts.

---

[59] Dietrich Bonhoeffer, *Discipleship*, ed. Victoria J. Barnett, trans. Barbara Green and Reinhard Krauss, Reader's Edition., Dietrich Bonhoeffer Works (Minneapolis, MN: Fortress Press, 2015), 19.

Indeed going to all the nations is commanded throughout the Bible (Ps 67; Is 49:6; Mat 24:14; Rom 1:5). The Scriptures are equally clear that once followers of Christ have gone into the world they are to proclaim and teach the truth (Ps 22:27-28; Is 42:1-4; Acts 1:8; Col 1:23). The concept going into the nations and making disciples s undeniably linked together throughout Scripture (Mat 28:19; Mar 16:15; Luk 24:47; Rom 10:18). Our purpose in the church is to make disciples for Jesus Christ and teach them to make disciples. Missions should never leave out discipleship.

Do not go on a mission trip to check the missions box. Go so you learn to have a lifelong burden for all the unsaved throughout the world. To disciple a new believer, to teach the lost, to mentor a brother, to share God's mercies - these are callings and honors for us all. Missions efforts that do not point to or ultimately increase discipleship are little more than moralistic tourism.

In order to disciple new believers we must first go, in order to go we must first be obedient. The desire here is not to decrease any kind of missions venture. The desire is to encourage churches to get more involved in missions efforts that make disciples. Preaching, teaching, theology books, seminaries, conferences; these are some of the ways disciple making is done. ESL, business as missions, medical, construction are not disciple making, but if they are done in such a way that they point nationals to a seminary, church, pastor or fulltime missionary they serve a valuable purpose. These important non-disciple making ministries are valuable if they result in new believers who are mentored and discipled in a Christ-centered, Bible-focused teaching ministry.

Many modern churches sacrifice teaching on the eternal wellbeing of others to make room for teaching that emphasizes temporary personal joy. Jesus' earthly ministry was not centered on teaching large crowds, but discipling 12 men. We too should pour ourselves into individuals.

In our reading of Christ's Great Commission, we can only find obedience in Matthew 28:18-20 if our church is going and sending to the nations. However, in order to comply with the entire command we must facilitate the making, baptizing and teaching of Christian disciples.

How to Disciple With a Book

As Jesus proclaimed the Great Commission (Mat 8:18-20) he provided four very simple yet significant instructions for all Christians. He closed out his earthly ministry with these instructions for taking his gospel to the world. The Great Commission is the charge that calls all believers to global evangelism.

The primary focus of the Great Commission, "make disciples," is a call for us to make followers and students for Jesus. This requires interaction with the unsaved and instruction on salvation. Making disciples can be done in many ways, but the end result is a new follower of Christ.

A disciple acquiesces to the teaching of a leader or belief system. A disciple can be thought of as an apprentice or someone who associates with a teacher for the purpose of learning from his instruction. Biblically, we find the word "disciple" almost exclusively in the Gospels and Acts, with other occurrences in Isaiah. Almost all references discuss disciples as followers of Jesus.

Disciples of Christ were the first true adherents to Christianity (Acts 11:26). Jesus explains, "If you abide in my word, you are truly my disciples" (Jon 8:31). The act of following Christ's teachings makes one a disciple. Disciples are easily identified as those who bear fruit (Jon 15:8) or who typify Christ-like changes in their lives. Disciples are filled with joy (Acts 11:52) through the knowledge they have of God's grace and mercy. And, disciples have a passion for duplication and a longing to create more disciples (Acts 6:1).

The possessive phrase "his disciples" occurs 113 times in the ESV New Testament. This clearly tells us when we become a disciple we become God's disciple. We belong to the Creator. You cannot become God's disciple unless you are utterly committed to him. A disciple of Christ puts his Savior ahead of himself. Willing to make personal sacrifice is what being a disciple is about. God calls us to be willing to give all we have.

Scripture tells us that there are costs associated with being a disciple of Christ. We must place Christ ahead of all we cherish, including our family (Luk 14:26). Christ says we must set aside all we posses and place nothing in front of Him (Luk 14:33). There will be sacrifice, persecution and even threats of murder for disciples of Christ (Acts 9:1).

There are countless ways to make a disciple, but it is imperative we understand what Christ intended of us. The authoritative "make disciples" is the central focus of the Great Commission. Making a disciple is a deliberate practice where individuals are evangelized and helped to grow in their Christian walk. Disciple making is intentional and must involve the salvation of the lost and equipping them to grow closer to the Father. The most favorable results come from face-to-face discipleship. Quality teaching takes place in person, with conversations and dialogue. Discipling can include other components, but must be centered on instruction. Making disciples can happen outside of the local church, but it must always point back to the local church. It was always Jesus' intent that disciplers would lead their disciples into biblical corporate worship.

As a frequent trainer of disciples I have seen few other tools have the impact of a Gospel-centered, Bible-based book in the hands of an obedient discipler. An experienced Christian using a book to lead disciples into a richer relationship with Christ has a lasting and deep impact.

I have experience discipling individuals and groups, youth and adults, educated and under educated. My discipling experiences have taken place in North American churches and around the globe. There are few occasions where my work for the kingdom has felt as impactful as when I have a theology book in one hand, a Bible in the other hand, a couple of chairs, a couple of newer believers and a shade tree.

Using a grace-centered, Bible-focused book in discipleship can educate better than most sermons, stir more passion than most songs and go deeper than any video. A book never takes a sick day, is always present, is inexpensive, can be shared or kept as a reference, and is easy to send.

No book, save the Holy Bible, is flawless. Every author is sinful and susceptible to bias, error and oversight. When a book is used as a discipleship tool it should always be accompanied by Scripture and centered on God's glory.

Here are some helpful tips on how to use books in discipleship relationships:

- Scripture - Have a Bible open and at the ready. When verses are cited, read them. Don't assume participants own or know the Bible. The book should always be used to point to Scripture.

- Sound - Use books which espouse biblical, grace-centered doctrine. Don't take a risk with an unfamiliar author. It must point to Christ and be supported by the Bible, or not used.

- Small - Discipleship groups should be intimate. One to five participants are ideal. People get intimidated in big groups. Encourage participation and limit know-it-alls. Depth is desirable.

- Speed - Neither too fast nor too slow is good. Be flexible with the schedule. Allow the interest level to dictate pace. Don't force completion of a chapter or section.

- Straightforward - If you don't know the answer say so and promise you will report back with the truth. Read the material in advance. Acknowledge difficult topics and stick to the relevant issues.

- Seek - Pray for direction from the Lord as a group and on your own. Open and close and smother the discipleship in pray. Listen to the Spirit and trust you will be guided.

Two true stories of using theology books for discipleship

Each week I was reading a chapter of the Spanish version of John Piper's *This Momentary Marriage* with a Latin American pastor. We read a chapter during the week and talked about the content each Friday. After several weeks of studying the book together the pastor asked if he could have an extra copy to use to disciple a couple in his church who were having marital problems. The following week the pastor asked for a second copy because the husband and wife refused to study together. After several weeks of studying separately the pastor went to the home of the wife for their weekly study through the book. To the Pastor's amazement he walked in to see the husband and wife studying the book together. Earlier that day the husband showed up at the door of his old home with tears in his eyes and the Piper book in his hand, "I have been doing marriage wrong," the man said to his wife, "Can we please read the book together?"

On another occasion I had the pleasure of leading three teenage boys through R.C. Sproul's *Now That's A Good Question*. Each week we would read a section and the four of us would gather together to talk and pray through what we had read. The boys came from separate backgrounds. One grew up in a legalistic home, one in a culturally Catholic home and the third in an unchurched home. As we sat in a circle each week the boys would challenge the content of the book, which was wildly original theology for each of them. The discussion topics were intimate, the shouting was loud and the tears were real. Two of the boys left the weekly study citing heresy, only to return weeks later. By the time we got through the book the boys collectively asked if I had another book we could study together. I continued to disciple the boys for years. After one of the boys shared the "new doctrine of grace" with his pastor, I was invited to preach the topic in his Pentecostal church.

The lifeblood of the church is to make disciples for Jesus Christ and teach them how to make to make disciples themselves. The church is a place to educate, instruct, and prepare its members to impact the world and share God's love, mercy, and truth. Pastor and Professor Reddit Andrews said, "'Go therefore and make disciples,' that is the mission of the church, as straight forward as it could ever be stated." Making a disciple who doesn't yearn to share the gospel with others is like making a sports car that doesn't ache for mountainous roads.

Dietrich Bonhoeffer, martyr for Christ, said, "Christianity without discipleship is always Christianity without Christ." Our business as Christians is to make disciples of all nations. It is our obligation to bring the lost into a saving relationship with the Lord and then grow them up in Christ. A theology book can be a discipler's best friend.

9 Ministries Which Satisfy the Great Commission

Matthew 28:18-20 is more commonly known as the Great Commission and it is centered on the imperative that the Christian church "make disciples." This non-negotiable mandate is frequently misconstrued as evangelism. This perspective does not correspond with the intent of the original text or the rest of Scripture. The making of converts through evangelism is clearly valuable and mandated in Scripture, but the Great Commission is about taking those converts are coming alongside them for a lifetime of learning God's ways. Discipling is the act of Christian believers who are being instructed by other Christian believers.

A conversion is a valuable beginning to a long journey. Disciple making is the lengthy, hard and messy process of transforming someone into a follower who finds their identity and worth in Jesus. Here are nine ways we can participate in the Great Commission and make disciples:

1. Bible Translation

The Bible is the perfect missionary. It never takes a furlough or gets sick. Scripture must be translated into new languages so God's people can learn what God teaches. God provided us his perfect Word for a very important reason. God wants his disciples to be dedicated to learning and living his ways, as found in his inerrant Scriptures.

2. Preaching

Dissecting Scripture and explaining it from the pulpit is a rare gift. Being able to explain God's inspired Word to a group of believers is a blessing to them and will benefit them, their families and their community. Speaking God's truth is the purpose, not entertaining man.

3. Small Group Studies

Providing intimate and regular opportunities to instruct believers is valuable. Frequent Bible studies for youth, kids, women, or men allow people to ask questions and learn in ways larger settings don't offer. Frequency and consistency breed intimacy and depth. Many people feel more free to ask hard questions in smaller settings.

4. Individual Discipleship

Sitting down with a new believer, one on one, is the most effective way to make a disciple. Whenever possible, this is the preferred way to make disciples. Intimate questions, tears and Bible instruction is what Jesus intended. This is a hard process that bears much fruit.

5. Seminary Instruction

Being able to train pastors and church leaders in an ongoing setting carries great valuable. Providing disciples with in-depth instruction enables them to teach and train in their own church and pays dividends for years. This is one of the most effective ways to combat the poor theology that is sweeping the developing world.

6. Theological Resources

Few Christians in the West understand the depth at which theological famine has gripped the rest of the Christian world. Bibles, theology books, radio programs, sermon audios, articles, e-books, and conferences are rare and coveted in the rest of the world. God has made the Western church the richest in the history of the world. Providing theological resources for developing Christian cultures may be one of the reasons.

7. Church Planting

Identifying, training and preparing local pastors and church leaders to start new churches is valuable. All things being equal, a pastor from a given culture knows better how to reach people from his culture better than any missionary ever will. Giving a local church the start and resources it needs to impact a community is a valuable blessing to God's kingdom. Scripture instructs us to worship together and tells us the local church is where disciples grow and learn.

8. Theological Conferences

Although, less intimate, the quality and depth is undeniable. Few Christians outside the Western world have ever had the privilege to sit in one place for several days and receive quality theological instruction brought to them. Two to five days of drinking from the biblical fire hose inspires and motivates Christians to seek further biblical knowledge and provides leaders with theological substance to share with their own churches.

9. Reproduction

The Great Commission is truly about making disciples who make disciples. Disciple making must include training Christians who are burdened to evangelize, plant churches and send out their own missionaries. No culture or church is exempt from participating in the Great Commission. Disciples of Christ must be instructed of the imperative to multiply. Every church exists for the purpose of reaching the lost.

Showing a film, handing out a tract, constructing a house, hosting a medical clinic, and feeding the poor are all biblical and Christ honoring ministries. There is nothing wrong with these or other biblical ministries on the mission field. However, to be considered fulfilling the Great Commission, every missional effort must support and guide people to an existing and ongoing disciple making ministry. Nothing written here should be considered denigrating any missionary, nor should this list be considered exhaustive. Any Christian who sacrifices comfort and safety to glorify God deserves our appreciation and prayer.

Jesus tells us a disciple is someone who abides in his word (Jhn 8:31). Therefore, the Great Commission is realized by the training of people who abide in the word of Christ. Making disciples is not simply evangelism or mercy, but the long-term investment in individuals to transform them into devoted disciples who dedicate their lives to teaching, learning and living the ways of Jesus Christ.

Theological Education: The Role of the West in Missions

The explosion of evangelical Christianity in the Global South in the past century is well documented.

In 1900, about 71 percent of Christians in the world lived in Europe. By 2000, that number shrank to 28 percent. Today, 43 percent of the world's Christians live in Latin America and Africa. In 1900, Africa had 10 million Christians, which was about 10 percent of the population. By 2000, the number of Christians in Africa was 360 million, about half the population of the continent. Mark Noll said, "In a word, the Christian church has experienced a larger geographical redistribution in the last fifty years than in any comparable period in its history, with the exception of the very earliest years of church history."

What is talked about less, in the phenomenon of the Global South, is the eruption of bad theology in Latin America, Africa and Asia. The theology that is taught from many of the pulpits in the Global South is so poor in can scarcely be recognized as coming from the Scriptures. The rapid spread of abysmal theology in the Global South is a detriment to the advancement of the gospel and the very people it is reported to be educating. Bad theology is poisoning many churches and it is spreading like a wildfire.

A contributing factor to the increase in bad theology in the Global South is that many US churches today would rather support nationals than send missionaries. This is a short-sighted financial decision which increases the probability of spreading bad theology. John Piper says, "Many people have embraced the uninformed notion that it is always more efficient and culturally effective to support ministries in the Global South to do the work of missions rather than pay tens of thousands of dollars each year to send Western workers."[60] Supporting those who spread bad theology as opposed to sending those with good theology is exacerbating the problem.

Western churches should increase their support of global theological education. Churches should support the translation and distribution of theology books, sending of theologically trained missionaries to teach and disciple nationals, Bible translation, and the development of grace based, in-country theological seminaries.

This concept is nothing new. For a thousand years the Christian church has been participating in the formation of formal schools of theological instruction around the world. What is new is the disparity of theological resources. Around the world churches hold services each day without enough Bibles for their congregants. In the West we have a multitude of theological conferences, articles, internet downloads and theology books. There should be no guilt over our bevy of theological resources, but, we should do everything we can to ensure our brothers and sisters in rapidly expanding churches have all they need to preach, teach and spread quality Bible-based theology. To disciple a new believer, to evangelize the lost, to mentor a brother, to teach biblical truth - these are callings and honors for us all.

As the wealthiest church in the history of the world, the Western Evangelical church should consider increasing support to ministries which provide grace based, bible believing theological training in the Global South. To combat the plague of bad theology in the Global South they need language appropriate seminaries, articles, books, e-books, conferences and more. The teaching of false doctrine should not be abided, but instead viewed as an affront to the majesty of our Lord.

Indeed, the Evangelical church in the Global South is growing rapidly. But, what good is a rapidly growing church with horrible theology? When thinking of the bad theology of the Global South, don't think of hymnals vs. modern music or ties vs. button down shirts. Christian churches in the Global South are spreading an array of bad theology which includes animism, works based theology, witchcraft and more. Millions

---

[60] John Piper, *Sermons from John Piper* (2000–2014) (Minneapolis, MN: Desiring God, 2014).

of people are "coming to the Lord" in a grotesque amalgamation of theological perversion that would make Satin blush. Never before in history have we had so many bibles in the world and yet so many biblically illiterate Christians.

God's Great Commission (Mat 29:18-20) instructs believers in Christ to "go." This is something, at which, the Western Evangelical church is doing an admirable job. However, at the heart of the great commission is the making of disciples. This is done, in part, by teaching the nations about Christ, his commands and his Scriptures. The Great Commission is fulfilled, not when we go, but when we go, make disciples, baptize and "teach them to observe all I have commanded you." When professed Christians around the world spread a false doctrine, Christ is not glorified.

The church is a place to educate, instruct, and prepare its members to impact the world and share God's love, mercy, and message. Much of the rapid spread of the "gospel" in the Global South in no Gospel at all. Our brothers and sisters around the world are in desperate need of theological education and our Western churches are in a prime position aide them.

The Importance of Planting Churches in Missions

The most efficient place to make self-replicating disciples for Christ, baptize them and teach them God's commands is within the walls of the local church. Missions is the implementation of God's plan for his glory among all people. Therefore, missions should center on the planting, training and equipping of culturally relevant churches around the world.

If Christians can grasp the concept that the purpose of man is to glorify God (Ex 9:16, Ps 106:7-8, Eze 20:9, 14), and God wants his disciples worshiping in a church (Heb 10:24-25, Acts 2: 42) and we as his disciples are called to spread his gospel (Mat 28: 18-20, Luk 9:1-6, Act 1:8), it is no stretch to conclude God's will for missionaries is to plant local churches for his glory around the world.

While the term "Bride of Christ" never appears in the New Testament, imagery of the Church and Christ connecting as the bride and groom appears throughout (2 Cor 11:2, Rom 7:1-6, Eph 5:21-33). Jesus venerates the local church and calls his disciples to love and respect her. Missionaries should esteem the local church the same way and teach nationals to honor her as well. What could be more honoring to the bride than duplicating her beauty?

Scripture is very clear how Christians are to view and interact with the local church. The local church is where we are to gather with others to experience Christ (Mat 18:20).

The local church is where we are to partake in the Lord's Super (1 Cor 11:23-26), worship in song (Eph 5:18-21) and serve each other (1 Cor 14:26). The local church is to be led by qualified leaders (Tit 1:5-9) who administer church discipline (Mat 18:17). Christ's bride is well defined by God's Word.

There can be countless ministries that can bring glory to God. Mercy, construction, education, microenterprise, and other missions activities are ways we point to Christ. However, if they are not done under the authority of a local church or done in order to drive people to the local church, their purpose should be reexamined. God can receive great glory if secondary ministries are done outside the local church. Nevertheless, educating, training and equipping nationals to do these ministries within the local church is more in line with God's Great Commission and our purpose as his disciples.

In culturally relevant, Bible centered, national run churches the leaders and pastors are better equipped to address the theological and physical needs of their congregants. A missionary who has served in China for 40 years is still not Chinese. He may become fluent in the language and understand the culture, but a Chinese Christian is more prepared to comprehend culturally appropriate Christ-centered solutions.

A missionary can teach and equip a national to provide countercultural Christian responses to uniquely cultural situations. The missionary does not change the gospel to fit the culture, instead helps local Christians to act as radical cultural insurgents for Christ. Martyn Lloyd-Jones said, "The glory of the gospel is that when the church is absolutely different from the world, she invariably attracts it." The church is a place to educate, instruct, and prepare its members to impact the world and share God's love, mercy, and truth. The missionary is someone who keenly situated to equip these disciples to glorify God in local churches across the globe.

The Western church is rich in resources, finances and quality theological education. Conversely, many of the Christians in the developing world lack those exact assets. Much of Africa is exploding with new believers, but suffers from the spread of poor theology. Much of Latin America is pocked with churches who don't have the resources needed to influence their own culture. And, much of the 10/40 window lacks the Christian leaders needed to disciple and mentor new believers in ways of the Lord. The Western church is in a position to equip local churches around the world and empower their pastors and leaders to spread the gospel throughout their own communities.

Western missionaries and local worldwide Christians can collaborate in such a way that the local, national run church becomes a beautiful biblically accurate, God honoring bride of Christ. Culturally appropriate and theologically sound churches that spread the liberty found only in Christ provide a powerful contrast to the world. Planting churches like this in other cultures shows that grace and mercy are not found in Western missionaries, but only in the blood of Christ.

Evangelical missions has a relevant and powerful place in today's sinful world. In fact, now more than ever a biblically healthy missions movement is needed to combat the global spread of works based theology, man centered pride and the health and wealth gospel. The role of the missionary is to help plant local churches and to train church leaders to enable them to participate in the fulfillment of the Great Commission in their own culture and across the globe.

Biblically Mandated Mercy

Man's pain and man's suffering originates from man's sin. Everything God made was good (Gen 1:31). The first man was tempted and sinned in a perfectly voluntary act. The contagion of sin spread throughout man and left no part of our being untouched. Man became utterly corrupt (Gen 6:5; Rom 7:18). Paul tells us that by one man death entered the world and passed on to all men (Rom 5:12). Sin causes man to turn against God and to turn against each other. With the addition of sin in our existence we have pain, sickness, death, suffering, poverty, racism, injustice, corruption, theft, starvation and other means of creating distance between us and our Creator.

The need for God's grace, mercy, and justice in the world are a direct result of the fall of man. Now, as a result, we are all needy recipients of the blessings provided by the Lord. The birth, death and resurrection of Jesus Christ were mandated by the sin of man. Through Christ alone is our sinful heart reconciled to God.

It is our sin that created a need for the mercy of Christ. It is also our hands which are called upon to disseminate God's love. Scripture commands disciples of Christ to show his mercy and justice to each other and to the lost. We are vessels for which his good work is poured out on others (2Tim 2:21). When we serve the poor, the widows and the orphans in Christ's name, they receive mercy, Christ receives glory and we comprehend justice. When we were poor, lost and destitute the Lord shared his mercy with us so we could share his mercy with the poor, lost and impoverished. Tim Keller said, "Because Jesus served you in such a radical way, you have a joyful need to serve."

Christ's disciples are called to dispense God's mercy and justice, not so we can be observed or glorified, but so that our Father can be glorified. Any action of mercy that elevates us as the provider is sinful. The dispenser of grace must always be seen as Christ. Those suffering must never see us as anything other than a willing vessel. The disciples of

Christ are called to give food to the hungry, drink to the thirsty, welcome strangers, clothe the naked, visit the sick and imprisoned (Mat 25:31-40). Those who do not do these things will be eternally punished (Mat 25:41-46). Serving the needy provides evidence we as disciples of Christ and have a truly altered heart. The love of Christ in our hearts compels us to show mercy to others, as we too have been shown mercy.

The term "mercy" (or merciful) appears over 200 times in the ESV. Of course, a majority of the mercy in Scripture refers to God's great mercy toward man. However, many occurrences of mercy relate to the actions we, as disciples of Christ, are to show to others so God can receive glory. The word "mercy" appears in Scripture (in all its Greek and Hebrew forms) more often than the words grace, justice, tithe, Sabbath, pray, church, baptism, and preach. Indeed mercy has great significance to our Lord.

Our thankfulness for the mercy God creates a strange conflict in our heart. We naturally desire to serve and comfort ourselves, but our new heart screams for us to show mercy to others. We feel a strange urge to show our love for Christ by showing his love to others. Micah 6:8 says, "He has told you, O man, what is good; and what does the LORD require of you but to do justice, and to love kindness, and to walk humbly with your God?" Charles Spurgeon wrote of this verse, "The prophet does not say, 'to do mercy,' but to 'love' it, to take a delight in it, to find great pleasure in the forgiveness of injuries, in the helping of the poor, in the cheering of the sick, in the teaching of the ignorant, in the winning back of sinners to the ways of God."[61]

James teaches that our faith is not real if it only results in wisdom and a warm heart and not in deeds of service. James 1:27 says, "Religion that is pure and undefiled before God, the Father, is this: to visit orphans and widows in their affliction, and to keep oneself unstained from the world."

Pray the God of Mercy will give you opportunities to provide justice to the oppressed and grace for the broken. Serving others isn't imparting our views, imposing our will or forcing our culture on others. It is sharing the joy and mercy of a perfect love. Answering God's command to share his mercy and love with the poor is a pleasure too few enjoy and too many disregard. Augustine implored us, "So give to the poor; I'm begging you, I'm warning you, I'm commanding you, I'm ordering you."[62]

---

[61] C. H. Spurgeon, "Micah's Message for To-Day," in *The Metropolitan Tabernacle Pulpit Sermons, vol. 39* (London: Passmore & Alabaster, 1893), 479.

[62] St. Augustin, *Sermons 51-94* (Brooklyn, NY: New City Press, 1991), 148.

Mercy Withheld Robs God of Glory

Our Savior is a God of mercy, grace and justice. He delights in disseminating his blessings to those in need. Indeed, he receives great glory when our actions of mercy point to his provision. We are called upon as disciples of Christ to provide the mercy of Christ to the hungry, sick and homeless. Withholding the mercy of Christ from the needy is not our choice to make.

Scripture tells us that it is the wicked, not the disciple of Christ, who withholds mercy. The Bible says believers are instructed to not withhold good (Pr 3:27) and that no mercy is found in the wicked (Pr 21:10). In fact, in much of the OT we see that mercy is withheld from those whom the Lord wishes to punish or eliminate. Withholding mercy is how the wicked are destroyed (Dt 7:2, Dt 28:49-50). Those who are marked by the Lord for destruction are to receive no mercy (Jos 11:20).

A disciple of Christ is merciful to others and a wicked man shows no mercy (Ps 112). James 4:17 also tells us that if we know the right thing and don't do it sin is in us. 1 John 3:17 goes as far as to question our dedication to the Lord if we withhold from the needy, "But if anyone has the world's goods and sees his brother in need, yet closes his heart against him, how does God's love abide in him?" Tim Keller echoed this theme when he said, "If you look down at the poor and stay aloof from their suffering, you have not really understood or experienced God's grace."[63]

Many well-intentioned Christians have elevated the concern over creating dependency above our biblical mandate to share the grace, mercy and justice of Christ with others. The concern lies in the belief that our dissemination of physical goods to the sick and poor can create a dependency upon the giver of the gifts. The belief is that it is more important to help the poor provide for themselves and to restore their dignity. The concern is if we provide for the destitute, they will never learn to provide for themselves.

The belief in not creating dependency is supported by many solid economic, philosophical and political viewpoints. Unfortunately, there is very little biblical reasoning to withhold mercy and justice to the poor and sick. When Christ walked the earth he sought to create dependency on himself. Christ never withheld his physical or eternal healing based on a fear of dependency. Never once did Christ say to the blind, paralytic or leper, "Wait, I am concerned that if I heal you, you might become dependent

---

[63] Timothy Keller, *Generous Justice: How God's Grace Makes Us Just, 1st ed.* (New York: Dutton, 2010), 96.

upon my grace and mercy." He desired to have his followers dependent upon that which only he could provide.

It is not our place to determine who gets mercy and who does not. And, it is not our place to determine why some receive mercy and some do not. Our job as disciples of Christ is to dispense God's mercy and justice to all who need it. We have not been entrusted by God to determine who is and who is not worthy. Christians dispense grace and mercy and let the Lord sort out who is lazy and who is industrious. All mercy comes from the Lord. Mercy, grace and justice bring glory to God. Choosing to withhold mercy from an individual is consciously deciding not to glorify God.

Disciples of Christ have been selected to disseminate God's mercy to bring him greater glory. When you give dignity, mercy, love, justice, charity and respect to others you are letting them see Christ in your words and actions. True justice and mercy is filled with the grace of God and is radical and offensive to the world. It is a radical concept in today's world to do justice for the needy when it is clear that there is no ability for them to repay you. A.W. Tozer said, "How utterly terrible is the current idea that Christians can serve God at their own convenience."[64]

Feeding the poor, clothing the hungry, serving the sick, these are not natural actions that flow from the human heart. It is unnatural for us to provide justice for the poor and homeless. The justice we dispense is an echo of the grace and mercy God gave us. The desire to serve grows from the grace of Jesus Christ in us. We provide a voice and aide to the poor and oppressed so they can receive the justice found only in Christ's love.

Mercy given separate from God's glory is sinful. Those who serve the needy and do not have Christ's glory at the center of their purpose are doing so to glorify themselves or their belief system. Disease, poverty and starvation are blessings if they help point us towards our greater need for Jesus. Only true mercy comes from Christ and only Christ produces true mercy.

By definition a disciple of Christ is someone who shares his mercy and justice with the sick and poor. Our calling is to bring God glory by sharing his mercy with the suffering.

The Value of Youth Ministry on the Mission Field

The biblical mandate to instruct children is important to Jesus and thus, should be vital to us. Youth ministry is an important way to change a culture. Be it children, high

---

[64] Lauren Barlow, *Inspired by Tozer*. (Ventura, CA: Regal, 1979), 164.

school or university ministries, discipling the young can be extremely valuable to long-term missions work.

Often times when entering into a new community a missionary can discover the adults are skeptical and slow to respond, but the children are more eager to interact. The innocence and curiosity of youth frequently causes kids to gravitate toward the new and interesting. Missionaries can make a large and swift impact on a community by first reaching out to children.

The Lord wants us to instruct the children (Deut 6:7; Prv 1:8-9, 22:6; Ps 78:1-7). Educating children in the ways of the Lord, for some kids, brings them their first exposure to the saving grace of Christ, and for others, affirms previous instruction from the home or church. Children are a gift from God and a blessing to us (Ps 127:3-5). The importance of instructing youth is clear in Scripture.

Ministering to children helps to counter the world's influence they are experiencing through sin, poverty and abuse. Discipling the youth of a culture will teach them how to love and forgive others in their lives. Kids in youth ministry are provided with valuable tools they need to glorify God in their own walk with the Lord.

The faith of children is an example for all adults (Mat 18:2-6, 18:10; 1Pet 2:2-3). Reaching kids with the gospel turns them into evangelists as they return home and share biblical truths with members of their family. John Piper said, "When we humble ourselves like little children and put on no airs of self-sufficiency, but run happily into the joy of our Father's embrace, the glory of His grace is magnified and the longing of our soul is satisfied."[65]

Reaching the youth of a culture helps missionaries to reach the entire family. Some parents are drawn back to the church by the faith of their kids. Children are a gateway to unchurched family members and provide a safe excuse to enter homes and talk about faith. Children are fearless and unimpeded evangelists. There can be fewer sounds sweeter than to hear the voice of a child say, "Here I am Lord, send me." Young people are not encumbered by the embarrassment and self-doubt that prevents many adults from sharing their faith.

The most impactful way to radically change a community is to alter a generation of its children. Reaching the youth of a community is changing the future leaders. Children have access to places that may be closed to most missionaries. Public schools, gangs and sports teams are all influenced by a kid who has a heart turned toward Christ. Andrew

---

[65] John Piper, *Sermons from John Piper* (1980–1989) (Minneapolis, MN: Desiring God, 2007).

Murray said, "Nature teaches us that every believer should be a soul-winner. It is an essential part of the new nature. We see it in every child who loves to tell of his happiness and to bring others to share his joys."[66]

If the next generations leaders are disciples of Christ an entire community can experience the grace and mercy of Jesus. The youth who are touched by the Lord today will be teachers, parents and police officers tomorrow. One missionary who disciples young individuals and small groups of youth can alter the DNA of a culture over time.

In churches all over the world there is a noticeable absence of young men and fathers. Too many children do not see biblical examples of men. Reaching the youth today will provide more qualified preachers and leaders in the years to come. Charles Spurgeon said, "You may speak but a word to a child, and in that child there may be slumbering a noble heart which shall stir the Christian Church in years to come."[67] Educating the youth creates a more biblically sound and engaged congregation in the future.

It is more impactful if the youth of a community are educated by national Christian leaders, preferably by a nationally run church. Ideally, a missionary will facilitate youth ministry and provide resources to national Christians so they can impact their own culture. A national run youth ministry that is pointing kids into local churches is the healthiest long-term solution for people group.

Christ calls us to reach the youth of a culture. Our Father instructs us to teach and value our youth. A missionary who is actively discipling the children in a community is planting seeds that will pay dividends for the spiritual health of future generations. Imagine, ten-years from now, an army of youth growing up to be theologically sound and Christ loving parents, teachers and pastors. Christ is glorified today and in the days to come through youth ministry.

Working with youth can be messy and hard. Kids are honest and fickle. Young people ask questions and demand sound answers. A Christ-centered youth ministry on the mission field can be one of the most productive discipling ministries to provide long-term change in a culture.

---

[66] John Piper, *Let the Nations Be Glad! Study Guide*. (Grand Rapids, MI: Baker Academic, 2010), 18.

[67] Thomas Nelson, *A Charles Dickens Devotional*. (Nashville, TN: Countryman, 2012), 111.

Teaching English as a Ministry in Missions

Missions is about making Christian disciples of the nations and teaching them God's ways. This should be the primary focus of any missional ministry. On the mission field, all ministries should either directly make disciples for Christ, or point the lost to a disciple making ministry. Teaching English in a foreign context can greatly enhance the disciple making efforts in missions work.

Teaching English is a natural and purposeful way to gain access, show mercy and build relationships with God's diverse creation. Used wisely English instruction can be a great foundational ministry and help missionaries expand the impact of their labors.

Before the Tower of Babel the earth had one language (Gen 11:1). Mankind had similar cultures and lived in close proximity to each another. Because of man's sinful heart and his desire to exalt himself above God, our Lord complicated man's plans to build the Tower of Babel. God gave man multiple languages and dispersed him throughout the globe (Gen 11:7-8). God separated the nations of man by distance, culture and language.

The Great Commission (Mat 28:18-20) is Christ's mandate and plan for his church to make disciples of the nations. The Tower of Babel was certainly one of God's earliest actions toward implementing that plan. The creation of varying tribes, while being a result of man's sin, was part of God's will to use man to call the elect to himself. In God's salvific mercy toward man, there is a straight line connecting the origin of languages to missions.

Teaching English can help a missionary gain admission he may not otherwise have. Entry can be gained at both the bureaucratic and the popular levels. Frequently, governments or universities grant access to English teachers which may not be provided to religious workers. At the popular level teaching English, may allow a missionary easy access to a community or group.

English is the third most popular first language in the world (behind Chinese and Spanish) and the most popular spoken language overall. English is the predominant language of the internet, media, and technology with most resources produced in English. English is the official language of over 50 countries. The most common second language taught in schools around the world is English. In short, much of the world desires to know English.

Teaching English for free in poor communities can help demonstrate the boundless mercy of Jesus Christ. Often, formal language study is expensive and out of reach for impoverished groups. By giving for free, what a community could not otherwise afford, a missionary could be providing additional employment or education opportunities which would not otherwise be available. Formal English instruction may be a lifelong pay raise for your students.

The compassionate and intentional instruction you can provide a group of students is often contrary to the learning environments in developing nations. Many education settings around the world are harsh, passionless and unproductive. Language lessons could be a wonderful way to show the selfless, joy and passion found only in Christ.

Wherever legally permissible, Bible reading is a great foundational resource to use in teaching vocabulary, grammar, reading, writing and listening skills. By using Bibles as the textbook for your English class, and then providing the skills needed to comprehend the text, an English teacher is placing the saving gospel into the homes of all his students.

Bible studies and Bible lessons are a great way to simultaneously teach English and the Scriptures. The Bible is full of diverse vocabulary, contains poetry, history, dialogue and narrative. The Bible was used for generations to teach English in U.S. public schools and it can be used as a teaching aide around the world.

English classes are wonderful and structured vehicles for building deeper relationships with groups of people. The organizational mechanism of meeting regularly, several times a week, is a natural way to get to know people and for the students and the teachers to develop substantive bonds.

Outings, home visits and other special events can be used as rewards and further educational opportunities. Shopping, meals and public transportation are all great ways to escape the classroom and teach useful vocabulary.

If a missionary promises a student or a government they will be teaching English, by all means, quality instruction of English should be provided. Don't deceive or misrepresent your intentions. Sufficient preparation should be made by the English instructor to guarantee God is glorified by your labors. No Christian missionary should ever invite the accusations of being dishonest.

Much of the world wants it and you've got it. Teaching English is a wonderful way to gain access to people with whom you may not otherwise be able to interact. Languages were created by man's sin. How glorious to imagine they can also lead to his salvation. God's mercy and the saving words of Scripture can be passed on. In the end, if you can speak it, many people desire to learn it and it can be a wonderful gateway for discipleship and the teaching of God's ways.

Chapter Seven

Missions and Suffering

There is a dirty little secret in missions. Most missionaries experience it, many senders expect it to be true, and few missions book teach about it. That secret; missions is hard. I mean, missions is really hard. Most missionaries understand this in theory before they depart for the field. It is not rocket science. A person grew up in a culture where they may have been articulate, successful, and fairly well educated. They then become a missionary and move to a new culture where they struggle to accomplish the mundane, they communicate like a small child, and they lack confidence. That is enough to make anyone feel small.

Only when a missionary arrives on the mission field do they realize they have lost most of their support structure. Life moves on for their friends and family, and supporters become less excited and interested each day following the day the missionary departed. When little things happen, and they will, the missionary then realizes most of their coping mechanism didn't make the trip with them. Marriage, family, spiritual life, ministry, confidence, and health all begin to break down, and those people you used to lean on are so far away. Your neighbors, friends, church, small groups, and accountability partners aren't around to kickstart your recovery or point you in the proper direction.

Then there is that unspoken adversarial relationship a missionary has with their financial and prayer supporters. Even though it is almost never true, every missionary believes (at some level) if the world finally finds out the missionary is battling depression, struggling with family life, or lacking confidence in ministry, the supporters will go elsewhere to find a missionary who truly has it all together. Most missionaries suffer in silence, but, at some level, all missionaries are suffering. Left unaddressed, and marriages, faiths, and ministries can be shattered.

Safety and Suffering in Missions

A quick search of the Internet produces a dozen missions organizations advertising "safe" mission trips. This is nothing they can guarantee nor do they have the biblical authority to do so. While these organizations make promises they cannot keep, the Apostle Paul was more honest with Christians when he said, "Indeed, all who desire to live a godly life in Christ Jesus will be persecuted," (2 Tim 3:12). Suffering is an expected element in Christian living and should not be hidden from the faithful.

It is sad how in recent years the words sacrifice, martyr and submission have become less popular and considered more extreme in evangelical churches. It is prevalent in our modern churches to teach believers to avoid pain and suffering, even if it means avoiding Christian service. Jesus himself told us, "Blessed are you when others revile you and persecute you and utter all kinds of evil against you falsely on my account." (Mat 5:11) In the next verse Christ said we should "rejoice and be glad" when we are persecuted. We were never promised a lack of pain or suffering, only the unwavering knowledge that the Creator of the Universe loves us.

In no way should this article be considered a call to place ourselves in harms way. Christians should not be foolish, dangerous or cavalier. Missionaries and all Christians should neither crave danger nor seek martyrdom. But, never forget, this body we covet and try to protect was not intended for our use, but God's glory.

Our modern church culture seeks false safety at the cost of service to God. What we are doing is making an idol of our control at the expense of God's sovereignty. If God is sovereign, and he controls all, there can be no tragedy or mistake, only the divinely orchestrated rolling out of his perfect will. Paul told the Philippians, "as it is my eager expectation and hope that I will not be at all ashamed, but that with full courage now as always Christ will be honored in my body, whether by life or by death." (Phil 1:20) If we were less focused on our comfort in this life and more focused on the kingdom of God, our idol of safety would not infest our decision to serve. In John Piper's Desiring God he tells us, "This is God's universal purpose for all Christian suffering: more contentment in God and less satisfaction in the world."[68]

God created us, breathed life into us and he has purposed us for his glory. The grace and mercy he gave warrants our love and obedience. Jesus Christ endured an inconceivable persecution and death to pay for our sins. Our response can only be the bold proclamation of his greatness.

---

[68] John Piper, *Desiring God* (Colorado Springs, CO: Multnomah Books, 2001), 265.

Missions is a form of sacrifice in the name of Jesus. However, not only missionaries are called to sacrifice. Sacrifice is the calling of every Christian. Dietrich Bonhoeffer, who gave his life for Christ during World War II, said, "A Christian is someone who shares the sufferings of God in the world."[69] God's love for us is deeper than any love we have known. The comfort and joy this provides should defeat all our fears and worry. Paul declares, "I appeal to you therefore, brothers, by the mercies of God, to present your bodies as a living sacrifice, holy and acceptable to God, which is your spiritual worship." (Rom 12:1)

The Bible never says missions is safe. In Isaiah 40:9 we are instructed in a single verse to both "herald the good news" and "fear not." Evangelism and suffering are again joined when Paul says, "As for you, always be sober-minded, endure suffering, do the work of an evangelist, fulfill your ministry." (2 Tim 4:5). We are called to make a sacrifice in our lives to facilitate the expansion of the gospel into the world.

Truly submitting to the gospel of Jesus can only result in a heart turned towards saving the lost, feeding the hungry and healing the sick. Charles Spurgeon, 19th century British Pastor alleged, "A man is not far from the gates of heaven when he is fully submissive to the Lord's will."[70] Sacrifice in the name of missions is not seeking martyrdom it is submitting to whatever the Lord wills in our lives.

Martin Luther said, "A religion that gives nothing, costs nothing, and suffers nothing, is worth nothing."[71] When we can acknowledge our perceived security is false and safety is an illusion we can begin to risk everything and accomplish great things for God's glory.

If you can manage your own life you've not sold out for Jesus. The life he wants for you is full of risk, peril & requires reliance on him. C.S. Lewis stated, "God, who foresaw your tribulation, has specially armed you to go through it, not without pain but without stain."[72] We are to trust God's sufficiency and serve him completely, no matter the cost.

Our life on this earth is only a blip in time. It should not be false safety and fabricated security we seek. Glorifying God should be our purpose. Life should be lived so that in

[69] Mark Water, *The New Encyclopedia of Christian Quotations* (Alresford, Hampshire: John Hunt Publishers Ltd, 2000), 982.

[70] C. H. Spurgeon, *Farm Sermons* (New York: Passmore and Alabaster, 1882), 214.

[71] Hillary Rodrigues and John Harding, *Introduction to the Study of Religion* (New York: Routledge, 2009), 133.

[72] Mark Water, *The New Encyclopedia of Christian Quotations* (Alresford, Hampshire: John Hunt Publishers Ltd, 2000), 982.

the end we are worthy of hearing, "Well done, good and faithful servant. You have been faithful over a little; I will set you over much. Enter into the joy of your master." (Mat 25:21)

Missionary, you Suffer for a Reason

Most Christian missionaries I know suffer in silence from a range of personal and spiritual issues. The weight of the conflict that rages in their hearts threatens to crush their ministry, family and faith. They oftentimes cannot see Christ at work and simply want the emotional pain to subside.

Missionaries are often unprepared to address the intensity of their suffering and this may threaten their ministry. Jesus and the Apostle Paul regularly promised we would suffer in our service to the Lord. It should not surprise us when it happens. If missionaries could better understand why they suffer, they may be better prepared to endure.

The sanctification process brings us closer to Christ and makes us more like him (Phil 3:10). Suffering turns us into the Christians we need to be to accomplish God's will. Our trials will never impact us beyond our ability to endure them and God will provide us with the capacity to endure and the aptitude to escape (1 Cor 10:13). John Calvin said, "You must submit to supreme suffering in order to discover the completion of joy."[73]

Our suffering is good for us (Ps 119:71), blesses us (Jas 1:12), makes us more holy (Heb 12:10) and prepares us for glory (2 Cor 4:17). Enduring trials makes us stronger and helps us to long more deeply for God. John Piper assures us, "This is God's universal purpose for all Christian suffering: more contentment in God and less satisfaction in the world."

It is sad how in recent years the words sacrifice, martyr and submission have become less popular and considered more extreme in our churches. This has resulted in a generation of Christians who are more concerned about their safety and comfort than they are about God's glory. Missionary Hudson Taylor said, "For our Master's sake, may He make us willing to do or suffer all His will."

When we suffer and lean harder into our Father it brings him glory (Rom 6:4). While we are not to be reckless and seek out danger we are to understand our pain and even death can bring God great glory (Jn 11:1-4). We are to rejoice in our trials bringing God glory (1 Pe 4:12-13). How fortunate to experience suffering that results in God's glory, pain that expands God's name, and persecution that points towards heaven. God's

---

[73] Fayek Hourani, *Daily Bread for Your Mind and Soul* (Bloomington, IN: Xlibris, 2012), 107.

love for us is deeper than any love we have ever known. The comfort and joy this provides us should defeat all our fears and pain.

Every disciple of Christ is a soldier (2 Tim 2:3-4). Missionaries, you are on the frontline of the battlefield. We should expect nothing less than spiritual attacks. When we read through Scripture we find two very important points about how Christ's disciples will suffer: 1) We will be persecuted, and 2) There will be an end to that persecution.

All who desire to follow Christ will be persecuted (2 Tim 3:12). When following Christ, we have been told that in this world we will suffer (Phil 1:29) and receive tribulation (John 16:33). Dietrich Bonhoeffer told us, "A Christian is someone who shares the sufferings of God in the world."[74] Everything in Scripture is clear that in this life following Christ will result in more pain, not less.

We are also promised our suffering will come to an end. God will deliver us from all of our afflictions (Ps 34:19). Our painful lives will become peaceful (Heb 12:11) and eventually death, pain and tears will be a thing of the past (Rev 21:4).

A flippant or callous response to suffering is dangerous. Scripture tells us how to respond to our suffering. Disciples are called to rejoice in our suffering (Rom 5:3-5), be joyful in our trials (Jas 1:2-4) and count ourselves blessed in our persecution (Mat 5:10). We were never promised lack of pain or suffering, only the unwavering knowledge that the Creator of the Universe loves us.

How sad for a Christian to live such a life that Satan feels no need to interfere. We have an enemy who is actively trying to stop the advancement of Christianity. Missionaries should expect spiritual attacks. If it is my pleasure or my anguish that brings God glory I pray it is more abundant in my life.

God created us, breathed life into us, and purposed us for his glory. The grace and mercy he gives warrants our love and obedience. Jesus Christ endured an inconceivable persecution and death to pay for our sins. In response, we should boldly proclaim his greatness to all nations.

Advancing the kingdom of God is a great privilege. However, our missionaries are paying an added toll due to their proximity to the frontline. Pray for them often. Remind them you appreciate their sacrifice. Missionaries, when you suffer, lean into God. Trust in his sovereignty and pray you are part of his will.

---

[74] Mark Water, *The New Encyclopedia of Christian Quotations* (Alresford, Hampshire: John Hunt Publishers Ltd, 2000), 982.

The Insufficient Missionary

Nearly every missionary I have worked or interacted with, at some level, views themselves as insufficient to the herculean task before them. Some, who might compare themselves to missionary greats, even view themselves as frauds. The daunting task of glorifying God in another culture seems too much to bare when you are on the inside looking out and all you see is your own sin and insufficiency.

Missionaries are some of the most self-deprecating, silent sufferers serving the Lord today. A typical missionary wrestles daily with the fact that, in comparison to his historical and contemporary counterparts, he is insufficient to minister cross-culturally.

Before missionaries can begin to heal and serve joyfully they must come to the freeing realization that, yes indeed, you are insufficient to the task for which God has called you. Your ability, skills and training are less important on the mission field than your willingness to serve others. You don't need training, certification or a job title to bring the gospel to the world. You only need an obedient heart inclined toward God. We must lay down our wisdom, our abilities, our strength and our victories and we must rest in the unmatched grace of God.

Disciples of God are to view our bodies as a living sacrifice (Rom 21:1). All our abilities come from God (Jas 1:17; 1 Cor 2:13; Is 41:10) and our God-given talents are provided for his glory (1 Pet 4:10). Therefore, when we despair because of our insufficiency we are to remember we can accomplish anything through God (Phil 4:13) and that in the end we will succeed in God for his advancement (Phil 1:6). Global evangelism is not always easy, but the Lord promises us that he has sufficiently prepared us and his purpose will be accomplished.

Missionaries, if we are in God's will we cannot and will not fail. No matter how badly we slow down the progress of the gospel or foul up the advancement of God's grace, God's will is guaranteed to be implemented. Look at the life of 19th Century missionary Hudson Taylor. This pioneering missionary to China would be declared by most everyone as a missionary success story. Yet, during his time on the mission field, he was beaten, became ill numerous times, and was robbed. He endured the death of five children, his first wife and dozens fellow missionaries. Hudson Taylor endured pain, but he knew he was being used by God for his glory. Taylor once said, "God's work done in God's way will never lack God's supplies."[75]

---

[75] Paul E. Brown, *Deuteronomy: An Expositional Commentary, Exploring the Bible Commentary* (Leominster, UK: Day One Publications, 2008), 205.

If God selected you for his work he will provide you with all you need. Go forward knowing our Father has prepared you for victory. When it comes to global mission you are neither a winner nor a loser of souls. You are a tool in the hands of a master carpenter. Let God work. God desires to utilize his disciples, but we must always remember, the gospel of Jesus Christ is the only thing that has the ability to truly change lives.

We have proven to be an insufficient source of wisdom. We cannot trust our fellow man. We must trust our labors to Scripture and God's perfect plan. We know God is sufficient and provides us with everything we need to succeed. So why do we continue to meddle in his perfect will?

God did not select you as a disciple because you were the wisest or most holly. He also did not set aside some to be missionaries because they were the best and the brightest. Missionaries are willing servants whose greatest attribute is they were intuitive enough to say "yes" when called to serve in cross-cultural missions. Our missionaries have been set apart, not because of their abilities, but because of their obedience. Dr. Martyn Lloyd-Jones said, "It was God's hand that laid hold of me, and drew me out, and separated me to this work."[76]

Missionaries, you were obedient when God called you to the field. Now, remain obedient when God asks you to endure hardship and allow yourself to be used for his glory. Embrace the fact you are insufficient for the task you have been called to accomplish. Find joy in knowing God is sufficient and he has prepared you to accomplish what he desires. You have been endowed, by God with great blessings which are to be used to bring him abundant glory.

We all have different experiences and abilities, trials and blessings. The question is, how are you using your life to bring glory to God? Go forward in confidence. God selected you to do his great work and he knew your flaws and limitations before he choose you. Like Paul and David and Moses before you, you are insufficient sinners who God has called and prepared for success. You are no mistake. You are exactly who God wants battling on the frontlines.

---

[76] David Martyn Lloyd-Jones, *God's Ultimate Purpose: An Exposition of Ephesians 1* (Edinburgh; Carlisle, PA: Banner of Truth Trust, 1978), 92.

Missionary Care for Yourself

Most missionaries are struggling. They battle emotional, physical and spiritual battles while on the field. Due to the fact they want to appear like a missionary worthy of support they typically hide their pain and keep their suffering private.

Certainly, supporting churches, friends, family and missions agencies should be caring for the missionaries they have pledged to support. However, the greatest benefit in a missionary's life comes when he is carrying for his own wellbeing. A missionary's support network can greatly influence the struggles the missionary is experiencing. But, to all my missionary co-laborers out there, you have the greatest impact on your own wellbeing. Missionary, you must care for yourself.

Too many believers do not realize our physical body is important to God. Sometimes we are so focused on the spiritual realm, that we do not acknowledge that God values our earthly bodies and wants us to care for them (1 Cor 3:16-17, 6:19-20; Eph 5:29). There is a well-known connection between and healthy body and a positive attitude.

Good diet, regular exercise and sufficient rest are important in ensuring we can serve at peak performance. Keeping ourselves healthy improves the odds we can give increased performance for God's glory. Stay healthy, not for vanity, but so you can better serve in God's name. Catherine Booth said, "I know not what He is about to do with me, but I have given myself entirely into His hands." Don't neglect time off and adequate preventative care. Proper care for your body improves longevity and improves the chances you will be able to serve longer on the mission field.

Missionaries experience spiritual battles and persecution at an elevated rate. Maintaining your faith and your walk with Christ is important. It is challenging for any believer who has a crisis of faith. When a missionary is overcome with spiritual doubt and questions his own faith it can mark the end of their ministry. As a missionary you must guard against spiritual dryness and dedicate yourself to frequent spiritual nourishment.

On the mission field there are fewer options when it comes to feeding your soul. Fewer conferences, guest speakers, DVDs or books are available outside the U.S. Missionaries need to daily place themselves in the study of God's Word. With few resources at their disposal a missionary will need to get creative to feed himself spiritually. Never neglect the reading of your Bible. In addition there are a bevy of electronic resources available via the internet. Use electronic books, simulcast conferences, internet study groups, theological blogs, podcast sermons, distance learning theology classes, prayer boards and more.

It is radically offensive to our selfish, me-centered culture to promote the idea that we need Jesus to save us and reconcile us to God. It is however true and magnified on the mission field. We must die to our cultural traditions and biases in our faith and learn to adapt our spiritual lives to the conditions we find ourselves. Giving our lives to God's service doesn't mean abandoning study and enrichment, it amplifies the need to lean on Christ. C.S. Lewis said, "Until you have given up yourself to Him you will not have a real self."[77]

If you, as a missionary, are immersing yourself in poverty, spiritual warfare, heavy workloads, high crime, suffering or cultural challenges this will take a toll on you. The constant barrage can truly do a number on your heart and mind. Emotional fatigue can impact your ministry longevity, spiritual life, physical health and family life. We must first die to what we consider "normal" and embrace the grace and mercy of Christ in order survive the emotional weariness. A.W. Pink said, "The first step toward a daily following of Christ is the denying of self."[78] Get up, shake off your fears, self-doubts, embarrassment and lack of confidence and do what God has sent you to this planet to do.

Don't be afraid to share your fears and concerns with others. Perceived weakness is not a statement against you, it is a statement about our need for Christ. When you are struggling don't hesitate to pray, seek help, cry and lean deeper into God. It is imperative to always remember the blood of Christ is the answer to your pain.

It is more common for a missionary to struggle on the field than to not struggle. It is preferential to receive care from others for your physical, spiritual and emotional struggles. Don't hesitate to ask your teammates, supporters and family to help you process and recover. But, dear missionary friends, you must first learn to make caring for yourself a priority.

Giving yourself over completely to God's will and following him into uncertainty is the mark of absolute dedication to his glory. A heart that avails itself to God's will is open to serve the Lord in whichever way he calls and is enthusiastic about sharing the gospel. Scripture confirms that pain and suffering is a frequent part of being a disciple of Christ. Lean into God's grace and mercy and know even your suffering is for his glory.

---

[77] C.S. Lewis, *Mere Christianity* (New York: Harper Collins, 2001), 227.

[78] Arthur Walkington Pink, *The Arthur Pink Anthology* (Bellingham, WA: Logos Bible Software, 2005).

Why Most Missionaries are Liars

No job description I have ever seen for a missionary includes the words "fast and loose with the truth." It is not my belief missions attracts the kind of people who are predisposed to being insincere. Unfortunately, I have seldom encountered a missionary who will tell the entire truth when asked important personal questions.

The questions which would cause a typical missionary to light up a lie detector include: "How are you doing?" "How is your family?" "How is your marriage?" "How is your spiritual health?" These personal questions are frequently asked by friends, family, and supporting churches. What gives a typical missionary emotional fits is juxtaposing an honest desire to receive help with the concern he or she may be perceived as a ministry failure.

The truth is most missionaries are suffering. They just don't want their supporters to know it. A typical missionary has an unspoken adversarial relationship with their supporters. It has to do with financial support. We missionaries think, at some level, if our supporters discover we are suffering, struggling or having a hard time while on the mission field, we will be viewed as a bad investment and our supporters will go find a better missionary who has his act together.

Two of the most discussed topics in the bible are sin & money. It should come as no surprise that money is at the core of much of our sin. Many missionaries are willing to suffer in silence for fear someone may discover we are ineffective servants. If the truth of a missionary's suffering was revealed someone may pull their financial support or a missionary may be called home for a season, or permanently. In a missionary's mind, what could be more painful than to be revealed as incapable of doing that which God has called and prepared them to do?

Missions is hard. Humans are weak. God is sufficient. What could be more unnatural than to leave a culture where you know the language, you are succeeding at life and are surrounded by people who support you, to live in a culture where you speak like a child, have no support group and fail daily? Missionaries leave for the mission field with visions of Amy Carmichael, David Brainerd and Jim Elliot in their heads. The reality is many missionaries spend some part of a typical day in emotional and spiritual anguish. Struggle and failure are typical items on a missionary's "to do" list. Tell your supporters and friends the truth. Get people to pray for you often. Let those who love you know you are in pain. When missionaries are honest, supporters don't run from you, they run to you. When you left for the mission field you asked individuals and churches to partner with you in ministry. Give others the opportunity to glorify God by serving you. You may be surprised how your honesty results in a deluge of compassion.

The church agreed to partner with missionaries. Now do it. This is not simply a financial relationship. It is not about the money. Care for your missionaries at least as well as you care for your stateside congregants. Ask them frequently how they are doing. Assume they are struggling and lying to you. Probe deeper. Ask them hard questions. Remind them frequently you are praying for them. They know you are praying, but they love to be reminded. Remember their family. Don't forget anniversaries and birthdays. One short e-mail or phone call will provide energy for months. You may not be called to go, but you are certainly called to pray for or support God's Great Commission. Every Christian is a participant.

Visit your missionaries on the field. Counsel them. Dive into their lives and invest in their spiritual health. Send them personal Christian resources. Conferences, books and CDs aren't as prevalent outside the U.S. Loving on a missionary isn't hard, but you'd be shocked at how few churches and supporters do it. Be the one to make a difference.

I have explained to dozens of churches I would rather see them invest sacrificially in two missionaries than superficially in two dozen missionaries. Instead of giving $100/month to two dozen missionaries and ignoring their personal needs, give $1000/month to two missionaries and pour your time, effort and soul into their personal wellbeing. Invest deeper into fewer missionaries instead of going a mile wide and an inch deep.

Missionaries, quit being so prideful. It is better for you to be spiritually healthy and able to serve for decades, than burning out after a couple of years. Be willing to be vulnerable so you can recover.

Sorry, to break the bad news to you. Most of your missionaries are lying to you. As they see it, they are sacrificing their personal wellbeing for the advancement of God's work. It is this type of self-sacrifice that makes them good missionaries. Let your missionaries know you love them and want to provide a safe place where they can heal their wounds.

9 Signs of a Missionary in Distress

The combination of heat, time and pressure can be productive in some cases. With just the proper combination of stressors, a hunk of coal can become a diamond or rotten bananas can become banana bread. Give too much heat and pressure to water and it can react like a bomb. But, give water too much time and it evaporates. In the same way, people respond differently to stressors. With the wrong combination of heat, pressure and time, one missionary may flourish, while another crashes.

Depression, burnout, stress and anxiety are all very different and can frequently be confused. The causes of each can vary, as can the treatments. The first step is to identify something is wrong. The next step is to seek professional input to ensure things don't get worse. Don't ignore or try to self-diagnose these complicated issues. Inaccurate treatment can be catastrophic.

The results of a missionary in distress can be horrible. Keep an eye on your missionaries. Here are a few examples of signs your missionary may be in distress:

1. Infrequent Communication

When life gets hard some people respond like a turtle and retreat inward where it feels safe. A missionary who withdraws from contact or communication may simply be busy. But, that missionary may also be avoiding others. If your missionary is observing lengthy periods of radio silence, it may be shame or depression causing them to evade interaction. If they don't have to communicate with others, they feel they don't have to answer hard questions or revisit pain. Encourage regular and open, two-way communication.

2. Emotional Outbursts

Burnout frequently result in mental or psychological impairment. In many people this may manifest in a verbal or emotional outpouring. Out of character verbal or emotional eruptions can be a sign of something worse just below the surface. More than grumpiness or irritation, when a missionary lashes out at teammates, nationals or family it can mean more than simply a bad day.

3. Indifference

Pessimism or a disregard for the legitimate suffering of others can be a red flag. Sometimes missionaries are surrounded by great amounts of poverty and misery. Seldom does a person become accustomed to witnessing the pain of others. A calloused heart is an unhealthy response. Nobody can say how much grieving is appropriate in the face of misery, but disregarding the pain of those around you is unnatural. Forgoing the mercy of Christ for the lost may be an indication of greater distress.

4. Critical Spirit

It doesn't take long for the honeymoon period to end in missions. Disillusionment toward the culture, fellow missionaries, a missionary's support system, or toward God are common responses. Instead of seeing God's glory a wounded missionary may focus on the negatives. A low view of self or others may cause a suffering servant to point out all that is wrong in missions. When the grace and mercy of Christ seems far off, everything may seem tainted.

5. Frequent Illness

No part of the body is immune from physical manifestations of emotional stress. Stress often displays itself with bodily damage. Sometimes a struggling missionary is frequently sick, other times they have illnesses which linger. The mental and emotional strain on a person can diminish the immune system and compromise unrelated portions of the body.

6. Excuses or Lies

When a missionary is struggling to keep his head above water he may dwell on the trivial while doing battle with the weighty. Forgetfulness or disorganization may cause mistakes. Admitting to those mistakes could force greater suffering and compel a person to address the root cause. In the moment, it may seem easier to ignore reality than to tackle the truth. The inability to focus and the use of poor judgment can be indicators of distress.

7. Disappearing Act

Avoidance can seem like the easiest path when a missionary is battling burnout or anxiety. Forgetting appointments, skipping meetings, missing deadlines or self-absorption may be the way a missionary fraught with distress avoids additional pain. Retreating and hiding is no way to address a problem, but is a great way of evading extra apprehension.

8. Guilt

The feelings of helplessness and hopelessness can result in placing the blame on oneself. Feeling personal responsibility for the failure of an event or the suffering of others can be common. A missionary who is in distress my feel accountable for the pains of others. When we struggle we take focus off of the sovereignty of God and place everything on our own shoulders.

9. Abnormal Change

When distress hits the heart of a missionary they may respond with abnormal changes in routines. A change in diet, sexual desires and sleep patterns are common biochemical responses to stress. Sudden and drastic changes in behavior can point to greater concerns.

Not all these signs are definitive indicators of a missionary in distress. A missionary suffering from burnout, stress, depression or anxiety may display combinations of several of these behaviors or none. Stressors impact different people, in different ways, at different times.

Understand your missionary friends have a high probability of being in distress. If ignored these issues can destroy ministries, families or lives. Love your missionary friends enough to help them heal. Reach out to the missionaries you love and support and help them get aide from professionals. Pray for your missionaries frequently and intervene when they show telltale signs of living with the time bomb of being in distress.

Struggling to Love in the Face of Evil

Even when life is "easy" it is hard to show mercy to our fellow sinners. When there is order and safety and congeniality serving others can still be a challenge. But, when you are drowning in poverty, murder, violence, lawlessness, sickness, injustice, pain and desperation, showing mercy to sinners amplifies the sin in yourself. Let's face it, as a sinner; it is difficult to love someone who doesn't return your love. But what do you do when the one you hope to serve desires to kill you?

Our fulltime team of a dozen missionaries serves in Honduras. This country is incredibly hard to live in, let alone minister to. For five years running Honduras has been the most murderous country in the world. Its people are the second poorest in the Western Hemisphere. The average first birth occurs at 15 years of age. Hospitals are closed, police are outgunned, pastors are driven from the country, babies starve, treatable illnesses lead to death and indifference and apathy are endemic.

Our fences have barbed wire, our windows have bars, our yards have attack dogs. The ladies on our team are not allowed to exercise outdoors or live alone. Our kids can't walk to the corner store or carry cell phones. Missionaries on our team have suffered burglaries, armed robberies and had guns put to our heads. Ministry is not easy in Honduras.

How on earth are we supposed to love a culture that refuses to love itself? And, more importantly to our sin nature, how are we supposed to show mercy to a people who want to do harm to us? Our mission team has been studying Acts together. You know, that ghastly book that has missionaries like Paul and Peter and Barnabas, who get chased out of town, beaten, stoned, imprisoned and continue to plant churches, preach the gospel and show mercy to those who disparage them. Yep, that book. The same book that

154

points out my sins and provides examples of a good missionary to whom I will never measure up.

The great theologians understood Christians are called to experience pain, and to endure it, because God is worth so much more than our fleeting comfort and pleasure. Dietrich Bonhoeffer, the World War II martyr for Christ, described a Christian as, "someone who shares the sufferings of God in the world." Augustine decreed, "It is not the punishment but the cause that makes the martyr."[79] And, John Calvin told us, "You must submit to supreme suffering in order to discover the completion of joy."[80]

Suffering is not a new concept, it is just new to us. Scripture addressed these issues long ago. God is by no means unaware of our pain (Exodus 3:7) and he calls us to endure our sufferings and continue in our service to him (2 Tim 4:5). We know God will not give us more than we can endure (1 Cor 10:13) and we understand the Lord prepares his servants for battle (Ps 144:1). The problem is God knows we can endure more than we think we can, we, on the other hand, have our doubts. Some days the battle just wears us down and even if we think we can endure another day, we just don't want to.

Our doubt, our pain and our discomfort does not absolve Christians of our responsibility to spread the saving grace of Christ and show his mercy to the needy. Tim Keller stated, "If you look down at the poor and stay aloof from their suffering, you have not really understood or experienced God's grace."[81] We were never promised lack of pain or suffering, only the unwavering knowledge that the Creator of the Universe loves us.

When we struggle with safety and security and still get out of bed every morning to toil in the name of Christ, he receives an extra measure of glory from our labors. How fortunate to experience suffering that results in God's glory, pain that expands God's name, and persecution that points towards heaven. Indeed, our bodies and souls belong to the Lord. Our worship of Christ includes offering our entire life to God. Our joy comes in service and our obedience is what is commanded.

Be it money, comfort, family or friends, mission work entails sacrifice. Being willing to make personal sacrifices is what being a disciple is all about. God calls us to be willing to give all we have. As all Christians are called to do, missionaries must die to self, forego

---

[79] St. Augustin, *Sermons: On the Saints* (New York: New City Press, 1994), 179.

[80] David Jeremiah, *What to Do When You Don't Know What to Do* (Colorado Springs, CO: Cook Publishing, 1994), 26.

[81] Timothy Keller, *Generous Justice: How God's Grace Makes Us Just*, 1st ed. (New York: Dutton, 2010), 96.

personal gain and submit to Christ. No matter the cost we are called to serve the Lord. Martin Luther told us, "They gave our Master a crown of thorns. Why do we hope for a crown of roses?"[82]

How Could God Use a Missionary Like Me?

Many churches sacrifice teaching on the eternal wellbeing of others to make room for teaching that emphasizes temporary personal joy. It is sad how in recent years the words sacrifice, martyr and submission have become less popular and considered more extreme in our churches. Willing to make personal sacrifice is what being a disciple is all about. God calls us to be willing to give all we have.

With these teachings in my heart I can't help but ask, how could God use a missionary like me? I turn to Scripture for answers and find Genesis 12:1 where we are told, "Now the Lord said to Abram, 'Go from your country and your kindred and your father's house to the land that I will show you.'" And, then in Matthew 28:19-20, Christ says, "Go therefore and make disciples of all nations, baptizing them in the name of the Father and of the Son and of the Holy Spirit, teaching them to observe all that I have commanded you. And behold, I am with you always, to the end of the age." And, the same question torments my mind, how could God use a missionary like me?

Returning to Scripture we find Romans 12:1, where Paul says, "I appeal to you therefore, brothers, by the mercies of God, to present your bodies as a living sacrifice, holy and acceptable to God, which is your spiritual worship." Then in Romans 10:14-15 he says, "How then will they call on him in whom they have not believed? And how are they to believe in him of whom they have never heard? And how are they to hear without someone preaching? And how are they to preach unless they are sent? As it is written, 'How beautiful are the feet of those who preach the good news!'" And, all I can do is ask, how could God use a missionary like me?

Doubts flood my soul and torment my thoughts. I am a missionary, but I am not a doctor, construction worker or pastor. What can I contribute? I became a Christian as an adult and I have a degree in Political Science. I am not a graduate of seminary or medical school. Daily, I look at my life and find nothing that points to the fact that I can be a good missionary.

---

[82] Mark Water, *The New Encyclopedia of Christian Quotations* (Alresford, Hampshire: John Hunt Publishers Ltd, 2000), 19.

I lived in a Latin country, in a culture that is not my own. For years I served as a missionary never feeling equal to the task. Always feeling I was an insufficient vessel for sharing God's good news. Yet, I have seen the sick healed, the hungry fed and the lame walk. I have watched as gang members lay down their guns and picked up a Bibles. I have witnessed blind children receive sight. I watched as a 13-year-old pregnant, rape victim shared the joy of Christ. I observed an abusive alcoholic father follow the Lord, put down the bottle and become a true spiritual leader in his home. However, I continue to ask, how could God use a missionary like me?

Throughout Scripture God uses insufficient vessels to bring himself glory. The great disciples in Scripture, the ones who stumble in their faith and return to God, they were just as insufficient to the task as I am. The great Moses was a murder. David, who was a man after God's own heart, couldn't keep his hands off his neighbors. And, the missionary Paul, began as a persecutor of Christians. Yet, all I can ponder is, how could God use a missionary like me?

Now, you have an important question to answer. How could God use a missionary like you?

- Pastors and church leaders: Are you preparing your flock to leave your church? Are you equipping them with the knowledge they need to share the gospel and the heart to take it into the world?

- Moms and dads: Are you preparing to send your babies into the world? Are you praying God will take them from you and place them in harm's way so he can be greatly glorified? If you are worried about sending your children on the mission field remember God had only one son and he sent him to be a missionary

- If you are NOT called: If you know God has not called you to missions, if you know he has called you to serve elsewhere, are you praying he would send your best friend, your boyfriend, your parents out into the world? If God is not currently calling you to serve as a cross-cultural missionary pray fervently for those he has called.

- If you ARE called: If you know God has called you to missions, if you are certain he wants you to leave your home, know this, God is worthy of sacrifice and he is calling his people to give all they have, even lay down their lives, so his gospel can reach the world.

- If you are scared: If you, like me, feel you are a called to be a missionary, but you are insufficient to the task, I tell you, brother, sister, embrace God's glory. Know that if you are called to be a missionary God has great plans for you. The great missionary C.T. Studd said, "If Jesus Christ be God and died for me, then no sacrifice can be too great for me to make for Him."[83]

Missionary Classism

Most of us are guilty of it. Senders and goers alike participate in it. That's right, we are missions classists. Most of us judge missionaries and missions work on the wow factor. We place a hierarchy on missionaries and global ministries based on whether it tickles our ears and not on Scripture.

Geography, danger level, pet-ministries, missionary lifestyles, and the tantalizing all play a major role in the missionaries we support and where missionaries are sent. Disciples of Christ must be careful to ensure we are not placing our personal preferences and views of missions ahead of God's mandates for global evangelism.

Let's take a quick quiz. Which missionary would you be most excited to read about or support?

Missionary A is a new seminary graduate who is about to start a new ministry in a predominantly violent and Muslim region of Qatar (located in the 10/40 window). Missionary A will live in a small village and will work on church planting and Bible translation.

Missionary B is a 65-year-old widowed woman who will serve on an Indian reservation within the US. Missionary B will take over all administrative work and accounting for an existing mission team of 10 other missionaries.

We all selected missionary A. Right? Why? Was our rational biblical? Was our decision based on God's glory? Is missionary B less qualified, less called, less competent? All missionaries are worthy of our prayer and respect.

Missionary classism is frequently perpetrated by churches or sending agencies toward missionaries. Also, from one missionary to another. It can be demining and offensive and it can cause missionaries to question their calling or worth within the kingdom of God. Creating a missions pecking order diminishes the sacrifice a missionary has made. If a missionary is truly called by God to serve, who are we to question the details?

---

[83] Roy B. Zuck, *The Speaker's Quote Book: Over 4,500 Illustrations and Quotations for All Occasions* (Grand Rapids, MI: Kregel Publications, 1997), 330.

Frequently we assign greater worth to missionaries who do work in locations which we approve. We say cities are more Pauline than rural missions and the 10/40 window is more valuable than elsewhere. Often a premium is placed on where modern missions is done that simply does not exist in Scripture.

Certain types of ministries are held in higher esteem. Frequently church planting, Bible translation, or mercy ministries are leaving accountants, construction workers and teachers left wondering if they are even worthy of the title of missionary.

Often we place added emphasis on how a missionary lives. A missionary serving in a dangerous area, incarnational living, or living in greater poverty truly excites us. In our eyes, suffering and discomfort seem to add more value to the missions experience.

Pastor, doctor, church planter or nurse, those are the real missionaries. All too often, missionaries who are untrained and under educated are made to believe they should stay off the mission field until they are "ready." Missionary Adoniram Judson said, "The motto of every missionary, whether preacher, printer, or schoolmaster, ought to be 'Devoted for life.'"[84]

Too often we have biblical (or so we think) reasoning to justify our preference for one type of missions work over another. We say, "That's what Paul did." Or, "That's where the unreached are." Or, "That's how missions should be done." Indeed, some missionaries or ministries can appear to be better suited for success. That does not then mean the other missionaries are not needed, useful or called.

If a missionary seeks the wisdom of the Lord and after great prayer, counsel and deliberation concludes he is called to a certain ministry, in a specific location he should be encouraged. No, you are not mandated to support him or even agree. But, refrain from belittling and criticizing his already difficult decision. David Sills said, "When God calls His child to live the life of a missionary, He gives him the desire with the calling."

Missionaries do it too. We eat our young by placing extra worth on sexy ministries or by belittling missionaries who do not live as we do. Missionary C.T. Studd reminds fellow missionaries, "Had I cared for the comments of people, I should never have been a missionary."[85]

Certainly there can be biblical or philosophical reasoning to support one missionary or ministry over another. But, take care not to disparage other missionaries in the process. Scripture tells us to, "Go" as we have been "commanded" (Mat 28:19-20) and if

---

[84] John Allen Moore, *Baptist Missions Portraits* (Macon, GA: Smyth& Helwys, 1994), 107.
[85] Wayne Vleck, *Dakota Martyrs: The Story you Never Heard* (Rugby, ND: Bunyan Family Books, 2004), 86.

we obey Scripture declares of us, "How beautiful are the feet." (Rom 10:15) A missionary should be appreciated for obeying the call and making the sacrifice few others are willing to embrace.

A missionary who leaves family, earning power, security and predictability for the mission field is worthy of our praise no matter her ministry or location. Guard the heart and emotions of those who serve on the frontlines by loving them and respecting their sacrifice.

What I Want for all Missionaries

I have often been asked, "How can our church, small group, or family better serve missionaries?" I get lots of churches that ask similar questions. They start with great intentions but have poor follow-through.

Missionaries, obviously, are human; we miss home, we sin, feel neglected, raise our kids poorly, have bad prayer lives, and so on. Just like we did when we weren't missionaries. The hard-to-swallow truth is that we are out of sight and out of mind. Our friends, family, and brothers in Christ don't see us every day, their lives move on without us, and we become forgotten by those who used to care for us and love us.

Most missionaries knew this would happen when we left for the mission field. People don't sign up to be missionaries for the fame, glory, and additional friends. It is no surprise, but I am shocked at how much it hurts me. I am surprised how much it hurts to be forgotten.

If I could ask for one thing of a church or small group or a family it would be for them to show some interest in my family and me. Send a small care package of stuff we miss twice a year. Give me a call once every other month. Send my kid an electronic iTunes certificate on her birthday and Christmas so I can be reminded someone other than me cares a little about her. Ask me about my marriage and my spiritual life, because both are probably suffering. Send me an occasional e-mail and tell me you prayed for my family today.

That being said, my family and I would continue to do missions work even if we never heard from another person in the United States. And I know the same goes for all eight missionaries on my mission team. But we want to be loved, and we want to know people are thinking and praying for us. If my team members were reminded that others care and pray for them, they would have strength to endure the hard days.

As leader of a mission team and a former elder in my home church, I would love to see each missionary on my team have at least one church that loves them and shows interest in them. In my four years on the field, half a dozen churches have told me that their church has a new plan to better care for their missionaries. They explain, "I have been assigned to care for your family." And few have followed through. I pray that each missionary serving on the field has one church, or small group, or pastor that shows interest in them, their lives, their faith, and their struggles.

When William Carey volunteered to be a missionary, he implored those who sent him, "Remember that you must hold the rope."[86] Missionaries must go, and senders of missionaries must remember to hold the rope.

---

[86] William Carey, "Rev. William Carey." The Gospel in All Lands, January 11, 1883, 15.

Chapter Eight

On the Mission Field

There are plenty of books, seminars, and sermons out there which teach the biblical basics of missions. Most are designed to motivate a Christian toward involvement in missions or teach them how to discern God's call. But once a missionary has been trained, raised their support, and landed in country, little can prepare a missionary for life on the field. Missions is frequently a school of learning by hard knocks.

Few things can prepare a missionary for a life and ministry full of increased sin, amplified demonic activity, and an abundance of cultural clashes. When the honeymoon period is over and the missionary settles into reality it is the mundane that shocks us. People still sin (including us), there is no operations manual, and your new home is not like your old home. This all makes sense. But, when a missionary and their supporters are imagining life at the cosmic level, the daily grind becomes shocking.

The on-field ministry is always different than originally perceived. But, while ministering in an ever changing and always sinning world, the missionary must establish foundations in God's glory and Scripture. Ministry can come in all forms, but all ministry should remain ground in God's instructions through his inerrant Bible. Minister creativity and with cultural contextualization, but minister as God commands.

Don't be a Missionary Tourist, be a Missionary

Before we get into discussing the pitfalls of being a missionary tourist, it is important we first attempt to define what is missionary tourist. However, being a missionary tourist is hard to describe by actions, as it is a condition of the heart. It is the purpose or the intent of a missionary which defines their actions, not the actions themselves.

A missionary tourist participates in missions for self-aggrandizing and humanistic reasons. They go on mission trips to be seen as compassionate or to experience the culture or to improve their résumé or to feel good about their service. By contrast a sincere

Christian missionary desires to be a sacrifice poured out so others can receive God's grace and mercy.

Because it is a condition of the heart it is hard for anyone but the offender to know if they are or aren't a missionary tourist. A missionary is not a tourist if they take selfies with poor kids or buy souvenirs or have fun while serving. These actions alone do not turn a missions servant into a missionary tourist. A missionary must examine his own heart and ensure his motives and purpose are pure and Christ-centered.

The purpose of missions is to get those throughout the world to focus on Jesus. The senders write checks and pray in the name of Christ, the goers make disciples for Christ and show his grace and mercy to others, and those who receive missionaries experience the glory of Christ's majesty. A missionary tourist draws attention away from Christ. A missionary tourist does what he can to make the experience about himself and thus elevates his own experiences above God's glory.

A missionary's actions must point to God first, last and always. A missionary tourist will take the credit and receive the praise and enjoy the attention given by others for their "good works." A missionary tourist relishes the attention their new fans give them and robs God of his due praise. A missionary tourist causes others to think, even for a season, that good things can possibly come from man. It is sinful to cause someone to focus glory anywhere but on God.

A missionary's pain, suffering, hard work and sacrifice should never be the focus of missions work. God's provision, glory and grace is where all missionaries should focus. As in any sin, the proof is in the heart and that is between the sinner and God. As an example, the same photograph of a youth group on a mission trip can be used by one person in the picture to bring God glory and by a second participant to promote themselves sinfully.

Many people cast dispersions on missionaries who take pictures, shoot video, blog or otherwise promote their missions experience. There is nothing inherently wrong with promoting missions work via electronic means or via social media. If social media posts cause more people to praise God or pray in the name of Christ, the result is God glorifying and should be replicated.

Much of the Internet and social media particularly has a tendency to be narcissistic and self-promoting for some. That does not mean a selfie or blog or missions report in front of your congregation, by definition, is sinful. Certainly, sinful man can use anything to rob God of his due glory and make it about himself.

Due diligence and prayer should be central to ensure the intent of the missionary is God honoring and not self-aggrandizing. As more and more people turn to the internet and social media for communication and to obtain their news, it is a natural progression to see personal glory promoted using these methods. A selfie stick does not a sinner make. However, a sinner can make anything sinful.

Few things could be more contrary to the human heart than missions. Nothing could be more inverse to our me-centered culture than to selflessly give of your time, talent or treasure to serve someone who can't repay you, and then give the credit to someone else. Because of this, much of missions incorrectly focuses on the efforts of the goers instead of the Creator who makes it all possible. This results in many missionaries receiving and accepting ill placed praise for their service.

In order to avoid becoming a missionary tourist a disciple of Christ must understand and embrace the theology behind missions. God takes sinful man and gives him a heart and gifts to share Jesus' grace and mercy with others who are equally undeserving. When this is understood, the missionary tourist can no longer take credit for God's work.

Missionary tourism is a result of missionaries, who do not themselves comprehend God's grace and mercy, being sent to disseminate it to others. Missionaries should humbly and reverently accept the calling to which they have been unworthily bestowed. Embrace God's Great Commission and bring him all the glory befitting the only true Savior of the lost.

It's Not Bad, It's Just Different

In the next 370-words I hope to address what is one of the most complicated issues in missions…cultural bias. It is imperative that missionaries not revert to mission tactics of the late 19th century and try to impose their "superior" culture on the people they have been sent to serve. The gospel is not American nor Western. The gospel changes cultures, the messenger should not.

Our landlord just had our house painted. The painters did their work in a very Honduran way, which in the U.S. would be viewed as lazy, sub-standard and unacceptable. White paint was on black paint, blue paint was on white paint, paint was on windows and there were few straight lines or right angles. And, here is the part that is going to get under your skin (and it would have me too a few years ago)…that's ok. The way they painted is not wrong. It just is. Why do we, in the U.S., insist on straight lines, right angles and non-touching paint? Yes, I know, you are screaming at your computer screen, "BECAUSE IT IS THE RIGHT WAY!!!"

As fulltime missionaries we have hosted hundreds of short-term missionaries and they see things through culturally biased glasses…as we all do. We have been asked many culturally biased questions; "Why are Hondurans so lazy?", "Why don't they care about their community and throw trash on the ground?", "Why are Hondurans always late?" These are questions that originate from the concept that our culture (no matter what culture it is) is better. We all believe that our way of doing things is best. And, that is normal, but not healthy in cross-cultural settings. The answer to all this is, "It's not bad, it's just different".

Missionaries are not sent to change cultures, but to deliver the life-changing gospel of Jesus Christ. When we as cross-cultural missionaries get bogged down in cultural bias we miss the point of missions. It is our job to enjoy, celebrate and sometime endure cultural differences without passing judgment. Christianity is global and our multi-ethnic family should rejoice in diversity and proclaim our unity in Christ. Let's not weigh down the purity of the gospel with our sinful biases.

Missions is People, Not Projects

Frequently missionaries report on the success of their ministry by listing off the schools built, churches erected, and roofs put on homes. This is not wrong or unbiblical. The concern is the focus must always remain on the people served and not the projects completed. Biblically, whether missionary, pastor, evangelist or congregant, our focus should be on people.

Projects are not wrong. The construction or renovation of clinics, houses or seminaries should not be considered sinful or a waste of missions resources. Projects are a great way to draw attention to a greater ministry and to the glory of Christ. A project that does not draw people in or provide an opportunity to share Christ is not focused in the proper place.

The purpose of constructing a house is to have intimate time with the family and neighbors so the love of Christ can be shared. The purpose of a medical clinic is to draw people in so the gospel and the mercy of Christ can be shared. The purpose of a new school is to attract people so the grace of God and the teaching of his truth. It is not about the building it is about the people who enter. A project brings great glory to the Lord when it is used to tend to the heart and soul of the people involved.

In the western world it is cultural for us to be focused on the project. To a westerner the experience of organizing and completing a project brings joy and satisfaction. To the rest of the world a project is an excuse to relate with people. Neither perspective is right or wrong. When we are involved in missions we must never forget that God did not send us to another culture to promote our own culture and views, he sent us to promote his culture and views. God's servants have always been sent because of the people.

In the time, it takes you to read this sentence eight more people have died and most of them don't know Jesus. Missions is that important. By anchoring your ministry in the matchless love of God you will discover people will become more important than programs and projects. Missions is an obedient servant taking a perfect message about a merciful Savior to a lost people. Keith Wright said, "Lost people matter to God, and so they must matter to us."

The Bible cries for the disciples of Christ to reach out to the lost and bring them the unmatchable truth of the gospel. Early Israel showed us people help each other glorify God (Ex 17:12) and that we are always to serve the poor (Deut 15:11). Jesus instructed his followers that helping people brings glory to God (Mat 5:16). Jesus wants us to give to beggars (Mat 5:42), treat the sick (Mat 10:8) and feed the hungry (Mat 25:35-40). James called us to visit orphans and widows (Jas 1:17) and provide for the needy (Jas 2:14-17). John told us to love (1 Jhn 3:17) and sacrifice (Jhn 15:13) for other people. And, throughout his epistles Paul instructed us to bare each other's burdens and to provide for the needs of others (Acts 20:35-38; Rom 12:13, 15:1; 2 Cor 8:9; Gal 6:2; Eph 4:28; Phil 2:4). Turn God's passion for the unsaved people of the world into your passion for the unsaved people of the world.

We are called to have a burden for people, not because serving others comes natural to our sinful heart. Instead, we are called to show God's grace and mercy to people because God first showed grace and mercy to us. God has called his disciples to reach into the lives of other people so his glory is multiplied.

Doing missions by focusing on a project can often be easier than focusing on people. Cinder blocks don't complain. Planks of wood don't cheat or steal. And, bags of cement are seldom ungrateful. But, it is these messy, deceitful, lying people God wants us to serve. Missionaries are called to risk their pride, gamble their health and jeopardize their lives so fellow sinners can grow closer to the Lord. The beggar, prostitute, drug addict, shut in, single mom and wino are people God has placed in your path so you can share his radical mercy. Frankly, projects are benign, people are toxic. God did not call us to minister to inanimate objects, but to sinners. And, guess what sinners do. Yep, they sin. And, if you get close enough they will sin all over you.

You've heard the joke…Missionary #1 asks missionary #2, "How is your ministry going?" Missionary #2 responds, "It's great. It would be better if it weren't for all the people." Why is that joke funny? It is funny, because it is true. Missions would be wonderful if not for all the sinners. Brothers and sisters, we have been called to dive into the muck and mire and engage sinners, not for our benefit, but for theirs. And, not for our glory, but God's.

Missionaries Mentoring Missionaries

One of the most valuable and biblical ways missionaries can increase the productivity of fulltime, cross-cultural ministry is to mentor other missionaries. However, in many cases, there is an insufficient willingness among experienced missionaries to mentor new missionaries. Sadly, the inverse is also true. Many new missionaries do not desire to receive guidance from those missionaries who have come before them.

Missions is hard enough without having to go through unnecessary pain and suffering. There are some priceless lessons to be learned in the school of hard knocks. Nothing teaches about the dangers of fire like placing your hand in it. However, sharing the experience which comes from an abundance of success and failure can also be an amazing teaching tool.

A missionary with years under his belt can be a great asset for newer missionaries. Veteran missionaries do not know everything, but when they are willing to share their insight it can benefit other ministries, and bring greater glory to God. Interestingly enough, not every seasoned missionary is eager to invest time and energy in younger missionaries. This is a sad reality, when it is God's glory on the line.

As weathered Christians, no matter where we are called to serve, is instructed by Scripture to mentor and disciple underdeveloped believers. The older generation are to instruct the following group (Ps 145:4) with humility (1 Pet 5:1-5). Faithful men are to teach other men (2 Tim 2:2) and older women are to teach younger women (Tit 2:3-5). As iron sharpens iron, so is one disciple to sharpen another (Pr 27:17). The experienced missionaries should be going out of their way to lend their time and background to the younger missionaries. This is not for individual accolades or pride, but so your pain and joy can bring greater glory to God's work through another servant.

The younger missionaries should seek out the counsel of men and women who have walked the path before them. Newer missionaries should humble themselves before the insight of experienced missionaries. This humility is a testament to being willing to place God ahead of personal pride. Seeking a veteran missionary who is enthusiastic to honestly share their suffering and knowledge is one of the ways God desires to sanctify his disciples. A humble servant who is willing to laugh at himself, share his tears, and help others grow is a priceless commodity.

Scripture tells us we become wise by walking with the wise (Pr 13:20) and when we consider the outcome of the lives of our leaders (Heb. 13:7). Followers of Yahweh are told to receive instruction, and insight in our dealings (Pr 1:2-3). A young missionary should not assume he already possesses all he needs to properly glorify the Lord in his ministry. It takes a modest and reserved spirit to admit one needs help. But, it is not our wisdom we seek to raise up, it is the provision God provides us through his Word and his disciples.

A journey together is how God intended his disciples to reach the nations. Throughout Scripture there are very few sojourners who went at it alone. Followers of Christ are called to humbly live in community and grow together for the benefit of the kingdom of God. As we set aside our arrogance and independence God's glory is magnified in the world.

In the end, it is not about a seasoned missionary's wisdom or the newer missionary's high energy. The final goal is for all missionaries to put aside man-centered pride to obtain great glory for Jesus Christ. There is no excuse for older missionaries to not pour their heart into the next generation of God's global servants. And, the younger missionaries are foolish to not willingly tapping into the resource of those who walked the path before them.

God has given us our experiences not only for our sanctification, but for the growth and benefit of our brothers in the trenches. Every elder missionary should strive to invest time and energy into the following generations of cross-cultural servants so those behind them can advance God's global call for the nations.

Our service in global evangelism can be so much more than the effort and years we put on the field. As a missionary ages, what he lacks in originality and stamina he makes up for in experience. God desires the old and young, new and experienced to grow together and learn from each other so his grace and mercy can be multiplied.

Older missionaries, reach out to your younger brothers and make their improvement part of your ministry. Young missionaries, humble yourselves by seeking the counsel of those who have succeeded and failed before you. Together, multiple generations of missionaries can learn from each other and more effectively bring glory to Christ among the nations.

9 Pitfalls to Avoid on the Mission Field

Missionaries have a hard job. Often their biggest fight isn't with their supporters or those they serve. Typically, missionaries are their own worst enemies. Odds are pretty good most missionaries or future missionaries won't learn from this list, I therefore commend the reading to their family, supporters and co-workers. Try to protect your favorite missionaries from these common on-the-field misstates.

1. Lone Ranger

The sin of pride causes too many missionaries to refuse help from others. Don't be a prideful recipient. God gave resources and abilities to others so they could use them for his glory. Don't prevent others from serving God by refusing their service. The "No, I've got this" mentality is me-centered and sinful. God intended missions to be a team sport. Don't rob God of his glory by trying to hog all the attention for yourself. You may think you are being honorable and pious, but by refusing additional workers, finances or help you are being prideful.

2. Too Connected To Home Culture

Communication with supporters and family is good. Checking the sports scores of your hometown team or staying up with friends on social media is fine. But, a missionary needs to strike a balance between the two cultures. Too many visits "home" for reasons other than health or training is dangerous. You will never be 100% here if you are still 50% there. Find local foods and events you enjoy. Invest in friendships with people from your adopted culture. Don't spend your time longing for your "home."

3. Too Immersed In Adopted Culture

This is just as bad as the inverse. Becoming more focused on your adopted culture than you are the gospel is never good. Fun and experiences should never become so important they interfere with your ministry. Don't become that missionary who leaves home for a few years and learns to hate his own culture. Never forget, all cultures are manmade and therefore sinful and inferior to heaven.

4. Do Nothing

Sometimes there is just so much to do you don't know where to start. If that is the case, start by doing something, anything. Other times you are frozen by the fear of failing. You believe your job is so big you'd rather do nothing, then something wrong. If you are doing nothing you are focused on you and how you are perceived. Never forget, missions is not about you. Missions is about God. He can do everything in your ministry without you. Try, fail, learn, improve, but glorify God in your actions.

5. Do Everything

One of the fastest paths to burnout and short-lived missions experiences is the missionary who can't say no. They don't comprehend the grace given to them by God. They are so performance driven they refuse to say no to those they serve, supporting churches or fellow missionaries. They try to "earn" the support of their financial partners by working 16-hour days, seven days a week. Every missionary wants to be a good investment, but working yourself sick or crazy is bad for everyone. Do the few things you do well. Stop thinking God can't do it without you.

6. Not Enough Resources

Too often missionaries work with insufficient help, resources and finances. They are too proud to ask for help, and don't want to be perceived as beggars. Their biggest problem is they forgot who supplies the resources. God controls everything. He wants you to ask so he can be glorified. Don't skimp, do without or do a poor job because you don't have the proper tools. Ask your supporters and those around you for help and watch the amazing things God does through them.

7. No Time Off

Nobody goes to the mission field for an all-expenses paid vacation. It is just not realistic. God rested and created the Sabbath for his elect. It is imperative for your mental health and that of our spouse and kids that you take time away. Get in the habit of unplugging one hour a day, one day a week, one weekend a month and one week a year. Turn off your phone and computer and enjoy God's creation. Remember your spiritual health and some occasional down time. Your longevity on the mission field depends on you caring for yourself and those you love.

8. Poor Language Skills

Few things are harder on a missionary than not being able to communicate. Missionaries who were intelligent, gregarious and articulate back at home become frustrated by being reduced to the communication level of an uneducated infant. Your language skills have a huge impact on the effectiveness of your ministry. No missionary has ever felt like they wasted their time by taking more language training before arriving on the field.

9. Bad Health

Missionary, care for yourself. Eat right, exercise, get rest and feed your soul. If you are sick and can't get the medical attention you need, go someplace you can. The story of the missionary martyr is really cool and God-honoring, but the story of the missionary who died because he was too proud to care for himself is just stupid. If you live a longer and healthier life, you get to serve God longer.

Avoid these pitfalls to help yourself and those you care for serve longer and more efficiently when fulfilling God's Great Commission. Increase God's glory by serving with joy.

Lying Missionaries and the Glory they Bring God

Telling a lie is viewed as unacceptable in almost all religious and secular belief systems. Christianity is firmly opposed to lying. The terms "bearing false witness" or "lying" are frequent themes in both the Old and New Testaments. From Genesis to Revelation liars are treated harshly (Ps 5:6; Rev 21:8) and hated by God (Pr 6:16-19).

Frequently, those who answer God's Great Commission (Mat 28:18-20) find themselves interacting with governments, cultures or individuals which are openly hostile to the saving gospel of Jesus Christ. Many missionaries are put in positions where they must contemplate lying in order to maintain their ministry, avoid punishment or preserve life.

Scripture and Christian prudence tell us lying is a weighty issue that should be approached with great prayer and study. Lying is always a sin and never condoned by God. However, it can be acceptable for missionaries to lie to bring glory to God and further his kingdom.

- Exodus 1:15-21 - The Hebrew midwives, Shiphrah and Puah, were instructed by the king of Egypt to kill all the sons born to Hebrew women. The midwives feared God and did not do what the king had instructed. When the king confronted them the midwives stated they weren't killing the boys because the Hebrew women were giving birth before the midwives could show up to assist. Scripture than says, "So God dealt well with the midwives." (Ex 1:20a). A verse later Scripture says, "And because the midwives feared God, he gave them families." (Ex 1:21). God was glorified by the results of lies.

- Joshua 2 - Joshua sent two spies to Jericho. The spies stayed at Rahab's home where she hid them. When confronted by the king's men Rahab lied about hiding the spies and then deceived the king's men into looking outside the city. Rahab acknowledged Yahweh as the true God, then schemed with the spies to save herself and her family. When Joshua destroyed Jericho he killed all in the city except Rahab and her family (Josh 6). The authors of both Hebrews and James mention Rahab favorably and her faith in God is remembered (Heb 11:31). God hates lies, but the results can bring him glory.

- 1 Samuel 16:1-5 - God instructed Samuel to anoint Jesse's son. When Samuel protested for fear of Saul's reprisal God instructed Samuel to "Take a heifer with you and say, 'I have come to sacrifice to the Lord.'" (1 Sam. 16:2b). When the elders confronted Jesse and his heifer he did as the Lord instructed then invited Jessee and his sons to the sacrifice. God gave Samuel a second truth to hide the first truth.

- 2 Chronicles 18:18-22 - Micaiah saw the Lord raising forces for divine battle. In planning for the death of Ahab and the defeat of the army the Lord was offered and accepted the services of a lying spirit to enter the mouths of the prophets to cause confusion. Scripture says, "the Lord has put a lying spirit in the mouth of these your prophets." (2 Chro 18:22). This is a difficult passage for those who believe lying is always wrong.

- Visas - In order to enter most countries a foreigner is required to receive an entry visa. Some countries refuse entry to religious workers or people attempting to share their faith. Missionaries have been known to request "tourist" visas or list themselves as "teachers' if they are pastors. Providing most of the truth and withholding some of the truth in order to advance the gospel is supported in Scripture.

- Bribes - What we call bribes in the West, the bulk of the rest of the world considers a daily way of life. Many taxi drivers, business owners and delivery personnel, in other cultures, make it a point to carry small bills in anticipation of being asked for money by government officials. A distinction must be made in the difference between paying a bribe to be left alone versus paying a bribe to advance your status. In the rest of the world, the former is a way of life, while the latter is contrary to Scripture.

- Tent Making - In order to get inside "closed" countries, some missionaries represent themselves as teachers, business owners or relief workers. They hold back their full intentions in order to conceal their Christian proselytizing from hostile governments or citizens. If a Christian missionary represents himself as an English teacher, he should regularly teach English as well. Lying is always wrong, but as God instructed Samuel, creating an acceptable reason to enter a hostile environment so God can be glorified in your other activities is acceptable.

Misleading behavior may not be desirable, but in many cases, it may be necessary behavior for missionaries who must disguise themselves in order to more effectively proclaim the gospel and live in cultures which are hostile to their God-honoring purpose. To many, lying is a black and white issue. However, lived and practiced in an imperfect world surrounded by sinful humans, missionaries must use situational ethics and a Christ-centered heart to determine if their words or actions bring greater glory or dishonor to God.

The weighty ethical dilemmas faced by Christians surrounding the issue of lying should be approached with great prayer and biblical study. Christian missionaries face the additional burden of attempting to contextualize Scripture in their adopted culture while continuing to carry the burdens placed on them by their home culture. If lying is not a black and white issue, cultural ambiguities blur the lines even further for missionaries. Lying is always a sin and is never condoned by God. However, it can acceptable for missionaries to lie in order to bring greater glory to God and the advancement of his kingdom.

Demonic Activity and Missions

Here it is, one of the least talked about, frequently avoided topics in biblically conservative circles. Demonic activity. Our Pentecostal and charismatic brothers love to talk about it. Christians around the world discuss it frequently. But, in the polite, conservative, churches in the suburban US we don't discuss it. We avoid the topic, even quietly dismiss it.

Covenantal Christians affirm the Bible is the literal word of God, and demons existed and were active in the pages of Scripture. It is acceptable to acknowledge demons existed 2,000 years ago, but today? Most of us are secretly skeptical or outright hostile to the idea that in our post-modern world, demons are alive and busy. Come on, that kind of hokum is for the uneducated, unenlightened masses, right? C.S. Lewis said, "There are two equal and opposite errors into which our race can fall about the devils. One is to disbelieve in their existence. The other is to believe, and to feel an excessive and unhealthy interest in them. They themselves are equally pleased by both errors, and hail a materialist and a magician with the same delight."[87]

That pervasive attitude is why few missionaries share their demon stories when making Sunday school presentations on furlough. But, secretly, privately ask your favorite missionary if they have ever experienced demonic activity. Not the plate fell off the table or I got a flat tire kind of demonic activity. But, the strong as a bull, speaking in foreign languages, unexplainable, horrifying kind of demonic activity. A large, yet admittedly anecdotal, sampling of missionaries leads me to believe most have experience with demons. Missionaries just don't want to talk about it because they fear you'll have them committed, or worse, reduce their financial support.

Studies indicate most Americans believe in demons, and demonic possession. A 2013 YouGov survey showed 57% of all Americans believe in the devil, while 86% of born again Christians believe in the devil. A 2012 Public Policy Polling survey found 57% of Americans believe someone can be possessed by a demon. The aforementioned YouGov survey said the number of born again Christians who believe someone can be possessed by an evil spirit is 72%. Even the areligious believe in the supernatural. A 2012 Pew survey showed 85% of those who considered themselves religiously unaffiliated, still believe in the spiritual or supernatural.

Of Americans who believe in demonic possession the YouGov survey found females (54%) were more likely to believe than males (49%). Republicans (54%) and Democrats (51%) were about equal. The South (59%) was more likely to believe than the Midwest (45%). Blacks (67%) and Hispanics (62%) were more likely to believe than Whites (47%). The average American believes in demons and demonic possession.

The Bible has plenty to say about the Devil and demons. The word "demon(s)" appears 77 times in the NT, and is mentioned in 19 of its 27 books. Scripture confirms demons exist (Deut 32:17; Ps 106:37; Mat 12:27). While God created everything (Jhn 1:3), he did not create evil (Jam 1:13; 1 Jon 1:5; 1 Cor 14:33). Demons were cast out of heaven (2 Pet 2:4; Jude 6) and Satan is their leader (Mat 12:24). All of our sicknesses, problems and accidents cannot be attributed to Satan and his demons, however, they are active in some problems. They can cause or exploit mental and physical illness (Mar 5:1-15; Luk 11:14). Demons have strength and knowledge (Mar 1:24, 9:17-27) and they fear Jesus (Mar 1:25, 3:11-12, 9:25).

---

[87] C.S. Lewis, *Screwtape Letters* (New York: HarperCollins, 2015), ix.

Demons can possess a person (Mat 9:32-33, 12:22, 17:18; Mar 5:1-20; Luk 22:3), but they cannot indwell a true disciple of Jesus Christ (Col 1:13; Rom 8:37; 1 Jhn 2:13, 5:18; 1 Pet. 1:5; 2 Cor 6:16). However, true Christians can be harassed and negatively impacted by demons (2 Cor 11:3-4, 13-15, 12:7, 1 Tim 4:1-5; 1 Jhn 4:1-3). Still, we have been given the power to resist them (Jam. 4:7). John Calvin said, "All that Scripture teaches concerning devils aims at arousing us to take precaution against their stratagems and contrivances, and also to make us equip ourselves with those weapons which are strong and powerful enough to vanquish these most powerful foes."[88]

So, why do missionaries see more demonic activity than do typical suburban church goers? Think of it like this...all Christians are active soldiers in a spiritual battle. Satan has a finite number of demons. Like any smart military tactician, Satan is going to send his troops to the frontline, where the gospel is advancing rapidly or into new territory. Christian missionaries have more experience with demons, than do other Christians, because missionaries are at ground zero of major battles. R.C. Sproul said, "The church is the most important organization in the world. It is the target of every demonic, hostile attack in the universe. Jesus personally guaranteed that the gates of hell will never prevail against the church. He made no guarantee that the gates of hell would not be unleashed against it, however."[89]

Don't let your missionary friends skulk in the shadows and hide their amazing stories of demonic activity. The mission field is not just a field for harvest, but a field for battle. Invite missionaries to unburden themselves with the horrible, amazing things they have seen on the frontlines. Allow your family, your small group and your church to be educated about the active work of demons and God's victories. Be open, be biblical and be prayerful for your missionary friends and their protection against demons.

Missionaries Should Communicate and Churches Should Demand it

On our last missionary furlough, I spoke with dozens of pastors and church leaders about their church's support for missionaries. In difficult economic times most churches were reducing their budgets and that included missions. Without exception, every single church that was cutting support to missionaries told me they were going to eliminate

---

[88] John Calvin, *Institutes of the Christian Religion* & 2, ed. John T. McNeill, trans. Ford Lewis Battles, vol. 1, The Library of Christian Classics (Louisville, KY: Westminster John Knox Press, 2011), 172.

[89] R.C. Sproul, *What We Believe: Understanding and Confessing The Apostles' Creed* (Grand Rapids, MI: HarperCollins, 2015), 184.

support for, "the missionary we have been supporting for years, but we just don't hear from anymore."

Eliminating support for non-communicative missionaries is a wonderful idea, for two great reasons: 1) churches must be good stewards of the resources they have been given and throwing money at a missionary who is not a partner with their church is foolish. And, 2) Missionaries must learn the importance of communicating with the partners in their ministry.

Missionaries, you have been called to leave your home and family and culture to go to far off lands and serve in the name of Christ. That is a beautiful calling and you should embrace it. The individuals who stay home and pray for your efforts and write checks to support your work are equally called by God to play their role. God has called the missionary to go and God has also called the supporters to remain home and make missions work possible. The calling is equal. Senders and goers are a team. Act like it.

I have met too many missionaries who view their supporters as a hurdle they must overcome before they can get onto the mission field and do what God has called them to do. When these missionaries are raising their financial support they say all the right things; "partner with me," "join the team" and "accept God's calling." But, as soon as their support is raised they forget about the team with whom God has surrounded them.

As Christians we are responsible to lift up our fellow believers and make it easier for them to glorify God (Deut 22:4; Pr 27:17; Gal 6:1-5). Working together to advance God's plan for the world requires prayers, givers and goers. A major part of our responsibility as goers is to provide the prayers and the givers with everything they need to better pray for us and the people we serve. If supporters of missionaries don't know what to pray for missionaries have not done their job.

Fellow missionaries have told me, "Doing all that communication work takes time away from ministry." They miss the point. Communicating God's glory and telling the world all the wonderful things he is doing in far off lands is not a burden, it is part of your ministry. "Let them shout from the top of the mountains." (Is 42:11)

Communication is not hard, expensive or time consuming. Most third world countries have Internet and smartphones. Resources like Blogger, Twitter, Facebook, YouTube, Zoom, etc. are very easy to use and all are free. Most entry-level digital cameras have both photo and video capability, as do most smartphones. Websites exist to manage your newsletter database or to send out personalized postcards and "thank you" notes. If indeed missionaries are doing the wonderful work that so many are doing, they should shout it from the cyber-mountaintops. There are very few excuses to be a poor communicator in this day and age.

It is not difficult for missionaries to communicate with their supporters. Write a couple of blog posts a week, take a picture every day, send out a 140-character tweet, e-mail out a short, picture filled newsletter once a month. If missionaries only communicated that much, supporters would feel like they are part of the ministry. When you share the stories of your work with the people who have committed to pray for you and support you then you are helping them to fulfill the Great Commission.

In our ministry in we know that we have supporters who don't subscribe to our tweets, or watch our videos or even open our e-mailed newsletters. That is fine. But, we also know that there are many people who are diligent readers and prayers and they want more information. They want to pray specific prayers for Antonio, they want to see Carlito's face and they want to know my wife is feeling better. They want to be connected. Communication is not intrusive or burdensome. If people don't have time or simply don't want to read about your ministry they can delete, unfriend or save it for later. But, if missionaries aren't sending out regular communication they are not giving their supporters the choice to get more involved.

Churches and individual partners, you need to insist that the missionaries you support are communicating with you. You are just as much a part of that ministry as the missionary is. Get passionate about your calling towards missions. Demand regular communication from your missionaries, but also communicate with them. Check in on them. Tell them you pray for them. Prove to them you've been reading their reports. Let them know their communication efforts are not in vain. Take your calling seriously.

Missions is a partnership. Missionaries and prayers and givers have all been called by God to join together in the expansion of his glory. Your mission team has many members who combine their talents to glorify God in the world. When missionaries communicate, what God is doing through the combined efforts of their team, the one who called them together gets the glory.

Biblical Reconciliation

Biblical reconciliation is a popular discussion topic among Christians. But, frankly, we do it poorly. It is frustrating, because many times we say we are reconciling, but mostly we aren't even getting close. By looking at the infrequency of true biblical reconciliation among Christians, you'd think we were trying to solve a Rubik's Cube, underwater, blindfolded. The truth is, biblical reconciliation is all right there in Scripture. But, are we interested enough to follow God's instructions?

God forgives us, even though we had no cause to sin against him. As it relates to repentance, we must forgive others as God has forgiven us. Gossip and hurtful words stir up evil and grieve the Spirit of God. (Eph 4:32)

The man renewed by the blood of Christ acts upon new principles. The believer is created new with a new heart. He is created in Jesus for the purpose of doing good works. We should strive toward the beauty of reconciliation for the glory of God. (2 Cor 5:18)

While we are still sinners God reconciled us to himself. He did not make us sinless first. We too are to understand that those with whom we are to reconcile are sinners, yet still beautiful to God. (Rom 5:10)

Biblical reconciliation begins with one person talking directly to the person who offended them. Reconciliation is our goal. Reconciliation glorifies God, while an angry, bitter heart robs God of his glory. God's glory is always more important than our ease and comfort. (Mat 18:15-17)

In the end it may not always be possible to be at peace with all people. Even when an effort is made a reciprocal desire may not be offered by the other party. Our responsibility is to do everything within our own power regardless of the response we receive. (Rom 12:18)

There is nothing biblical about consulting a third party regarding someone who has offended you instead of talking to the person who offended you. When we "seek wisdom of others", "bounce the idea off of a friend" or "compare notes" we are attempting to justify our sin of gossip. There is no "moral high ground" in the sin of gossip. All we are trying to do when we talk to others about a third party is slander him in the eyes of others and thus justify our actions or hardened hearts. Your gossip about the offender is just as sinful as his perceived offense and you should seek forgiveness from him for your gossip against him.

A gossiper can do much more harm to a church than a drunk or an adulterer can. A drunk or an adulterer will typically only hurt a handful of people while a gossiper can single handedly take down an entire church or ministry. A gossiper demonstrates he is absent the grace of Christ when he pours his cruelty out on others.

If you are angry at a person because a third party relayed something to you, the third party has clearly sinned in gossip and you should aide him in repentance of his sin and apologizing to the person against whom he gossiped.

The Bible's opposition to the destructive practice of gossip is clear (Lev 19:16; Ps 41:7; Pr 11:13, 20:19, 25:23).

According to the Journal of Personality & Social Psychology we misunderstand the tone of e-mails 50% of the time. The more your day-to-day communication is done off-line the better off you will be. All efforts at conflict resolution and reconciliation should be done off-line. Face to face is always the preferred method.

- Communication styles differ from person to person. Don't assume intent.

- The purpose of conflict resolution is not to assign blame, but to reclaim a brother in Christ.

- Accepting forgiveness means the issue is over. The incident is not to be recalled to others or held in your heart.

- While forgiveness is mandated, there is no requirement to be best friends after.

- If conflict occurs and another person is 90% at fault and you are only 10% at fault, you must be 100% responsible for your 10%.

There is little room for interpretation on this issue. The biblical model for reconciliation is quite simple and direct.

1. If you believe you have been sinned against pray about it. Ask the Lord to separate your perceptions, biases and sensitivities from the action so you can clearly discern the spoken words from your perception of the intent of the offender. Is it possible the offense was not intended?

2. Before consulting others ask the person to meet you face to face in private. Without pointing fingers, assigning blame or attacking you should say; "You said X and that hurt me. When you said X did you mean X?" If the person asks for forgiveness you must accept it. Your forgiveness is not optional. Remember, this is to be a reconciliation moment and not a blame moment. It is intended in the Bible to be a sweet time. If it is not, check your heart.

3. If the person refuses to acknowledge his part, and refuses to apologize you are to bring a third party into the situation (example: church Elder, neutral third congregant, pastor, etc.). Preferably an authority figure. Do not choose a third party based on biases, but rather on neutrality. With the same calm and loving

tone the facts are presented. If the person apologizes you must accept it. Your forgiveness is not optional.

4. If the person does not acknowledge his part, and refuses to apologize you are to bring a larger group into the discussion (church leadership, community group, etc.). With the same calm and loving tone the facts are presented. If the person asks for forgiveness you must accept it. Your forgiveness is not optional.

5. If there can be no reconciliation at that point, walk away.

Biblical reconciliation is God-honoring, commanded by Scripture and very rare in today's Christian church. Biblical reconciliation was so important to our Lord that he spelled it out very clearly for us. It falls upon all disciples of Christ to honor our Father by loving our brother.

What Does a Healthy Missionary Furlough Look Like?

Missionary furloughs are misunderstood and misused by most missionaries. Because missionaries don't want to appear lazy to their supporters they usually take too short of a furlough and pack in too many events. The result is, furloughs are usually periods of high stress, little rest, lots of travel, and excess anxiety. Many missionaries say they can't wait to get back on the mission field so they can rest from their furlough.

That is not how furlough is supposed to be. Furlough should be a time of joy, recuperation, and preparation. If a missionary is running around exhausted and giving insufficient time to convey God's glory to those who sent him, the missionary is not properly serving himself, his senders or his Savior. While churches can certainly help make furlough restful and productive, the burden falls on the missionary to do furlough well.

Missionaries are sent by churches (Acts 13:3-4) and they should report back to those churches (Acts 14:26, 28; 18:22-23). When on furlough a missionary must share with those who partner with him and explain their successes and struggles so God can be glorified and prayers can be better directed. Provide ample notice of your speaking schedule and invite outsiders to come hear your presentations.

Don't feel pressured to visit with every family individually. Ask churches or friends to host lunches so you can talk to lots of people and be more efficient with your presentations. Avoid individual meetings when possible and let your friends and supporters know you don't have time for anything but large group visits. You have hundreds of people to visit, while most of your supporters have only one missionary to listen to. You've traveled 99% of the distance from your home to the church, ask your supporters to travel the final 1% to come to you. And, give your family a rest. Your spouse and kids don't need to attend every event. Be honest and let supporters know your family needed extra rest, so they didn't make this trip. People will understand.

Some missionaries are ashamed to admit they need rest and recreation. Honestly, most days on the mission field are simply exhausting. Paying bills, shopping, and maneuvering foreign governments can be frustrating and draining. Booking several weeks of doing nothing on furlough is often needed just to reach baseline.

Plan some time away with just the family. Vacations and alone time are important to put on your calendar and treat as sacrosanct. Do fun things you can only do in your culture. Eating healthy, proper sleep, and regular exercise are important. Don't forget your soul. Conferences, small group studies, and individual counseling are imperative. Also, plan a few Sundays where you are not presenting at church and you are simply able to worship the Lord in community. The word rest appears 347 times in the ESV Bible. Our rest is important to God (Ex 33:14; Is 28:10-12; Ps 23:1-6; Mar 6:32; 1 Chron 22:9). Make real rest a priority for you.

During a missionary's time on the field, they learn just how great the needs are and just how unprepared they are to address all of God's work alone. Part of a missionary's report and presentation should be dedicated to growing the missions community. Get others excited about serving the Lord of all nations. Be a cheerleader to encourage others to serve God globally, in your context or elsewhere.

Recruit new fulltime missionaries to come serve by your side. Have conversations with other potential missionaries and counsel them to take the plunge to serve on other fields. Ask churches to prayerfully consider sending a short-term mission team to work by your side. Solicit new financial and prayer partners to join your team and serve God by giving time and money. An experienced missionary is a great way to get others excited about God's Great Commission.

As sinners, we covet what we know. Our food, our culture, our traditions, and our way of worship are important to us. If we go too long without experiencing things the way we like them it impacts us negatively. Go ahead and unashamedly bath in worshiping of God in the way you in which you are familiar. Attend music concerts, speakers, and special events to soak in the grace and mercy of Christ in the ways you like best. And, don't feel guilty for it.

God is the Lord of all cultures, countries, and languages. But, he knows we love things that touch our heart and stir our memories. Attend your favorite restaurants, sporting events, and Western conveniences. If we aren't living for or worshiping these trappings, God is pleased for us to find joy in them. Enjoy your time on furlough.

Furlough must be a time of connecting with your supporters, increasing focus on God's glory, and raising additional support. But, do not neglect yourself or your family. Focus on your physical, mental, and spiritual health. Heal, recuperate, and learn how to enjoy worship and service again.

Use your furlough to regain your joy for your adopted culture and your joy for service. Share the good and the bad with people and embrace some down time so you can create longevity in your ministry. Rediscover your joy in Christ.

Chapter Nine

Missions and your Family

Few things can inspire us and simultaneously confound us as our family. Marriages, singleness, kids, and our extended family all have huge impacts on our hearts and ministry. Scripture is clear that our family will be impacted by following Christ. How we interact with family and the issues surrounding family is clearly outlined in Scripture. We are instructed to prioritize God's glory above all, but God is also clear he wants us to care for those in our inner circle.

Some missionaries deprioritize their familial relationships to the detriment of God's glory. Others elevate their family to a status above God in their lives. Children, extended family, and marital status should not suffer due to ministry, but, they also should not become idols to the missionary.

Placing Christ above all is important for all Christian disciples, but paramount for a missionary who strives to serve the lost. Your familial situation and how your respond to adversity can be an amazing testimony to those you serve. The world is always watching you and judging Christ through your actions. Address you family in a way which Glorifies God, and still honors him by serving those you love the most.

Your Family – Your Most Important Ministry on the Mission Field

Missionaries comprehend, more than the average disciple of Christ, that there is a price to pay for following the Lord. This is a joyful sacrifice every missionary is willing to make in order to bring God's glory to the nations. But, what are you willing to give? Your health? Your life? Your family? All?

Some missionaries are needlessly paying a sacrifice that has not been asked of them. God has entrusted you with your family. You are called to care for your kids and your spouse and to raise them all in a God-honoring home. Missionaries must learn the difference between being willing to sacrifice your family for God's glory and neglecting your family under a performance based mentality.

Missionaries, like others, can become workaholics. They can needlessly put ministry ahead of family in an unhealthy way. Yes, you are willing to sacrifice your family, but don't needlessly give up on your family. Missionary, your family is your first and most important calling. You have no business doing ministry outside the home if your own household isn't in spiritual order.

The Bible is the guide and test for every believer. As a missionary you heard and accepted your call from the Lord to go to the nations and make disciples in his name (Gen 12:1-3; Acts 1:8 Mat 28:18-20; Mar 16:15; Luk 24:46-49). As he promised, God provided you with all you needed to accomplish his will (1 Tim 6:17; Ps 107:9; Heb 13:21; 2 Pet 1:3). Indeed, the Lord has declared your feet beautiful because you carry his message (Isa 52:7; Nah 1:15; Rom 10:15). God has also promised you that you will be persecuted in his name (Mar 13:9; Luk 21:12; Rev 2:10). That is not all. The Bible has more to say about your life, family and ministry.

In the Pastoral Epistles (1 & 2 Timothy and Titus) Paul outlines the credentials for church leadership. In contrast to leaders of the world, leaders in the church are defined by their character. The requirements for church leadership are specifically outlined in three locations (1 Tim 3:1–7, 3:8–13; Tit 1:5–9). While these three passages specifically refer to officers of the church, it can easily be inferred that similar characteristics are beneficial for all Christian workers and servants of the gospel.

Noticeably present in all three passages is the significance placed on the condition of a Christian leader's family. According to these passages a Christian leader will, "manage his own household well, with all dignity keeping his children submissive" (1 Tim 3:4), "be the husband of one wife, managing their children and their own households well" (1 Tim 3:12) and be "the husband of one wife, and his children are believers and not open to the charge of debauchery or insubordination" (Tit 1:6).

Why is the condition of a potential leader's family such an important issue? 1 Timothy 3:5 clarifies that, "if someone does not know how to manage his own household, how will he care for God's church?" In short, if a disciple of Christ cannot manage his most important ministry (his family) how can he be expected to manage the affairs of the Bride of Christ? 1 Timothy 5:8 even takes it a step further when it says, "But if anyone does not provide for his relatives, and especially for members of his household, he has denied the faith and is worse than an unbeliever."

In the Pastoral Epistles we see that a Christian laborer is to first be a servant leader. The heart of Christian servant is not manipulative but caring. John Piper says of 1 Timothy 3:1–7, "What Paul is saying is that the way a man manages his own household is a good test of whether he can provide what the church really needs, namely, leadership that has a caring heart, and a caring heart that has the strength to lead." Paul looks at a man's children as the indication of whether he delivers leadership at home and can properly serve the church.

Indeed, we must trust our family, our health and our very lives to the Lord. Dedicate all you have to his service and the expansion of his kingdom. But, a Christian servant must first care for his family. John Calvin says a Christian leader, "should be content with his wife, should set an example of chaste and honorable family life, and should rule over his children and household with holy discipline."[90]

Missionaries must never forget the standards and priorities God has established for them. Yes, sellout for the Lord. Give your all for his glory. Entrust everything to him. However, this does not mean to foolishly neglect the spiritual, emotional and physical health of your family.

Take time to serve your family and let them know they are a priority. Take time off from ministry and focus on your family. Prioritize your kids and your spouse so they see how much they matter to you. Missions ministry begins in your own home. A healthy ministry begins with a healthy family.

Loving Your Children Enough to Send them Into Missions

Too frequently I have heard from parents that their pastors and churches are discouraging them from allowing their kids to enter the mission field. Helicopter parents are being trained by pastors, who are themselves helicopter parents, that the right thing to do is hold onto your children, protect them from danger and keep them away from uncertainty. This teaching is contrary to Scripture. It is a result of a generation of overbearing parents who are willing to embrace the sovereignty of God, except in parenting.

A healthy, God-honoring church would welcome parents into their church by explaining, "The purpose of our church is to help you raise your children in the ways of the Lord and send them out into the world, into harm's way, so they can glorify God." Indeed, children are a gift from God (Ps 127:3), but not for our pleasure. Instead, our children are for God's glory.

---

[90] John Calvin, *1, 2 Timothy and Titus, Crossway Classic Commentaries* (Wheaton, IL: Crossway Books, 1998), 59.

Our children have not been given to us so we can incase them in bubble wrap and protect them from the world. Our children have not been given to us so they can get the best college education or be trained for a white-collar job. Our children belong to the Lord and he has entrusted us with them for a short time so we can train them in his ways (Pr 22:6; Joel 1:2-3; 1Pet 5:3; Dt 4:9-10, 11:19). Parents are to discipline their children, but this discipline is not about good behavior or house chores. Parents are to discipline their children to be obedient to the Lord's commands (Prov 13:24, 19:18-19, 23:13, 29:15, 29:17; Eph 6:4).

In training our children we are to encourage them to live their lives and sacrifice their lives for the Lord's will. If we are training children to dedicate their lives to the Lord, up to the point of discomfort, but no further, we are not training our children in the ways of the Lord. Our lives are a living sacrifice to the Lord (Rom 12:1). Our children should be raised knowing that a disciple of Christ lives his life as a living sacrifice to the Lord, no matter the cost.

Christian parents raise our kids so they know that God commands them to honor their father and mother (Ex 20:12; Dt 5:16). The assumption of this commandment is that a child is being raised by a God-honoring parent. Nobody would suggest that a child should obey a parent who tells their kid to walk into traffic. Children are to honor parents who are teaching them the ways of the Lord. Obeying parents is ultimately about obeying the Lord. When a parent tells a child they should (contrary to Rom 12:1) not live their life as if it were a sacrifice to the Lord, should the child obey?

Children are to receive and obey Godly training (Pr 1:8-9, 10:1; Eph 6:1-4; Col 3:20) from God-honoring parents. Why then are there so many parents training their children to avoid fulltime ministry, stay off of the mission field, and obey the Lord as long as it costs them nothing? A parent who advises his child to stay off the mission field because it is hard, dangerous or scary is worthy of disobedience from their child.

Parents should be thrilled to have a child who wishes to live a life dedicated to service in the Lord. A child who wishes to serve the Lord in a dangerous location is a child who has been trained that their life is to be dedicated to God's glory. The only reason parents have been entrusted with God's children is to raise them so they understand they are here to bring God glory (Gen 18:19; Ex 20:12; Lev 19:3; Ps 78:2-8; Jos 4:20-24; Luk 1:17; Acts 2:28-39; 1Tim 5:3-4).

If our children are raised to be God-honoring we should be thrilled when they commit their lives to missions in a risky way. How beautiful to know that we as parents have done our job so well our children are willing to give all for God's glory.

Deuteronomy chapter six instructs us on the Greatest Commandment. We are called to love the Lord, not unenthusiastically, but with all our heart and soul and might. The Lord's instructions are to be on our heart and we are to teach the Lord's will to our children. God's words are to be a lifelong dedication to all disciples of the Lord. We should never forget the Lord, nor place anything ahead of him. And, we are to instruct our children to dedicate themselves to the Lord.

Moms and dads, grandmas and grandpas, aunts and uncles, you have been entrusted with a child of God. You are to love them and teach them the Lord's ways, not the ways of the world. Your love for your child is not in question. However, the focus of that love is. Do you love your child enough to send them into to missions? Do you love your child enough to help them pack their bags and drive them to the airport so they can serve the Lord in a closed country? Do you love your children enough to trust them to the Lord?

Are you Messing Up your Missionary Kids?

Many missionaries, at some level, struggle with taking their kids on the mission field. Many people around them, as well as their own parental guilt, question the wisdom of raising their kids in a foreign land. For many missionaries, this is one of the hardest aspects to reconcile of the missionary life. We are willing to sacrifice in our own lives, but should we truly risk handicapping our children by raising them in another country?

Before leaving for the mission field many friends and family, Christians and non-believers openly questioned the wisdom of my wife and I taking our daughter with us to live and serve in a third-world country. We were told, "If you want to throw away your life that is one thing, but to risk a child is reckless." Another person close to us said, "Taking a child who has experienced the United States and putting them in a third world country is child abuse." And, a leader in a church told us, "You are taking your faith too far by including your child in your calling."

Few people could comprehend our desire to leave the US and embrace a calling to a poor and violent country. Fewer still could condone us involving our child in missions. Coupled with our own self-doubts, we were certain our obedience to the Lord's Great Commission was ruining our daughter's future. It became abundantly clear to us that most other missionaries felt the same as we did.

However, our time on the mission field and our experience with hundreds of other missions families has showed us that taking our children on the mission field isn't the horror it was cracked up to be. In fact, there are many lifelong and eternal benefits for missionary kids.

By taking your child onto the mission filed you are teaching them unwavering obedience to Christ. They will see you suffer and struggle on the mission field, but they will see you endure the difficulties by embracing the love of the Lord. Your child will grow up living a life sold out for God's glory. Whether or not they choose to return to the mission field as adults, they will better comprehend how to live a life dedicated to God's glory.

Your missionary kids will have a better grasp on the grace and mercy offered only through Jesus. The mission field is a place where God's laborers witness and acknowledge God's miracles daily. You and your kids will also have a working knowledge of evil and spiritual warfare. I child growing up witnessing, first hand, the amazing grace of our Father is bound to live a life benefiting the kingdom. Contrary to popular belief, our job as parents is not to shelter or hide our kids from the world. Our job as Christian parents is to teach our kids, when they experience the sin of the world, they are to respond with the grace found only in Christ. The mission field is an amazing place to teach your child to embrace and share the mercies of Jesus.

While there is nothing wrong with raising our children in the United States, statistically it is not normal. The US population accounts for 1/20th of the world's population and frankly, the rest of the world doesn't live like US citizens do. This is not a negative statement against living in the US. Helping your children experience the world and observe other cultures is something very few people get the opportunity to do.

If your child grows up in another culture, speaking another language they will have a very unique life experience. When our daughter started her freshman year of college in the US, she was fluent in two languages and intimately knew two cultures. This gave her a perspective that less than 1% of US college students could share. Her diversity was so coveted by college admissions departments that she was offered substantial scholarships simply because she was a missionary kid.

The diversity and global perspective a missionary kid has is a rare commodity. Your children's experiences will not only be coveted by future colleges, but employers. Their global viewpoints will be useful in their future employment experience, no matter what profession they select.

Your children are not missionary kids. Instead, consider them as kid missionaries. Our children see and understand more than we give them credit for. The dedication your children have for the Lord and their involvement with the local culture will almost guarantee they have more Christ-honoring impact on your adopted culture than their parents do. In school, sports or at the market, your children will also be active missionaries on the mission field. Give them the freedom to embrace the calling they have been given in a new culture.

If you are worried about sending your children on the mission field remember God had only one son and he sent him to be a missionary. Keith Green said, "You would never be foolishly 'neglecting' your family's needs by obeying God's call to go. God will show you the way."

Education and your Missionary Kids

Every parent worries about providing their child with a quality education. Every Christian parent frets concerning giving their child a biblical foundation. Every missionary agonizes over turning their child into a social outsider. By extension, a Christian, missionary, parent is burdened with the reality that by following Jesus call into missions they may have just sacrificed their children in order to be obedient to God.

The education of our children, before and during missions, causes great anxiety for many missionaries. Lots of God's global servants wrestle with the reality that by obeying God's call to live in another culture they may have just ruined their child's education opportunities. And, this concern isn't lessoned by the fact that many secular and Christian friends are reinforcing their doubt. Missionaries need to remember; our God promises he will care for your kids better than you can. Never forget, the future of your children is far more important to Jesus than it is to you.

Still, parents must prayerfully contemplate what academic options they have for their children. In modern missions, there are lots of education choices for missionary kids.

Schooling your children from home, while serving on the mission field, is a great way of providing quality, individualized education for your kids. Now, more than ever, the internet and technology make homeschooling a quality option. E-books, video conferencing, and electronic databases ensure a child can receive amazing resources anywhere a descent internet connection is available.

Living in a foreign country can optimize social studies and language acquisition for missionary kids. It is a huge opportunity to take advantage of that rare opportunity to expose your child to foreign art, historical sites, food, culture, and governments. The hands-on possibilities open to your child cannot be duplicated and will enrich their lives.

Boarding schools are becoming less prevalent, but international schools are expanding in popularity. International schools draw third culture kids from parents who are military, diplomats, business executives, and missionaries. These schools frequently have kids from many cultures attending. The exposure to varying cultures is an experience which is hard to replicate.

Often, international schools can be expensive and are frequently attended by kids of upper-class families. While the cost can be prohibitive for missionaries, the quality of education and rare cultural diversity are often undeniable. Typically, these schools only exist in metropolitan cities and can be hard to find in developing parts of the world.

The downside of a national school hinges on the quality of the school and the education standards of the country in which a missionary serves. To assume all non-U.S. education is substandard would be an error. However, due diligence must be given to determine the quality of education at any school which a parent is unfamiliar. Educational quality and curriculum varies, not just from country to country, but school to school.

However, the benefit which can be gained by a missionary kid attending a national school is truly a one-of-a-kind experience. By immersing your child into a national school, your child will gain language and cultural acquisition like few other children on the planet. Your child could leave their experience fully comprehending two cultures and two languages. This would give them exposure to life few of their peers could ever comprehend. Kid missionaries, when attending national schools, also have a wonderful opportunity to share the gospel with their peers.

The college application process can be confusing when being done from another culture. But, with the help of the internet, it can all be completed from anywhere in the world. College applications, scholarships (private and institutional), and the Free Application for Free Student Aide (FAFSA) applications are all daunting, but can be done 100% online. The ACT/SAT tests are the only part of the process which must be done in person, but these standardized tests are frequently offered in foreign countries.

Interestingly, being educated in a foreign culture is seen as a benefit to many college admissions offices. Many colleges, especially Christian colleges, appreciate the diversity a third culture kid brings to their campus. Some colleges do require foreign transcripts to be verified (at your cost) by an independent vendor, but even that is rare. Some colleges, again, especially Christian colleges, offer scholarships to missionary kids because their worldly experiences add to the overall learning environment.

Going away to college is no longer obligatory. In this modern age, missionary kids can attend college classes from a laptop. Many brick and mortar colleges offer full undergraduate and post-graduate degrees 100% online. College-aged third culture kids can complete some or all of their college education from anywhere in the world.

Answering God's call to missions, is not nearly the burden or sacrifice it once was for missionary kids. In fact, being educated on the mission field can provide lifelong benefits your kids couldn't acquire living in the U.S. Educating your missionary kids while serving in a foreign land can be a great kingdom and personal benefit to your children. If God has called your family to missions, know he will provide your kids with everything they need to serve him in the future...including a quality education.

The Hardest Job in Missions: Missionary Mother and Wife

The most complicated position on the mission field is not the church planter, doctor or Bible translator. Indeed, the most conflicted calling on the mission field belongs to the missionary mother and wife. Seldom have I experienced a demographic so filled with anxiety and internal struggle over the role they play in global evangelism. Few women have grasped the elusive balance of being simultaneously content with their efforts given to their family and their ministry.

The missionary mother and wife possesses an internal pendulum which swings between family and ministry. She seldom finds joy in her service to family and ministry at the same time. These women too often feel that when their families are flourishing, they are neglecting their ministry. And, when their ministry is thriving they are forsaking their families. This struggle results in a never ending cycle where the missionary mother and wife perceives she is either failing at home or failing at missions.

Throughout Scripture women played a vital role in the global advancement of the gospel and the spreading of God's grace and mercy. Miriam led the women in worship (Ex 15:20-21). Women were gifted by God to use their skills to construct the tabernacle (Ex 35:25-26). Deborah judged Israel (Ju 4:4-5). Huldah prophesied (2 Chr 34:22-27). Anna served in the temple (Luk 2:36-38). Lydia's heart was opened by God to pay attention (Acts 16:16). Phoebe was recognized by Paul as a servant in the church (Rom 16:1). Priscilla was a fellow worker of Paul's and a teacher of Apollos (Acts 18:26; Rom 16:3). Eudoia and Syntyche were laborers in the gospel (Phl 4:2-3). Junia was an imprisoned disciple (Rom 16:7). No doubt, many of these woman also simultaneously raised children, kept a home and supported the work of their husbands.

Women have a proud history in modern missions. In 1812 Ann Judson became the first female missionary from the United States. Until her death in 1826 Ann both helped translate the Bible into Burmese and cared for her home and family. Today, according to David Barrett & Todd Johnson, women account for 46% of all missionaries.

Women on the mission field should not simply learn to be content with their discontentment. Enduring an unsatisfying role in global evangelism is unacceptable. Women receive a calling to participate in the Great Commission that is all their own and not always linked to the calling received by their husbands. However, the role and contributions of women is too often devalued. It is incumbent upon missionary leaders, mission sending agencies and churches to champion the role of women and treat them like co-laborers for Christ. It must never be forgotten that women too are made in God's image and are equal in dignity and worth. We must affirm the unique gifting and contributions only women can make.

Women have so many ways they can contribute to God's glory and the expansion of a ministry. But, women who choose to focus on raising their children and keeping their home should also not be viewed as less of a contributor. Andy Stanley said, "Your greatest contribution to the kingdom of God may not be something you do but someone you raise."[91] Women must rejoice in their giftings. Likewise, missionary partners must celebrate the varying ways women contribute to missions. In her book Let Me Be A Woman, missionary mother and wife Elisabeth Elliot exclaimed, "It is a naive sort of feminism that insists that women prove their ability to do all the things that men do. This is a distortion and a travesty. Men have never sought to prove that they can do all the things women do. Why subject women to purely masculine criteria? Women can and ought to be judged by the criteria of femininity, for it is in their femininity that they participate in the human race. And femininity has its limitations. So has masculinity."[92]

All too often we concentrate on what women can't do more then we facilitate what they can do with their God given gifts. Missionary mothers and wives should be mentored, discipled and trained to accentuate their strengths.

Women must celebrate and respect the undeniable fact God made men and women different. If a woman is called to be a fulltime mother she should do that with joy to the glory of God. If it is fulltime missions she seeks, she should serve wholeheartedly. If a missionary mother and wife desires to do both jobs simultaneously she must avoid self-ridicule and unrealistic expectations. Rejoice in your role ladies. God made you abundantly capable of being a mom or a missionary or both. Pray, plan, balance and don't feel like a failure if you have to step away from missions work to serve your first ministry calling, your family.

---

[91] Chrissie Chapman, *The Night the Angels Came* (Oxford, England: Lion Hudson, 2016), 177.
[92] Elisabeth Elliot, *Let Me Be a Woman* (Wheaton, IL: Tyndale House, 1976), 65.

A change of heart must not fall solely to the women. Fellow missionaries, supporting churches and sending agencies must be proactive and supportive. Women bring a different set of skills to missions than do men. In many ways, the skillset of a women is precisely what is called for to advance the Gospel. Too frequently we prioritize male dominate traits above female traits. This is unbiblical. Every missionary is called to serve God to the fullest of his or her ability. No missionary should be evaluated in comparison to others. Women have a unique value as disciples of Christ. Those who send and support missionaries must strive to keep the missionary mothers and wives involved and properly utilized and not treated as if they were lesser missionaries.

Let's pray missionary mothers and wives feel the freedom to balance their roles on the mission field as they see fit and the rest of us are encouraging and supportive of our sister servants.

9 Ways to Care for your Family on the Mission Field

Missionary you are on the front line and in harm's way. You, your spouse and kids struggle as you labor for Christ in your adopted culture. Your support network is far away and the emotional, spiritual and physical toll on your family is high. You are the human who can most positively impact the struggles of the ones you love. Glorify God and serve your family by making their care a priority for you while serving in missions.

To those fulfilling the Great Commission, or about to, here are a few practical ways you can decrease the burden missions can inflict on those closest to you:

1. Family Vacations

Spend some time away from daily ministry and relax. Remind your family members they are at least as important to you as those to whom you came to minister. Have fun together and laugh with the special ones with whom God has entrusted you. Turn off your cell phone and put someone else in charge of your daily ministry for a few days. You don't have to travel far or spend lots of money to have a family getaway.

2. Cultural Experiences

God has called you to serve him in a culture that is not your own. Learn to enjoy the culture in which you live. Explore and learn about the people, food and life together. Your ministry is made easier if you understand the culture of those to whom you minister. When you see the culture through the eyes of your spouse and kids you comprehend deeper the people you are discipling.

3. Date Night

No matter your station in life, never forget to date your spouse. Remind yourself how special your spouse is and remind them they still matter to you. Get out of the house, away from kids and away from daily ministry and enjoy each other's company. Go to special and intimate escapes together. Continue to fall in love no matter how long you have been married or what country you live in.

4. Prayer

Pray together and pray for each other. Let your family hear you pray to God for their wellbeing. Petition your Father to help your family members feel loved, safe and valuable. Remember to pray for your spouse and kids in your private prayers and family prayer. Teach them to pray for each other and those you serve. Pray for your first ministry, your family.

5. Language Acquisition

Make sure your spouse and kids receive adequate formal language instruction. A stay at home spouse or homeschooled kids still must participate in commerce, interact with neighbors and contribute to the ministry. A family member who struggles at their new language may feel marginalized and less relevant to the family. Practice together and help each other improve in language in a nurturing environment.

6. Traditions

Maintain family traditions and holidays. Use family traditions to help you feel connected to those far away from you. If your resources are limited celebrate Thanksgiving by eating a chicken or decorate your Christmas palm tree. Remember your old culture and embrace your new one. Combine old traditions with new flavor. Remembering your home and the culture you came from does not dishonor your new calling.

7. Seek Counsel

As you, your spouse and kids are struggling, seek the guidance of a spiritual advisor or therapist. There are possibly both in your new culture, but if not, use technology to communicate with professionals back home. Seek guidance from trained experts. Do not feel negative stigma or weakness for seeking help. Allow your family to grow with Godly marriage, individual or family counseling. We all struggle, only the honest seek help.

8. Minister Together

Include your kids and your spouse in your ministry as often and appropriate. Allow your missionary kids to be kid missionaries. Make sure your spouse has opportunities to minister as his or her time and abilities allow. Don't force your family to embrace your ministry, but instead, find ways they can minister that allows them to utilize the gifts God has given them. As is possible, minister side by side.

9. Familiar Contact

Use letters, Skype, e-mail, phone calls and social media to maintain communication with your friends and extended family back home. While encouraging your family to get to know people in your new culture, do not discourage interaction with those you left behind. If those back home can experience your ministry and familial love they will be more supportive of your missions work and know better how to pray for your family.

Caring for yourselves and your family is healthy, biblical and increases the probability you will serve longer on the mission field. You and your family are already paying a price, don't make it worse by neglecting each other. You have no business ministering to another culture when your own family is suffering.

Do not allow your kids and spouse to be casualties of your missions work. As you would back home, care for the special needs of your family while you involve them in your missions work and adopted culture. You may be surprised what a Godly witness a healthy and loving family is to the culture you have been sent to serve.

Being Single and a Missionary

Today about a quarter of evangelical missionaries are single, and most of those single missionaries are women. Most estimates state that above 80 percent of all single missionaries are female. These single missionaries bare all the same struggles as married missionaries, plus a few complications that are unique to singles. Single missionaries have increased struggles with issues like chastity, loneliness, misconceptions by others, parental desires, housing, safety, unwanted matchmakers, contentment and more.

Many missions agencies and churches have estimated that singles tend to last a shorter time on the mission field than do their married counterparts. The additional stress, the desire to get married and perceived or real ineffectiveness in their ministry takes a toll on these suffering servants.

Specifically, single women often find it hard to be fruitful in ministry to cultures that do not value women as much as they are valued at home. Many cultures simply do not esteem women at the same level as they do men, single women, even less. Many singles find their ministry more difficult and even less effective than their married peers.

The struggles of single missionaries are prevalent and real. In fact, there are enough missionaries that wrestle with being single that in March of 2014 a new website was launched. Called Together (calledtogether.us) is a matchmaking site specifically for single missionaries and it boasts thousands of members.

The great missionary Paul was very clear on his views towards singleness. Paul was single and viewed being single as a good thing (1 Cor 7:8). He wished that others could be like him (1Cor 7:7). Paul said that being both married and being single are good, but he enjoyed the fact that a single person was more free to serve the Lord (1 Cor 7:25–35). He stated we are all prepared, gifted and conditioned in different ways and that we should not long for change, but embrace what we have be given and use that situation for the Lord (1 Cor 12).

In his first letter to the church at Corinth Paul references the "unmarried" four times. He notes that being unmarried can, but shouldn't be a form of stress. Paul believed that remaining single can provide great advantages for kingdom work. He embraced his singleness and encouraged the same for others. It is what the Lord had given him, therefore it was good. Dedicating one's life exclusively to the advancement of the gospel is a great blessing. Paul acknowledged that singleness is not an option for everyone, and that it was better to be married than to be burdened by lustful temptations.

Marriage in a Christian union is beautiful and God-honoring. But, there is also great God-honoring beauty found in an unmarried life of service. There are ways we can use our bodies and our lives to glorify Christ in marriage and in singleness. It is important that neither marrieds nor singles look down on each other as sinful, less committed or less of a servant.

The kingdom of God grows by both sexual activity and through the justification of the lost. Singles can certainly help God's family grow. Christian relationships are more permanent and valuable than biological families. A brother in Christ is forever. While marriage is beautiful, it is temporary. A relationship with the Lord lasts forever.

Some the greatest missionary servants in history have been singles who dedicated their lives to service in Christ. David Brainerd was a single missionary to the American Indians in the 18th century. His life was short, but his influence on missions was great. Those missionaries who claim to have been driven to the mission field by Brainerd's life story reads like a who's who of evangelical missionary heroes.

Gladys Aylward was a single missionary in the 20th century. She served 16 years in China. Her life and amazing work has been retold in numerous books and the 1958 Academy Award nominated film The Inn of the Sixth Happiness.

Amy Carmichael served in India in the 19th and 20th centuries. She opened an orphanage, founded a mission, wrote more than a dozen books and served over 55 years without ever taking a furlough.

Single missionaries are capable of serving and excelling in nearly all areas of mission work. Singles should not fear entering the mission field nor be prevented from doing so. Singles should neither limit themselves nor be limited in where and how they can serve.

Churches and mission agencies should be aware and accommodate the unique struggles of single missionaries. Field leadership should talk to their single missionaries openly about their struggles and should not pigeonhole singles into specific work.

Every missionary should embrace their gifting and situation in life. God has every missionary on the field at the exact time and location he wants them. If you are called to missions as a single missionary embrace the privilege and know our sovereign Father has plans for you. Do not be burdened with what you do not have but instead, rejoice for what God has given you and use all your gifts and every circumstance to bring glory to God through missions.

Are you too Old for the Mission Field?

As the Baby Boomers continue to pass into retirement age more mission agencies and churches have had to rethink the concept of people moving onto the mission field at a later stage in life. The typical first-time missionary is still a twenty-something new Bible school or seminary graduate, but more and more people in their 40s, 50s and 60s are taking on missions for the first time.

Missions is statistically a young person's game. With youth comes enthusiasm, energy and a heart for adventure, all great qualities to have on the mission field. But, with age comes experience, wisdom and patience, also great qualities for a missionary. Yet, too often we assume older Christians are not cut out for missions. Occasionally, it is even offered that seasoned Christian disciples shouldn't waste the resources by going on the mission field. Older Christians should be encouraged to prayerfully consider their role in missions, and if they feel a strong calling to the mission field our churches should pray for and support them.

Scripture affirms there is an esteemed place for older Christians in our church ministries. The Bible tells us wisdom and understanding (Job 12:12) allow Christian disciples to bear great fruit into old age (Ps 92:14). Grey hair is a crown of glory (Pr 16:31) and a splendor for and older believer (Pr 20:29). Both older men (Tit 2:2) and older women (Tit 2:3) have important roles to play for the kingdom.

The Bible values the contributions made to the local church by older Christians. Nothing says the mission field should be any different. If missions is a corporate mandate for the church, every member of the church should be allowed to make a contribution as their giftings and resources allow.

Many have questioned if the traditional western view of retirement is a biblical option for Christians. Did God provide us with a lifetime of blessings so we could spend the final 30 years of our lives collecting sea shells, hitting golf balls or playing bingo? We will not venture to tackle that question here, but instead refer readers to John Piper's book "Rethinking Retirement." In that book Piper says, "Live dangerously for the one who loved you and died for you in his thirties. Don't throw your life away on the American dream of retirement."[93]

There is no question a Christian who saved and invested for decades could greatly glorify God with the additional time and financial security God has provided him. How glorious to use a pension, 401(k) or IRA toward God's glory. A Christian who has the extra time, flexibility and financial security to dedicate to fulltime missions is a great benefit to the kingdom.

God provided you with your education, job, and financial blessings. God did not provide you with all that so you could add to your personal comfort and security. Certainly a financially secure retired Christian can benefit and serve the local domestic church, but, how glorious to give all that earned experience and wisdom for the reaching of the nations.

God is calling fewer younger Christians to the mission field and more older Christians. Those who send missionaries have been forced, in recent years, to rethink their views on sending older missionaries and most organizations have developed "second career" or "retired missionary" programs. "Most mission agencies are trying to work with this trend that 20 years ago was unwelcome," said Todd Johnson, director of the Center for the Study of Global Christianity. "Today, most realize it can be useful to their work."

Many Christians are realizing in their older years, not that they wasted their youth, but that God was preparing them for their later years. "The Lord didn't design us to

---

[93] James H. Grant Jr., *1 & 2 Thessalonians: The Hope of Salvation*, ed. R. Kent Hughes, Preaching the Word (Wheaton, IL: Crossway, 2011), 201.

coast out on flowery beds of ease, but to make some sort of difference," said Nelson Malwitz, founder of Finishers Project, "There is a full spectrum of mission opportunities, both at home and abroad, both short-term and long-term." Older Christians are answering the call to fulltime missions and mission agencies and churches are responding with open arms.

Our western culture flies contrary to Scripture when it comes to our plans for old age. The world tells us, "you earned a break," and "you deserve a rest." That is in conflict with God's biblical call to serve him. Quitting your job, selling your home and moving closer to your grandkids are all wonderful options. While God has set up our lives so we could have more time, he never wanted us to use that time for selfish gain, but to glorify him and expand his kingdom.

God provided for every step of your life, how glorious to live our final years serving the next generation of Christians. Missions is a viable option for Christians of every age. Older Christians have much to offer and should be encouraged to embrace the call to global evangelism. Allow the Lord to work through you no matter your age, and lend your worldly experience and financial flexibility to the reaching of the nations.

On the Mission Field with Aged Parents at Home

Your parents gave you life and love and it is natural for a child to desire to care for his parents as they get older or sick. Adult children with aging or infirmed parents are blessed to be afforded the opportunity to care for their mothers and fathers in the final years. Sharing the grace and mercy of Christ with our parents in their twilight is a privilege not all are able to enjoy.

Scripture is clear when it says Christian disciples are to honor their parents (Ex 20:12; Dt 5:16; Mat 19:19; Mar 7:8-13; Eph 6:1-3) and to care for members of their family (1 Tim 5:8; Gal 6:10). Scripture is also clear Christians are to go into the world and disciple the nations (Mat 28:18-20; Acts 1:8). How can an obedient Christian care for aging parents when he is half a world away sharing the gospel of Jesus Christ in a foreign culture? What is a missionary to do when those commands appear to be in conflict?

As your parents get older it is understandable for them to desire the company of their children and grandkids. The importance of our family comes into greater focus the older we get. As a missionary, your obedience to the Great Commission, deprives you and your parents with the close, meaningful relationships desired by most families.

It is painful for a missionary to absorb the reality their departure results in greater loneliness for their parents. Even if a missionary's parents say they understand, the missionary knows their parents are forced to sacrifice quality time with their kids and grandkids.

As the health of your parents declines familiar concerns are raised, but are magnified when an adult child is a missionary. Ensuring proper care is made more difficult by the distance. Sharing the time and financial burden with siblings becomes a near impossibility. Other relatives are forced to carry the extra load created by the missing missionary.

Inevitably, when the death of a parent becomes a reality the grief and self-doubt are multiplied for the missionary. The missionary is overwhelmed by a sense that their pursuit of God's glory in a foreign land took too much of a toll on their family and the shame of not being around enough at the end is almost unbearable. The spoken or perceived sense that the missionary abandoned their parents in their greatest time of need is profound.

If the parents of a missionary do not have a saving relationship with Christ, the missionary agonizes over the assumed contradiction that they are laboring for the souls of perfect strangers while their own family is without Christ. The missionary places too great a responsibility on himself to save his parents. Yet, self-deprecation and the perspectives of other pain the heart of the missionary who has lost a parent for eternity.

The missionary feels a crushing guilt and even shame for not being around their parents in the final years or during prolonged illness. The missionary may have a firm theoretical grasp on the unwavering sovereignty of God and truly know our Savior is in control of everything. Yet, while that fact absolves the missionary of any real culpability, it doesn't always address the palpable guilt a missionary feels by being away from family in times of need.

The joyous reality is, when a missionary is called by God to serve in another culture, God has accounted for and ordered every related detail. The Creator knew the timing of illness, salvation, and death of your parents long before you put on your missionary training wheels.

God is very clear in his Scriptures. Our family does not come before the Creator of the Universe (Mic. 7:6; Mat 10:34-37; Luk 14:26). The glory of the Lord is the ultimate purpose of each disciple. We are called to place Christ ahead of our own life and health and ahead of every member of our family.

Whether your parents understand it or not, the best gift and example of Christian service a missionary can offer, is obedience to the Lord's calling to go into the nations. Love and honor your parents and share with theme the mercy and grace of Jesus Christ. But, obey your eternal Father before all. The call to missions carries with it many burdens the missionary is asked to carry. Being separated from elderly parents while laboring in a foreign land excises a surprisingly heavy toll on a missionary.

Remind your earthly parents your love for them is great and you will honor them by obeying Jesus, no matter where he sends you. Communicate with your parents while on the field and help them to be part of your journey. Visit when you are on furlough and invite them to experience your new life. Ensure them, that our sovereign Lord has control over them and he can provide for them far better than you. Provide your parents and extended family an example of unwavering obedience to God, and show them an example of steadfast submission to a perfect Lord.

When your Extended Family Doesn't Support your Call to Missions

There are many difficult choices in missions, but what could be harder than being forced to choose serving God and his glory over the family God has given you. In many instances missionaries are faced with extended families who do not support their call to global missions. Christian as well as non-Christian relatives have been known to oppose and even stand in the way of a missionary's departure to fulfill God's will.

How is a missionary to respond when parents, siblings, grandparents and cousins are not on board with missions? Should a missionary depart if extended family does not echo their call to missions? And, how does a missionary honor his father and mother if parents do not support their missions work?

This is a battle which far too many missionaries must face when moving toward the mission field. Never be surprised who Satan will enlist to discourage you from dedicating your life to serving God.

In 1 Samuel 20 Jonathan was placed in a difficult situation by his father. Saul asked his son Jonathan to put his father, his family and even his own future reign ahead of God's glory. Jonathan choose to honor God over obeying his father Saul. Jonathan protected God's chosen son David, instead of doing what his own father asked. Jonathan's decision was more than a choice between his father Saul and his friend David. Jonathan was asked to select God's glory or his own happiness and his family's name. When Jonathan's father forced him to choose the honor of his family over God's glory, Jonathan did not hesitate, he chose God.

Make no mistake, it grieved Jonathan to no end to disappoint his father. But, he did not hesitate to place God's honor above the happiness of his family. Scripture is clear that following God will cost us those things dear to us. A disciple of Christ cannot serve both God and something else, even family (Mat 6:24; Luk 14:33, 16:13, 26:13; Jon 12:25; Acts 20:24; Rev 12:11). A follower of Christ cannot place his family ahead of God (Dut 13:6-8, 33:9; Mat 10:37; Luk 14:26). In Jonathan's case, following God cost him a relationship with his father. What has following God cost you?

When put in a place to choose God or family a disciple of Christ must always select the Creator of the Universe. Yes, it is hard when family forces Christians to make such decisions. But, our relationship with the ones who gave us biological life, can never supersede our obedience to the one who gives us eternal life.

If your friends and family are counseling you away from fulltime ministry service they are not focused on God's glory. You can provide no greater witness to your family than your obedience to God's calling.

Throughout Scripture God commands us to honor our father and mother (Exe 20:12; Lev 19:3; Dut 5:16, 27:16; Eze 22:7; Mal 1:6; Mat 15:4, 19:19; Mar 7:10, 10:19; Luk 18:20; 1Tim 5:4; Eph 6:2). How does one honor their father and mother if your parents don't support your call to missions? The Bible tells us to love our neighbor, love God and love strangers, but Scripture reserves the word honor for our parents. There is no one else who the Bible commands us to honor.

Honoring our parents teaches us to honor moral authority, yet God is an even higher moral authority than our parents. There are many ways to honor parents. They get special treatment. Parents are biblically unique and deserve to be treated in a unique way. Pray for your parents, be patient with them, provide a God-honoring example for them. Find a way to love your parents through the missions process.

Missionaries do not get a pass. They must honor their parents even when parents disagree with missions. But, missionaries must worship, obey and glorify God. There are no perfect family members, but there is a perfect God who is to be unconditionally followed.

Don't delay your calling to missions because of family. You can provide them no better witness then going when God calls you. We must trust our family, our health and our very lives to the Lord. Dedicate all you have to his service and the expansion of his kingdom.

To whom should we submit? With whom should we side? Friends, family, co-workers and neighbors or the one true God? Will we side with Christ only up to the point of discomfort or are we willing to sacrifice everything for his glory? When a choice is to be made between obedience to God and the ones we love, we must never hesitate and embrace God's glory.

Family is important. Idols can be made of the very things which are good in our lives, those things given to us by God. But, idolatry toward a good thing is still idolatry. God's glory must come before all. We must give our allegiance to the one who's kingdom has no end. If your extended family does not support your call to missions, choose God, choose missions.

Chapter Ten

Theory of Missions

Missions is serious business. But, there continues to be lots of philosophical and theological thought that has and will continue to go into the study of missiology. While the heart of missions lies in the practical applications of the work, we must explore the theoretical relevance of some of the major issues. This discussion shouldn't be done only by scholars, but practitioners must have a voice.

Every would-be missionary should be knowledgeable and conversant on prominent missions topics. It doesn't matter if a theoretical missions topic doesn't touch your ministry today, it may in the future. It is healthy to prayerfully contemplate those topics which impact missions and missionaries. Christian disciples should be aware of past, present, and hypothetical missiology issues.

Continuing to hypothesize about missions keeps us sharp and ahead of the curb. On the ground missionaries should work together with theoretical missiologists to guide the trends of missions to better glorify God in the nations.

A Missionary Afraid to Die Will Never Live

No missionary, no disciple of Christ should seek death. No fool hearted person should pursue danger or peril. Physical harm is not the measure of a good Christian. However, nobody who has dedicated their life to the glory of Christ ought to fear physical or emotional harm. If servants of the Lord shy away from those things which may cause temporary pain we risk missing our full purpose in Christ.

Too often Christians ignore a call to missions because a pastor, parent or friend convinces them of the danger or difficulty they might experience. Prospective missionaries are frequently ambushed by those who claim to serve the Lord and are convinced to embrace safety and avoid risk. A Christian friend who had what is best for the kingdom in mind would help you pack your bags and drive you to the airport so you could go serve God in a dangerous country.

No disciple of Christ should embrace the security in this temporary life at the cost of the eternal glory of God. A Christian who encourages a missionary to avoid danger, risk and hardship does not fully comprehend the sovereignty and kingship of God. Missionary Amy Carmichael said, "Missionary life is simply a chance to die." God is supreme and he can and will call you home when he sees fit, on the mission field or in the perceived safety of your home.

While the advice of other Christians may do much to confuse and dissuade us about risk and possible martyrdom, the Bible is very clear. We are told throughout Scripture that being a disciple of Christ is full of risk. We are told the godly are persecuted (2 Tim 3:12). Christians are to glorify God in our suffering (1 Pet 4:14-16). A follower of the Lord should not fear death (Mat 10:28-33). We are instructed to glorify Christ with your suffering (2 Cor 12:9-10). And, to rejoice in your suffering (Rom 5:1-21). Throughout the Bible we read about fellow believers who were tortured and killed for their dedication to God; Abel (Genesis 4), John the Baptist (Mat 14:1-12), Stephen (Acts 6-7), James (Acts 12: 1-2) and more. Why should we view ourselves as above what is outlined for followers in the Bible?

It can be argued that a Christian who fears death does not understand the purpose of his life. Our temporary life is to be used to glorify God, and not to bring ourselves comfort and security. As disciples of Christ our lives should be dedicated to his service and glory. We must never place our personal wellbeing and safety ahead of the primary purpose we have been placed on this earth.

Embracing ease and an aversion to risk in this life at the expense of God's eternal glory guarantees we will not embrace our fullest potential in our ministry. A timid, safety-seeking service to the Lord is not what we are called to give. If we are looking over our shoulder, making safe decision and avoiding risk we are not giving everything we have to the Lord. Dietrich Bonhoeffer said, "When Christ calls a man, he bids him come and die."[94]

Living in this world is risky. Safety is an illusion. But, of all people, Christians should know the true risk of death without Christ. Today over 150,000 people will die and most won't know Jesus. We can look the other way but you can never again say you weren't aware. The world says a smart person avoids death and suffering. But, a Christian knows a temporary body in this life is worth risking for the eternal soul of a stranger. Jesus, the King who died for us, is worth giving your life for.

---

[94] Dietrich Bonhoeffer, *The Cost of Discipleship* (London: SCM Press, 1968), 79.

Again, let it be stressed here that nobody is encouraging Christians to foolishly place themselves in harm's way or martyr themselves for a better lot in eternity. However, being a disciple of Christ means we are to place glory and service to Christ ahead of our personal security. Do not make a decision based on your benefit, but the benefit to the kingdom. Your temporary body was intended to be used to advance the gospel. Simply believing in Christ is insufficient. He wants your unconditional love. We are to be obedient unto death and glorify him no matter the cost.

This article is not intended to result in guilt and shame, but freedom. Break free from the shackles of temporary safety and security and embrace your calling to bring eternal glory to the Lord. Do not limit your service for fear of death but, embrace a life of service. This is not for your fame, but for that of the Lord. Ignatius said, "I would rather die for Christ than rule the whole earth."[95] If God is calling you to stay home or serve in a safer location, it is my prayer you embrace that calling. However, if you hear a calling to serve in risky or dangerous conditions, amen.

Be Gone Perfect Missionary

Like Dr. Frankenstein I have occasionally tried to assemble the perfect missionary from spare parts. Unlike the good doctor, I have only ever tried this experiment in my mind. What does this perfect missionary look like? The creature must be an orator with the skills of Billy Graham. It is a necessity he have the exegetical skills of Charles Spurgeon. It is essential the perfect missionary have the stamina of an Olympic athlete and the driving skills of a NASCAR driver. He must have the bedside manner of Florence Nightingale and the ability to engineer something from nothing like the Myth Busters. Needless to say, this grotesque amalgamation of a missionary does not exist. That, however, does not prevent Christians from judging real life missionaries by this perfect missionary.

As should be the case, missions minded Christians read great missions biographies. We learn from these amazing Christ-centered missionaries of yesteryear. Mention missions to a typical disciple of Christ and visions of the greats dance in their heads. The result is that every missionary is compared to Jim Elliot, Hudson Taylor, Amy Carmichael and David Brainerd.

The result is evident. All too frequently missionaries and supporters of missions compare today's suffering servants to a standard to which they never can nor ever will

---

[95] Elmer L. Towns and Vernon M. Whaley, *Worship Through the Ages* (Nashville, TN: B&H), 66.

achieve. Missionaries view themselves as failures if the lives and their ministry are not worthy of a feature film, or at least a short book.

Playing a part in world evangelism, be it going, sending or praying, is not for the super Christian, it is for the obedient Christian. God does not set aside the special or more qualified disciples for missions work. The late Vance Havner once said, "The primary qualification for a missionary is not love for souls, as we so often hear, but love for Christ."[96]

In the Bible there is little in the way of traditional qualifications for a missionary. They aren't required to be seminary trained, hyper spiritual or have a didactic memory for Scripture. According to the Bible a missionary must be willing to go (Is 6:8). A missionary must be ready to endure hardship (Mat 10:16-31) and must be willing to serve, not from obligation, but from love (2 Cor 5:14-21). More is said in the Bible on how a missionary serves, than what makes a good missionary.

Missions is an obedient servant taking a perfect message about a merciful Savior to a lost people. More is said in the Bible about a missionaries willingness and obedience than their abilities. Christianity has been advanced by some very sinful and flawed individuals. Moses was a killer, Paul was a persecutor of Christians, David couldn't keep his hands off his neighbors. God can use all of us for his good.

There is nothing good in us and we can bring nothing of value to God. Our eternity depends only on the grace and mercy we receive from God. God receives great glory when flawed and imperfect vessels serve him. Imagine if God only called the perfect Christians to be missionaries. If they succeeded it would be expected and God's glory would be diminished. On the other hand, as God calls flawed, sinful and struggling servants to the mission field his glory is magnified. When much is accomplished by suffering servants the world sees more clearly that God was in control. We struggle with our imperfection because we only see it in contrast to God's perfect will. Perfect love is God choosing to have a relationship with us while knowing in advance just how flawed and selfish we would turn out to be.

Missionaries should not agonize over not reaching the unachievable model of perfection. Instead, we should embrace our flawed nature. Like the Apostle Paul, we should admit our faults and then use our faults to point to God. We should brag about God and tell the world the only reason anything good happens is because of the grace he

---

[96] Leonard Ravenhill, *Why Revival Tarries* (Minneapolis, MN: Bethany House, 1987), 116.

has given us (2 Cor 12:7-10). Don't hide how flawed you are, but use your flaws to point to the glory of the Lord.

Yes, my fellow missionaries, you are flawed. You are not now, nor will you ever be, the perfect missionary. In fact, those missionaries we all read about, they too were flawed and sinful. They had doubts, failures, struggles and trials. They questioned their abilities and contemplated calling it quits.

Persistence, patients, prayer and relentless reliance upon God is what makes a good missionary. Hudson Taylor, missionary to inland China, said, "There are three indispensable requirements for a missionary: 1. Patience 2. Patience 3. Patience." Wait in the Lord and his perfect timing.

A missionary who trusts in his own abilities may occasionally succeed. A missionary who spends time on his knees and seeks the Lord's direction cannot fail. A missionary dedicated to the perfection found only in the Lord Jesus Christ has already succeeded, no matter the outcome. Imperfect missionaries who trust in God's perfect grace and mercy are exactly what is needed to bring glory to the Lord.

Crawling Through the 10/40 Window

For more than two decades much of the Christian world has been turning its gaze toward the 10/40 Window. Increasingly the North American Evangelical church, the richest church in the history of the world, has been redirecting its missionaries and missions resources toward the darkness within the 10/40 Window. The goals are highly commendable, but are our methods prudent?

Argentine-born evangelist Luis Busch coined the phrase "10/40 Window" in 1989. The Joshua Project currently defines the 10/40 Window as those 69 countries that sit between 10 and 40 degrees north latitude in North Africa, the Middle East and Asia. This is the heart of Islam, Hinduism and Buddhism. It has been estimated that 90% of the 4.4 billion people living in the 10/40 Window are unevangelized; yet only 10% of our global missionary force serves there.

Is the answer to this missions conundrum to redirect an increasing amount of our North American missionaries and resources to the 10/40 Window?

According to the Center for the Study of Global Christianity, in 2010 the U.S. sent out 127,000 of the world's estimated 400,000 missionaries. It is wonderful to see U.S. churches accepting their role as senders. However, missionaries sent from the U.S. may not be the answer to opening the 10/40 Window.

In the current geo-political environment the United States and its citizens are not favorably viewed by a majority of the governments in the 10/40 Window. Of the 10 countries in the world that are classified as hardest for U.S. citizens to receive visas, seven of those are located in the 10/40 Window. In much of the 10/40 Window missionary visas are simply not granted to foreigners.

The U.S. Department of State has issued "Travel Warnings" for 23 of the countries located in the 10/40 Window. Due to safety concerns the State Department recommends U.S. citizens avoid travel in those countries. The Open Doors World Watch List ranked the top 10 most dangerous countries for Christians in the world. All 10 of those dangerous countries are located within the 10/40 Window.

Women account for a disproportionately large percentage of U.S. missionaries. Single women outnumber single men 4 to 1 on the mission field. While our culture views the involvement of women on the mission field as a blessing, much of the rest of the world disagrees with us. In fact, many of the cultures contained within the 10/40 Window are hostile to women, especially Western women.

The United States and its missionaries are simply not welcome in much of the 10/40 Window. With this knowledge, should U.S. citizens then fold up our missions tents and ignore the billions of unsaved in the 10/40 Window? Absolutely not! Jesus promised us hard times, "Blessed are you when others revile you and persecute you and utter all kinds of evil against you falsely on my account." (Matthew 5:11) John Piper echoed this same sentiment when he wrote, "If you live gladly to make others glad in God, your life will be hard, your risks will be high, and your joy will be full." Nobody said missions was easy.

In recent decades we have seen an eruption of Evangelical churches in Latin America and Southern Africa. New churches and individual conversions are exploding in the Global South. Many of these newer churches now have a generation or two of spiritual maturity and are sending out their own missionaries.

As churches in the Global South have developed, many U.S. missionaries and churches have been forced to change their approach to these regions. U.S. churches are beginning to transition into supporting roles in the Global South. Churches in Latin America and Southern Africa are now seeking theological resources, biblical training and assistance in forming seminaries. In these regions U.S. missionaries are focusing more on discipleship and theological training.

Already missionaries are going out from these regions. But, why not send more? Latin passports can gain access to countries that U.S. and Western European passports can't. Missionaries originating from the Global South can gain easier access to countries in the 10/40 Window than U.S. missionaries.

It may be time for churches in the United States to embrace the shifting landscape. The role of the sending church in the U.S. may need to change.

As we can still find ways, we should continue to send U.S. missionaries into the 10/40 Window. The 10/40 Window is the heart of evil in this world and must be evangelized with ferocity. But, churches in the Global South are ready to play an increased role. This is not about danger or ease of passage. The lives of our U.S. missionaries are no more valuable in God's eyes than their Latin and African brothers and sisters.

This is about wise use of the resources God has given us. Churches in the U.S. possess a wealth that is unmatched in Christian history. Those vast resources would be best-used sending U.S. missionaries into the Global South and providing discipleship and theological training to our brothers and sisters in Latin America and Southern Africa. Let's give the churches in the Global South the training, resources and financing they need to reach the 10/40 Window. Churches in the United States and churches in the Global South can partner together to evangelize the billions of lost souls in the 10/40 Window.

We in the Western world may need to take a more supportive role and let our brothers in the South handle the face-to-face evangelism. But, in the end, if we are able to crawl through the 10/40 Window and share the gospel with billions of lost who are not being reached, God will receive the praise and the glory.

Missions Through Red, White, and Blue Colored Glasses

One of the hardest things to overcome in missions is cultural bias. It is natural for every person to judge a new culture by comparing it to their own culture. This is not an American problem, it is a condition of the sinful human heart. As we experience life in a new culture we evaluate it with what we know, and that is our way of life.

Missionaries, both long-term and short-term, must never forget, we are not fulfilling the Great Commission by teaching someone to be a good American. In fact, teaching other cultures about the "American Dream" or "American Work Ethic" can hamper our primary purpose. Missionaries should not travel to other cultures to teach better time management, hard work, direct communication, pride in appearance or driving etiquette.

Tim Keller said that, "to reach people we must appreciate and adapt to their culture, but we must also challenge and confront it."[97] We are to confront the culture of others, not by using our culture as a standard, but instead by measuring every culture to Christ.

Jesus tells us in Matthew 28:18-20 that the primary purpose of a missionary is to teach them, "to observe all that I have commanded you." A missionary is called to teach God's ways to other cultures. Anything shy of this is not a fulfillment of the Great Commission.

The American way of life has prospered for over 200 years. Western culture has been dominant for several centuries. And, Western philosophy pre-dates Christ. However, these schools of thought are man-made. They are thus sinful and inferior to Christianity. In fact, no man-made culture or philosophy is worthy of being propagated when compared to the observance of God's ways.

The Great Commission is clear; make disciples, baptize and teach God's ways. God's ways do not improve if they are mixed with our own cultural biases. Our own thoughts, whether personal or collective, hinder the advancement of the gospel. True, unfiltered Christianity is perfect and gains nothing by adding cultural biases.

It is very common and expected for us to add our own cultural biases to global evangelism. Sinful man sees everything through the filter of what he knows. This is one of the hardest aspects of sharing the gospel of Christ in a cross-cultural setting. No man-made philosophy should ever be viewed as equal to Christianity in any way. Teaching that focuses on the best qualities of man ignores the extent of our depravity and discounts the urgency of our need to be rescued. Gresham Machen said, "Modern culture is a mighty force. It is either subservient to the gospel or else it is the deadliest enemy of the gospel."[98]

The Lord certainly understood his followers would be burdened by the culture, time period and historic context in which they lived. This was a challenge God knew all men would face. The Crusades, the Inquisition, witch hunts, and indulgences were all actions of sinful men who allowed their own biases to supersede the truth of Scripture. Cultural bias was as real for the people in Scripture as it is for the people reading Scripture today.

This world is not our home and as Christians we should anticipate a level of uncomfortableness entrenching ourselves in this culture. The Christian is called to engage and confront the culture we live in, not immerse ourselves in its trappings. Missions isn't

---

[97] Tim Keller, *Center Church* (Grand Rapids, MI: Zondervan, 2012), 24.
[98] J. Gresham Machen, *Christianity and Culture* (Fort Worth, TX: Religious Affections Ministries, 2012), 13.

imparting your views, imposing your will or forcing your culture on others. It is sharing the joy and mercy of a perfect love found only in Christ.

The purpose of this article is not to point out the flaws of America, Westernism or other cultural standards. It is however intended to drive home the point that God's ways are superior to and different from any culture embraced by man. Even the church itself has become stained by the sins of man. Certainly, every way of life or culture, other than Christianity itself, must be viewed as inferior and must never be blended with the gospel. The views that one culture is either superior or inferior to another are both offensive to God's supremacy and an affront to his free grace.

Disciples of Christ do no service to the Lord when they evaluate a person or culture through the lens of their own worldly biases. We must ask God to help us see all men through his eyes. When we look through the unfiltered lens of the gospel we see all men as God does; broken and in need of a Savior. No sinner receives benefit from becoming more Americanized. A good American without a saving relationship with Christ goes to the same hell as a Muslim, Buddhist or Hindu.

9 Must-Read Books on Missions

If you are on the mission field, contemplating missions, or a disciple of Christ who wishes to expand your understanding of missions these books should be in your personal library. The combined content of these nine books will boost your understanding of God's passion and mandate to make disciples among the nations.

1. The Life and Diary of David Brainerd

This is a biography of missionary David Brainerd written by theologian Jonathan Edwards. First published in 1749 the work was edited from Brainerd's diary. Such missionary greats as William Carey, Hudson Taylor, Adoniram Judson and Jim Elliot acknowledge being greatly influenced by this book. Brainerd served as a missionary to the American Indians in modern day New York, Massachusetts, Delaware, Pennsylvania, and New Jersey. His missionary service and life ended when he died of tuberculosis at the age of 29.

2. The Hole in Our Gospel

Richard Stearns tells us that if our individual faith in Christ has no positive outward expression then our faith has a hole in it. As Christians, we committed our lives to following Christ and living in such a way those watching would see a reflection of God's love, justice and mercy through our actions. Stearns takes a challenging look at followers of Christ. For many of us the problem with our faith is we have ignored, rewritten or lied about what the gospel says regarding poverty and justice. Much of the gospel is about serving the poor and the needy as Christ has called us to do.

3. Let the Nations Be Glad

This is a theological and biblical defense of God's supremacy in missions. It makes it clear missions is not simply a good option, but a mandate for all Christians. We must be senders or goers. John Piper shocks the reader by explaining we cannot take our own comfortable lives and make them the measure of what we allow the Bible to mean. God's glory is man's chief end. Missions exists because worship doesn't. It is our call to spread the worship and glory of God through missions.

4. On Being a Missionary

Thomas Hale wrote this landmark book on missions. Every prospective missionary would benefit from reading it before leaving for the field, and every Christian should reread it regularly. It is challenging and fascinating. The author pulls from his experience as a missionary in Nepal. Hale explains about being a missionary, what it's like, the problems, the challenges, the heartaches and the joys.

5. The Spiritual Secret of Hudson Taylor

Taylor was a pioneer missionary who spent the last half of the nineteenth century serving in China. He provided an example of faith and prayer that was unequaled. He spent more time in prayer than any other activity. His level of faith in God was unshakable. Taylor knew God would honor his work as long as Taylor continued to honor God. This book is worth reading if only to catch a flavor of the depth of faith possessed by Hudson Taylor.

6. Book of Jonah

This short Old Testament book tells the story of the Minor Prophet who served as a reluctant missionary to Nineveh, the great capital of the ancient Assyrian empire. This short, four-chapter, book helps the reader see how our sovereign God uses a sinful and imperfect man to accomplish his glory and the salvation of the lost. This insightful work helps disciples of Christ experience how God can and does use his imperfect servants.

7. Evangelism and the Sovereignty of God

J.I. Packer has written a great book addressing the topic of evangelizing in the name of our sovereign Father. It is a privilege to evangelize and tell others of the love of Christ, understanding that there is nothing they need more then to know the saving grace of

God. The world is full of people who are not aware they deservedly sit under God's wrath. It is urgent we try to arouse them and show them the way to be free of our well-earned punishment.

8. Through Gates of Splendor

In 1955 five missionaries entered the jungle in Ecuador to bring Christ to a violent and primitive tribe. They were massacred by the very people they went to serve. Elisabeth Elliot uses interviews, articles, journals and personal accounts to take the reader to the jungles of Ecuador. This book and these five men have done more to advance Christian missions then almost any event in the past 100 years. This story caused a swell of men and women willing to give their lives to Christ in missions and still influences missionaries into action 60 years later.

9. Finish The Mission

A collaborative book written by some of the top modern theologians. The book focuses on God's call for his followers to be engaged in missions. The book has contributions from John Piper, David Platt, Michael Oh and other heavy hitters. The six primary authors each wrote a separate chapter focusing on a different facet of missions.

There are many great biographies and books on the practice and theology of Christian missions. This must-read list will provide a foundation to better understand God's mandate for missions and the role his disciples are called to play.

Predestination and Missions, the Perfect Match

Predestination is a biblical doctrine. Both the unconditional election and reprobation of man are spelled out in the texts of God's ordained Word. So too are the commands that Christians are to share his gospel with the lost around the globe. To many, the concept of a sovereign deity who chooses those who are elect and those who are reprobate and then mandates his followers to reach out to the lost and share Christianity sounds conflicting, or at least confusing.

Indeed, the same God who commands missions clearly spells out predestination. This is not an inconsistency. Predestination unifies and clarifies the gospel and missions leaves humanity without an excuse. The doctrines of predestination and missions are not at odds, but elegantly complementary.

Some claim predestination creates an unnecessary barrier for missions. Dissenters ask, how can a Bible believing Christian espouse predestination and have a zeal for missions?

If God has determined who will be saved, they believe, there is no need to engage in missions. However, the strong union of predestination and missions has some very valuable results. Much that is man is diminished and all that is God is amplified.

Disciples of Christ share the gospel, not because they are gifted, but because they are commanded to do so (Mat 28:18-20). Even though God is the one who reclaims the sinner, he has ordained his effectual call of the elect will occur via the dissemination of the gospel message and not without it (Jhn 17:20; Acts 26:16-18; Rom 1:16; 1 Thes 1:4-5; 1 Cor 1:23-24). The missionary cannot be puffed up with pride if his actions do not determine the result. Only a fool could become conceited by performing actions which the Creator commanded him to execute.

If God is the only one who is involved in the salvation of an individual, God is the only worthy of being consulted on the matter. Disciples of Jesus are to pray to Christ for the salvation of the lost. Christians are instructed to pray for the those separated from Christ. Increased prayer in the name of God brings increased glory. When we pray to God we are acknowledging two very valuable points; we can't and God can. The Christian diminishes himself so as to elevate his Father. An increase in missions and prayer for missions point to the fact God is about to unleash something miraculous.

Missionaries are to gain boldness through predestination. Hearts of men and people groups who were previously thought closed to the gospel have been seen to be opened to God's grace in a way which can only be attributed to God. It is incredibly freeing to the missionary to know a person, culture or country is closed only if God wills it so. John Piper preached, "The great biblical doctrines of unconditional election, and predestination unto sonship, and irresistible grace in the preaching of Christ are mighty incentives to venture forth into a Muslim or Hindu or Buddhist or tribal culture where people seem hard as nails against the preaching of the gospel." The hardest of hearts are cleaved wide open by God and provide assurance to the missionaries who labor in his name.

Far from being a deterrent to missions, God's sovereign election and reprobation have historically been energizing to those who acknowledge the doctrine of predestination. Reformed and covenantal preachers and missionaries have been some of the most passionate in history.

John Calvin sent missionaries into France and as far off as Brazil. Calvin was not deterred from sending missionaries even after many were martyred. Calvin once said predestination was, "the eternal and unchangeable decree of God by which he foreordained, for his own glory and the display of his attributes of mercy and justice, a part of the human race, without any merit of their own, to eternal salvation, and another part, in just punishment of their sin, to eternal damnation."[99]

George Whitefield was at the center of the First Great Awakening. He was believed to have preached more than 18,000 sermons and traveled across the Atlantic more than a dozen times. Whitefield once said, "Man is nothing: he hath a free will to go to hell, but none to go to heaven, till God worketh in him to will and to do his good pleasure."[100]

Charles Spurgeon was arguably the most influential preacher of the 19th century. In his life he preached 3,600 sermons and published 49 volumes. Spurgeon said, "We must have the heathen converted; God has myriads of his elect among them, we must go and search for them till we find them."[101]

D. James Kennedy founded Evangelism Explosion, which is believed to be the most used evangelism training in history. Kennedy once wrote, "God is determined to save His elect and He is perfectly succeeding in doing just that."[102]

Predestination is no hurdle to missions. Instead, truly understanding the biblical doctrine of predestination, is motivation for missions. Without God being the prime mover and man being a subordinate instrument, no sinner could be saved.

Predestination is the merciful and loving outpouring of a just and perfect Creator. Our good and sovereign Lord identified the elect for mercy and the reprobate for justice. The missionary is an obedient disciple who God uses to call his elect home. Together, predestination and missions bring glory to God and obedience to his followers.

The Culture War and Missions

Christian missionaries are encouraged to embrace their adopted cultures. Immersing oneself into the culture where a missionary serves is said to help the missionary better understand the people he is trying to reach. Indeed, learning the nuances of a culture helps a missionary comprehend how to convey and contextualize the grace and mercy of Christ.

---

[99] Philip Schaff, *The Creeds of Christendom, with a History and Critical Notes: The History of Creeds, vol. 1* (New York: Harper & Brothers, Publishers, 1878), 452.

[100] Arnold A. Dallimore, *George Whitefield: God's Anointed Servant in the Great Revival of the Eighteenth Century* (Wheaton, IL: Crossway, 1990), 70.

[101] C. H. Spurgeon, *Lectures to My Students: Addresses Delivered to the Students of the Pastors' College, Metropolitan Tabernacle. Second Series.*, vol. 2 (New York: Robert Carter and Brothers, 1889), 67.

[102] D. James Kennedy, "Why I Am a Presbyterian" Christian Observer, March 3, 1989

The danger for any missionary, any Christian for that matter, is making the gospel secondary to the culture. All cultures, be it your adopted or your home culture, are derived by man and therefore sinful. Every culture in this world, modern or historic, is superficial and wicked when placed alongside the kingdom of our Father.

No missionary, indeed no Christian, should idolize or embrace the cultures of men. The Christian is called to engage and confront the culture we live in, not immerse ourselves in its trappings.

This world is not our home and as Christians we should anticipate a level of uncomfortableness entrenching ourselves in this culture. The focus of a missionary should be to help man see how wicked this world is, and not encourage others to embrace it. Scripture clearly cautions disciples of Christ against worldly adoration. We are advised against being transformed by the world (Rom 12:2), and loving the world (1 Jhn 2:15-17).

There is little profit in embracing a worldly culture which despises that which is good. It is radically offensive to our selfish, me-centered culture of man to promote the idea that we need Jesus to save us and reconcile us to God. Few things could sound more repugnant and contrary to any modern cultures than a faith which believes man is fallen and his ways are wicked and only by diminishing himself and exalting Jesus can he be saved from eternal torment.

No missionary should be shocked he is giving his life for a culture which despises him. The Bible assures believers we are not of this world (Jhn 15:19). Disciples of Christ have been warned that the world hates those not of the world (Jhn 17:14) and more to the point, the world hates you (1 Jhn 3:13). Count yourself in good company Christian, because the world first hated our Lord (Jhn 7:7, 15:18).

The Christian missionary must make a choice. He must decide if he will embrace the things of man and forgo Christ, or if he will embrace Christ and forgo the things of man. Christ did not sacrifice his son and send his missionaries into the world so those missionaries could inform the world that it is just a little bit sinful and that its culture has great value. We have been made a completely new creation in Christ (2 Cor 5:17, Rom 6:4, Jhn 3:3) and the world and its trappings should be repugnant to us. Missionaries are going into the world to transform it, not to coddle it.

When we are in love with this world we are in danger of deserting our true calling (2 Tim 4:10). Obedient missionaries are not to embrace the cultures of the world, but embrace the holy conduct of Christ (1 Pet 1:14-15). Disciples of Christ must make a choice.

Christians are not called to spurn the world like the Hare Krishnas or Brahma Kumaris. Christians are called to live among the lost and share with them the joy found only in Christ. Nineteenth century preacher Charles Spurgeon said, "The Christian, while in the world, is not to be of the world."[103] Disciples of Christ are called to stand out, not blend in (Mat 5:13-16).

Missionaries should engage, walk in and confront the culture to which they have been sent. Christ descended to walk among humanity and show the world he was different, not to embrace the humanity around him. Missionaries too have been sent to provide a contrast which points to Christ.

Eat the food, wear the clothes, live among the people. Travel as they travel and experience what they experience. Live the daily life of the nationals to whom you have been sent to minister. Rejoice in their victories and shed tears for their pain. But, missionaries are not anthropologists, they are warriors. A Christian is to show the world it needs something radical. Whenever a Christian embraces a culture, his own or one foreign to him, he lends approval to the ways of man. Help the culture in which you live to see Jesus is all that is worth embracing.

The Only Place a Missionary Should Serve

When missionaries are raising support, or traveling around sharing their ministry they learn that every church and nearly every Christian has an opinion on where missionaries should serve and what they should be doing. The cause célèbre or the sexy missions venture changes every few years. Some new website pops up all of a sudden there is a new missions cause every missionary MUST participate in.

Ask your Christian friends. Everyone has an opinion about the 10/40 window, unreached people, sex trafficking, Muslim ministries, When Helping Hurts, tent making, or business as missions. Many people will tell you that one of the above ministries is where we need to focus all missions resources. Before, you go to the bottom of this article and write a nasty comment, about my ignorance of the importance of your pet cause, let me clarify. There is nothing wrong with the amazing ministries I mentioned in this paragraph. But, they are not the only valid ministries or methods that exist. Blanket statements like, "Missionaries should only go to…(fill in the country)", or "Our church will only support missionaries that…(fill in the ministry)" can usually be chalked up to a

---

[103] C. H. Spurgeon, *Morning and Evening: Daily Readings* (London: Passmore & Alabaster, 1896).

new fad or new book or charismatic speaker. All or nothing approaches to missions is faddish, short-sited and not in line with Scripture.

The arbiter of whether a ministry or missions destination is appropriate should be left to Scripture and the guidance of the Holy Spirit. In the Bible we see the will of the Lord has been metered out by bodyguards (1 Sam 28:2), carpenters (2 Ki 12:11), counselors (2 Sam15:12), doorkeepers (2 Ki 22:4), hunters (Gen 10:9), masons (2 Ki 12:12), soldiers (Jon 19:23) and writers (Ps 45:1). Similarly, in Scripture we witness God's servants doing his work in dozens of cities and countries. Where and what ministry disciples of the Lord participate in varies with wondrous variety. The Lord has shown he enjoys using the diversity of his followers to accomplish his will all over the world.

Scripture calls all disciples to take part of the dissemination of God's glory and truth throughout the globe. All believers are to play a part. One would think with billions of Christians on the earth today we would have plenty of room to embrace the diversity of the calls that exist among missionaries and evangelists.

If a missionary has prayerfully sought the will of the Lord and consulted the leadership of his church who are we to question the answer the Lord has given. If they say they have sought to discern the Lord's plan and through great prayer and consternation they have come to a clear understanding of where and how they are called to serve, we should rejoice. How glorious it is to witness an obedient servant. A.W. Tozer said, "Our Lord told His disciples that love and obedience were organically united. The final test of love is obedience."[104]

Missions work and the decision to go is gut wrenching enough without a missionary being questioned by others who have likely not put nearly as much thought into the process as the missionary himself. Some Christians wrestle for great lengths of time to discern the Lord's will for their lives'. The rest of us should praise God when we learn he has provided a clear calling to a missionary about their future. Instead of hearing "praise God for your service" too many missionaries hear "Why don't you serve in another country?" or "This other ministry is more important." If people in your life don't support your call to missions never forget it is not them you are ultimately trying to glorify.

Every missionary should serve proudly wherever they are called. If you seek the Lord, avail yourself to his will and follow him where he calls you, you are serving in the correct ministry. Satan uses those who we admire and respect to put doubts in our mind. If you

---

[104] A. W. Tozer and Anita M. Bailey, *That Incredible Christian: How Heaven's Children Live on Earth* (Camp Hill, PA: WingSpread, 1964), 164.

are following the Lord's direction for you onto the mission field don't let the finger wags and opinions of others dissuade you or rattle your resolve. The call to missions has more to do with the condition of our heart than it does the location of our feet.

The shepherd's sheep have been scattered throughout the world. He has called us to find them and tell them it is time to come home. Christians worship a God who requires unwavering obedience and calls us to participate in a mission that warrants extreme commitment. David Sitton said, "We are called to Christ. If we are called by Christ then we are called to his mission." It is my prayer that all Christians embrace their call to serve God fully and completely as we have all been called to do.

There Can Be Only One - Religious Pluralism in Missions

Is there only one true track that directs man to God or do many paths lead explorers up the mountain where they all reach the top, no matter the route they take? The biblical beliefs of Christianity exclusivity claim there is but one way to commune with God and that is by having a personal salvific relationship with is son, Jesus Christ. As the secular culture and her cousin, secularized Christianity, continue expansion, religious pluralism threatens the purity of the Christian faith as outlined by God in his inspired Bible. How should the new face of tolerance on the old sin of religious pluralism impact our preaching, missions and evangelism?

From a purely philosophical perspective it is acceptable to believe in either religious pluralism or it is acceptable to believe in the Bible. It is, however, inconsistent to believe there is more than one way to God and to simultaneously hold to the exclusive claims of the Christian Bible. A person who believes the Bible is the inerrant, infallible, unchangeable word of God must believe in the exclusivity of Jesus Christ. To believe in religious pluralism is to deny the Scriptures.

Paul's letter to the Colossian church is a result of false teachings before the church. Paul attempts to warn the readers to avoid false teaching and focus only on Christ as the one way to God. In his letter to the Colossians Paul writes Christ is the Lord of creation (1:15-17), is the knowledge of God's mystery (2:1-5) and to not let anyone convince them that Jesus isn't the only way to God (2:8-15). He told the church to be aware of false teaching (2:16-23) and to focus on Christ (3:1-4). Don Carson said of Paul's letter to the Colossians, "Thus, against the claims of other intermediaries, Colossians insists not only on the supremacy of Christ but also on the exclusiveness of his sufficiency."

The Bible tells us, unequivocally, Jesus is the Savior of the world (Acts 4:12; 1 Jhn 4:14). Scripture says, Jesus is the one mediator between God and man (1 Tim 2:5) and that Christ brings us to God (1 Pet 3:18). Also, through Jesus we have access to God (Eph 2:18). The Bible is clear that those who believe are saved (1 Cor 1:21), but those who don't believe the gospel perish (2 Cor 4:3; 2 Thes 1:8-9) and those believing in anything other than God are fools (Rom 1:22-25). Also, teaching Jesus is not the way results in damnation (Gal 1:8).

The seminal verse in all of Scripture pointing us to a mandate of exclusive faith in Jesus Christ is John 14:6, which says "Jesus said to him, 'I am the way, and the truth, and the life. No one comes to the Father except through me.'" John Calvin wrote of this verse, "So all theology, when separated from Christ, is not only empty and confused but also mad, deceitful, and spurious; for although philosophers sometimes come up with excellent sayings, they contain nothing but what is ephemeral, and even mixed up with perverse errors."[105] There could be no clearer claim by Christ in support of his exclusivity.

Christian preachers and missionaries must anchor themselves in the fact that to be saved a person must follow the gospel of Christianity and have a relationship with Jesus Christ. This is nonnegotiable. If there is perceived wiggle room or other alternatives to this, why is it we do missions? A jungle tribe must hear the gospel and follow Christ. A "good" person in New York must repent and follow Jesus. A Mormon, Muslim or Sikh must abandon false religion and embrace Jesus Christ.

The consequences of religious pluralism are becoming more radical and pervasive. Yes, we should tolerate other beliefs, but no, we should not condone them. Christian preaching and global evangelism must be clear that Jesus is the only way to God. In the face of religious pluralism Bible believing churches must respond resolutely. Derrick Mashau stated, "Although the influence of secularism and pluralism has been devastating, it is my Reformed conviction that a missional church can bring about change in this regard by propagating a Christian worldview that seeks to penetrate every society with the life-giving gospel of Jesus Christ who sovereignly reigns through his Word and Spirit."[106]

Christian exclusivism is a compassionate and merciful response in the face of the sinfulness of man. Religious pluralism espouses multiple paths when God has made clear there is only one. How entrenched in sin must a man be to purposefully lead another

---

[105] John Calvin, *John, Crossway Classic Commentaries* (Wheaton, IL: Crossway Books, 1994), Jn 14:6.
[106] T. Derrick Mashau. "A Reformed Missional Perspective on Secularism and Pluralism in Africa." Calvin Theological Journal 44 (2009): 126.

away from the mercy of Jesus. Christian exclusivism is the one way God has given man to avoid punishment for his sin. Carl Braaten said, "There is no need for many ways of salvation, because the one way God has revealed in Jesus Christ is sufficient for all." The true compassion rests in the truth that no soul will perish unless it is separate from Christ.

Religious pluralism is a dangerous and evil lie loved by Satan and perpetuated by sinful man. Christian exclusivism is a loving response to the otherwise impossible burden of atoning for our own sins. Christian preachers and missionaries must strive to lead others from the darkness of religious pluralism to the light of exclusive faith in Jesus Christ.

We are All Missionaries

The primary point of missions is not to train pastors, build houses, or teach VBS. The purpose of missions is to glorify God. God created the world to bring himself glory. Everything exists to bring praises to God and missions seeks to exalt God's name.

As Christians, the purpose of our life is to seek God's glory throughout the world. Scripture tells us, "May he have dominion from sea to sea, and from the River to the ends of the earth! May desert tribes bow down before him, and his enemies lick the dust! May the kings of Tarshish and of the coastlands render him tribute; may the kings of Sheba and Seba bring gifts! May all kings fall down before him, all nations serve him!" (Ps 72:8-11)

We begin to understand why we are here when we first begin to live our lives as a tribute to God. When we view our home, possessions, family and even our life as a gift from God, we will begin to view ourselves as a living sacrifice to the Lord. We must live our lives daily willing to return all we have to the one who gave it to us. Richard Sibbes, a sixteenth and seventeenth century English theologian, eluded to 1 Cor 10:31 when he said, "The whole life of a Christian should be nothing but praises and thanks to God; we should neither eat nor sleep, but eat to God and sleep to God and work to God and talk to God, do all to His glory and praise."[107]

The book of Romans supports the idea that we are called to give ourselves for God's glory. "I appeal to you therefore, brothers, by the mercies of God, to present your bodies as a living sacrifice, holy and acceptable to God, which is your spiritual worship. Do not be conformed to this world, but be transformed by the renewal of your mind, that by

---

[107] Richard SIbbes, The Complete Works of Richard Sibbes, Vol 7, ed. Alexander Balloch Grosar (Edinburtgh: James Nichol, 1942), 185.

testing you may discern what is the will of God, what is good and acceptable and perfect." (Rom 12:1-2) This encapsulates what it means to live for God.

In his acclaimed book on missions, Let The Nations Be Glad, John Piper explains, "Missions exists because worship doesn't. Worship is ultimate, not missions, because God is ultimate, not man. Worship is the fuel and goal of missions."[108]

We are all a sinners saved by God's grace. The fall turned the world away from its' true purpose, and the cross is God's sacrifice to reclaim this world for his glory. Missions is Christ on earth. God saved each of us with missions and missions is why he is using us now.

Throughout history the world has coveted strength, but God has always used weakness. When trying to conquer the world the Nazis sent brute force, the Romans sent skilled warriors, but God is sending the weak, poor & uneducated. We are all sinners and bring only disappointment as our contribution to our relationship with God. Christians are nobodies with nothing to offer, but our God is everything. Romans affirms this assertion by reminding us, "for all have sinned and fall short of the glory of God" (Rom 3:23)

Even with our imperfections God delights in using us to obtain glory via missions. Our sin only works to magnify his splendor. If God can accomplish great wonders while using chipped and broken vessels his glory is increased. Hudson Taylor, pioneering nineteenth century missionary to China said, "The Great Commission is not an option to be considered; it is a command to be obeyed."[109]

We are all missionaries. Throughout scripture Christ's followers are called sojourners, pilgrims and strangers in a strange land. We do not belong and have been sent out only to spread God's glory through evangelism and missions. We are missionaries in our own home, in our town, in our schools, at our jobs, across the street and around the world. The Prince of Preachers, Charles Spurgeon, left little room for debate when he said, "Every Christian is either a missionary or an impostor."[110]

God's mission is to grow and expand his kingdom throughout the world, which means in your hometown and around the world. This is not a physical kingdom, but a

---

[108] John Piper, *Let the Nations Be Glad: The Supremacy of God in Missions* (rev. ed.; Grand Rapids: Baker, and Leicester: IVP, 2003), 17.

[109] Tim Koster and John Wagenveld, *Take your Church's Pulse* (Sauk Village, IL: Multiplication Network Ministries, 2014), 120.

[110] John Dickerson, *The Great Evangelical Recession* (Grand Rapids, MI: Baker Publishing, 2013), 211.

spiritual one that is reclaiming souls from the gates of hell. Missions is God's victory march towards his eternal triumph, and the battle is being waged wherever God has placed his followers.

We are told that God will give us resources and ability and we are to use them to expand his kingdom to every point on the globe. "But you will receive power when the Holy Spirit has come upon you, and you will be my witnesses in Jerusalem and in all Judea and Samaria, and to the end of the earth." (Acts 1:8)

Missions is not something that a select few are called to do. Every Christian is called to share God's love and mercy wherever God has placed us. The call to missions has more to do with the condition of our heart than it does with the location of our feet.

In his book, *The Missionary Call*, David Sills said, "If someone does not have a missions heart at home, nothing magical happens when they buckle the seat belt on the airplane."[111] Missions does not only occur on foreign soil. You do not need a passport to be considered a missionary. What you need is obedience.

As followers of Christ our lives were never intended to seek our own comfort, joy and entertainment. We are all missionaries and every Christian is called to share the love of Christ. Some of us are called to go far away and others are called to stay local, but we are all called to participate.

---

[111] M. David Sills, *The Missionary Call* (Chicago: Moody Publishers, 2008), 29.

Index

For more information contact:

Mike Pettengill
C/O Advantage Books
P.O. Box 160847
Altamonte Springs, FL 32716

info@advbooks.com

www.TheBeautifulFeetOfMissions.com

To purchase additional copies of this book visit our bookstore website at: www.advbookstore.com

Longwood, Florida, USA
"we bring dreams to life"™
www.advbookstore.com